Related Books of Interest

Developing and Hosting Applications on the Cloud

By Alexander Amies, Harm Sluiman, Qiang Guo Tong, and Guo Ning Liu
ISBN: 0-13-306684-3

The promise of cloud computing is that centralization, standardization, and automation will simplify user experience and reduce costs. However, achieving these benefits requires a new mind set. *Developing and Hosting Applications on the Cloud* covers these aspects of application development and operation and provides practical guidance, giving numerous code examples and demonstrations of system utilities for deployment, security, and maintenance.

This title makes special reference to the IBM SmartCloud Enterprise, but the principles explained are general and useful to anyone planning to automate management of IT infrastructure using the cloud. Developers using cloud management application programming, architects planning projects, or others wanting to automate management of IT infrastructure will value this end to end story for why they would want to develop a cloud application, how to do it, and how to make it part of their business.

The Business of IT
How to Improve Service and Lower Costs

By Robert Ryan and Tim Raducha-Grace
ISBN: 0-13-700061-8

Drive More Business Value from IT…and Bridge the Gap Between IT and Business Leadership

IT organizations have achieved outstanding technological maturity, but many have been slower to adopt world-class business practices. This book provides IT and business executives with methods to achieve greater business discipline throughout IT, collaborate more effectively, sharpen focus on the customer, and drive greater value from IT investment. Drawing on their experience consulting with leading IT organizations, Robert Ryan and Tim Raducha-Grace help IT leaders make sense of alternative ways to improve IT service and lower cost, including ITIL, IT fi nancial management, balanced scorecards, and business cases. You'll learn how to choose the best approaches to improve IT business practices for your environment and use these practices to improve service quality, reduce costs, and drive top-line revenue growth.

Related Books of Interest

The Art of Enterprise Information Architecture
A Systems-Based Approach for Unlocking Business Insight

By Mario Godinez, Eberhard Hechler, Klaus Koenig, Steve Lockwood, Martin Oberhofer, and Michael Schroeck

ISBN: 0-13-703571-3

Architecture for the Intelligent Enterprise: Powerful New Ways to Maximize the Real-time Value of Information

Tomorrow's winning "Intelligent Enterprises" will bring together far more diverse sources of data, analyze it in more powerful ways, and deliver immediate insight to decision-makers throughout the organization. Today, however, most companies fail to apply the information they already have, while struggling with the complexity and costs of their existing information environments.

In this book, a team of IBM's leading information management experts guide you on a journey that will take you from where you are today toward becoming an "Intelligent Enterprise."

The New Era of Enterprise Business Intelligence:
Using Analytics to Achieve a Global Competitive Advantage

By Mike Biere

ISBN: 0-13-707542-1

A Complete Blueprint for Maximizing the Value of Business Intelligence in the Enterprise

The typical enterprise recognizes the immense potential of business intelligence (BI) and its impact upon many facets within the organization—but it's not easy to transform BI's potential into real business value. Top BI expert Mike Biere presents a complete blueprint for creating winning BI strategies and infrastructure, and systematically maximizing the value of information throughout the enterprise.

This product-independent guide brings together start-to-finish guidance and practical checklists for every senior IT executive, planner, strategist, implementer, and the actual business users themselves.

 Listen to the author's podcast at:
ibmpressbooks.com/podcasts

Related Books of Interest

Enterprise Master Data Management
An SOA Approach to Managing Core Information

By Allen Dreibelbis, Eberhard Hechler,
Ivan Milman, Martin Oberhofer,
Paul Van Run, and Dan Wolfson
ISBN: 0-13-236625-8

The Only Complete Technical Primer
for MDM Planners, Architects, and
Implementers

Enterprise Master Data Management
provides an authoritative, vendor-
independent MDM technical reference for
practitioners: architects, technical
analysts, consultants, solution designers,
and senior IT decision makers. Written
by the IBM® data management innovators who are pioneering MDM, this book
systematically introduces MDM's key
concepts and technical themes, explains
its business case, and illuminates how it
interrelates with and enables SOA.

Drawing on their experience with
cutting-edge projects, the authors
introduce MDM patterns, blueprints,
solutions, and best practices published
nowhere else—everything you need to
establish a consistent, manageable set
of master data, and use it for competitive
advantage.

The Greening of IT
How Companies Can Make a
Difference for the Environment
Lamb
ISBN: 0-13-715083-0

Executing SOA
A Practical Guide for the Service-
Oriented Architect
Bieberstein, Laird, Jones, Mitra
ISBN: 0-13-235374-1

Viral Data in SOA
An Enterprise Pandemic
Fishman
ISBN: 0-13-700180-0

IBM Cognos 10 Report Studio
Practical Examples
Draskovic, Johnson
ISBN-10: 0-13-265675-2

Data Integration Blueprint and Modeling
Techniques for a Scalable and
Sustainable Architecture
Giordano
ISBN: 0-13-708493-5

Is Your Company Ready for Cloud?

Is Your Company Ready for Cloud?

Choosing the Best Cloud Adoption Strategy for Your Business

Pamela K. Isom
Kerrie Holley

IBM Press
Pearson plc
Upper Saddle River, NJ • Boston • Indianapolis • San Francisco
New York • Toronto • Montreal • London • Munich • Paris • Madrid
Cape Town • Sydney • Tokyo • Singapore • Mexico City
ibmpressbooks.com

The author and publisher have taken care in the preparation of this book, but make no expressed or implied warranty of any kind and assume no responsibility for errors or omissions. No liability is assumed for incidental or consequential damages in connection with or arising out of the use of the information or programs contained herein.

Note to U. S. Government Users: Documentation related to restricted right. Use, duplication, or disclosure is subject to restrictions set forth in GSA ADP Schedule Contract with IBM Corporation.

IBM Press Program Managers: Steven M. Stansel, Ellice Uffer

Cover design: IBM Corporation

Associate Publisher: Dave Dusthimer

Marketing Manager: Stephane Nakib

Executive Editor: Mary Beth Ray

Publicist: Jamie Adams

Senior Development Editor: Christopher Cleveland

Managing Editor: Kristy Hart

Designer: Alan Clements

Project Editor: Jovana San Nicolas-Shirley

Copy Editor: Geneil Breeze

Indexer: Larry Sweazy

Compositor: Gloria Schurick

Proofreader: Sheri Cain

Manufacturing Buyer: Dan Uhrig

Published by Pearson plc

Publishing as IBM Press

IBM Press offers excellent discounts on this book when ordered in quantity for bulk purchases or special sales, which may include electronic versions and/or custom covers and content particular to your business, training goals, marketing focus, and branding interests. For more information, please contact:

U. S. Corporate and Government Sales
1-800-382-3419
corpsales@pearsontechgroup.com.

For sales outside the U. S., please contact:

International Sales
international@pearsoned.com.

The Library of Congress cataloging-in-publication data is on file.

Text printed in the United States on recycled paper at R.R. Donnelley in Crawfordsville, Indiana.

First printing: June 2012

ISBN-13: 978-0-13-259984-9

ISBN-10: 0-13-259984-8

This book is dedicated to our soldiers of war and peace and our special forces; I cannot imagine life without your support, your courage, your strategic thinking, and steady intervention.

To the military families, thank you for your strength.

I am sending a special shout out to the Vietnam veterans; thank you for what you have done and continue to do for me and our nation; you are loved, most appreciated, and always, always remembered.

Contents

Acknowledgments

The book was written in acknowledgment of several passion points of mine. The first is my clients: I find you interesting and I thank you for being you. The second is strategy, which is what I focus on to keep my clients satisfied. The third is cloud computing, which is an exciting process enabler and business technology. And the fourth is enterprise architecture (EA)—there is something about that holistic, integrated approach to anticipating the need for change and solving business problems that I find extremely valuable. I hope you find my experiences insightful as you read this book. I thank God first and foremost for the ability, and for doing great things for me.

I thank my family for unwavering support. To my darling husband and Vietnam veteran, Frank, well, first of all thank you for your service. I love you and I appreciate you, your encouragement, and your amazing faith. I am so glad you came home. *And then came you, Frank, and then came you.*

I thank my baby girl, Talea. What an amazing and beautiful young lady you are. I am so very proud of you, your intelligence, your stamina, and your ability to remain genuine and true to your word. These combined characteristics are and will continue to take you far so hold on to them. And you know something else, Talea, thank you for keeping me positive while I worked on this book and your insights on supercomputers—only my girl can do that!

I am thankful for my baby brother, Sgt. McCoy; I am so glad that you made it back from two wars. I know you don't mind serving, but I hope you stay home! To the rest of my family you are special, and you are loved and you know it.

Claus, thank you for co-authoring Chapter 7—there certainly is a lot to think about when it comes to planning the transition to cloud. Thank you, Althea Hopkins, Robert Carter, and James Jamison, for reviewing content; Omkhar Arasaratnam, I appreciate your insights when it comes to both managing and mitigating risk (Chapter 6); Chris Molloy for making the time as well as for your contributions to Appendix A; John Caldwell, Tina Abdollah Martin Jowett, Rob High, Hector Hernandez,

Steve Stansel, Mary Beth Ray, Sham Vaidya, Faried Abrahams, Sugandh Mehta, Sue Miller-Sylvia, and Ruthie Lyle; Emily Koenig, and the entire corporate executive board for graphics that you shared to help enforce some key messages; Mark Carlson from Oracle Corporation; Lydia Duijvestijn and husband for your contributions to the financial chapter; the late Mark Ernest for including me in the cloud adoption framework development initiative at IBM; Jeffrey Caldwell from SonicWALL— what a friend you are indeed; Elisabeth Stahl for your support and contributions to the financial chapter; Susanne Glissman, for your perspectives on component modeling and cloud, which landed in Chapter 4; John Lamb, for your case study that is referenced repeatedly and elaborated in Appendix B; I also appreciate Ms. Hayes-Angiono and my students of 2011, Talia, Julissa, Kayla, Natalia, Jacque A., Jacquelyn V., Lizbeth, Vivian, and Esmeralda; yes, it is possible!

—Pamela Isom

I want to acknowledge my two sons for their spirit and love: To my oldest son, Kier Holley, for his maturity, kindness, intellect, kindred spirit, and paving a road that always reminds me that the future is bright. As a freshman in high school, he is beginning to build his future, and I am quite proud of him. Quiet in disposition, always thinking, he will be brilliant at whatever he decides to do in life. I love him dearly and watching him expand his horizons is pure pleasure. His love of mathematics, science, and the arts is most excellent.

To my youngest son, Hugo Holley, for his old soul spirit, his sweet soul, who torched the road ahead for me in writing, and makes my soul shine whenever he says, "You are the best dad ever." I love his critical thinking and optimism. His love for his brother and mother warms my heart. I love him with all my heart. It is a pleasure to see him excel in mathematics and science.

To my brother, Laurence Holley, for his support throughout my life, and my late sister, Lynette Holley, whose love and support has always created a steady path in my life. It is to her memory that I dedicate this book.

Finally to Sue Duncan, founder of the Susan Duncan Children's Center, for creating a world I could live in as a child and making the road I travel today possible.

—Kerrie Holley

About the Authors

Pamela K. Isom is an executive architect in IBM® Global Business Services® and a chief architect of Complex Cloud Integration and Enterprise Application Delivery in the Application Innovation Services, Cloud Solutions Practice. She is a member of the IBM Academy of Technology where she leads initiatives on smarter cities and cloud computing in highly regulated environments. On the client front, Pamela leads complex cloud adoption, gamification, and integration projects as well as initiatives that attribute to a greener, cleaner environment. Her passion is helping clients develop cloud product and implementation strategies and establish partnered relationships so that the adoption of cloud solutions are optimized. She looks across the enterprise and thinks end-to-end when it comes to cloud adoption. She works with all stakeholders from the CEO to delivery practitioners where her ultimate strength is driving client value. In addition, Pamela is a leader of SOA and enterprise architecture. Within IBM Pamela manages the GBS patent board where she has filed and received issuance of patents with the U. S. Patent Attorney's office.

Externally, Pamela is a graduate of Walden University where she is an active alumni and plans to teach other students; she is an active member of IEEE, The Society of Women Engineers (SWE), The Open Group™ where she represents the cloud steering committee and leads the Cloud Business Use Case (CBUC) team, TMForum, the National Society of Black Engineers (NSBE), The American Legion where she and her husband connect with and support the military and their families, and Pamela is a frequent speaker at global, industrywide conferences. Pamela is a two time recipient of the Black Engineer of the Year Award for Modern Day Technology Leaders and a contributor to numerous publications on *Intelligent Enterprise Architecture, Smarter Buildings,* and *Maximizing the Value of Cloud for Small-Medium-Enterprises, an Open Group Guide;* and she is a key contributor to three books: *The Greening of IT* by John Lamb, also an IBM cloud offering, *SOA 100 Questions Asked and Answered* by Kerrie Holley and Ali Arsanjani, and *Cloud Computing for Business* by The Open Group where she also resided on the editorial board.

Kerrie Holley, IBM Fellow, is the global CTO for application innovation services in IBM's Global Business Services (GBS). His responsibilities include technical leadership, oversight, and strategy development, consulting, and software architecture for a portfolio of projects around the world. He also provides technical leadership for IBM's SOA's and Center of Excellence.

IBM's CEO in 2006 appointed Kerrie to Fellow, IBM's highest technical leadership position. It is the highest honor a scientist, engineer, or programmer at IBM (and perhaps in the industry) can achieve. Thomas J. Watson, Jr., as a way to promote creativity among the company's "most exceptional" technical professionals, founded the Fellows program in 1962. Since 1963, 238 IBM Fellows have been appointed; of these, 77 are active employees. The IBM Technical Community numbers more than 200,000 people, including 560 Distinguished Engineers.

IBM Fellows have invented some of the industry's most useful and profitably applied technologies. Few computer users may realize how much of this group's innovations have created the computer technology we take for granted.

Mr. Holley's expertise centers on software engineering, software architecture, application development, business architecture, technical strategy, enterprise architecture, service-oriented architecture, cloud computing, and cutting-edge network-distributed solutions.

Mr. Holley is an IBM master inventor, and holds several patents.

Mr. Holley has a BA in mathematics from DePaul University and a Juris Doctorate degree from DePaul School of Law.

Preface

Written by Pamela K. Isom, Executive Architect, IBM

While numerous books in the market describe implementation details of cloud computing, this book emphasizes the need for a cloud adoption strategy offering guidance on cloud investment decision making as well as how to evolve your strategy so that it remains relevant during changing business conditions.

We have had the pleasure of working with companies that are business-centric when it comes to cloud decision making as well as those that are more technology-centric. The business-centric consumer tends to focus on ensuring that cloud investments will strengthen the company's presence in the marketplace; these companies are concerned with establishing the right business portfolio that encompasses cloud and understanding the buying behaviors of targeted consumers. The technology-centric consumer on the other hand tends to lean on cloud services to build up IT capability and improve business performance. In both cases increasing profitability and agility are at the forefront of business objectives.

When it comes to developing your cloud adoption strategy a mixed business and technical strategy is significant, and that is why we wrote this book—to share experiences and insights on how to integrate business and information technology (IT) decision points as well as offer holistic, companywide considerations in an effort to guide development of an effective strategy that generates sustainable business outcomes! Written from a cloud consumer's point of view, this book offers cloud service providers insight into how to motivate consumption of their cloud services, while both consumers and providers will learn how to go about developing an effective cloud adoption strategy tailored for their business.

Business Influence and Cloud

Having 25 plus years of experience in IT, I have worked with a vast array of executives, business leaders, and practitioners from small, midrange, and large companies that face challenges of varying degrees. I enjoy working with clients, and I really enjoy getting to know the teams so that we solve business problems together and in such a way that identified changes are actionable and easier to embrace. Examples include ensuring that adequate sourcing strategies are understood and put in place within organizations, as well as ensuring that appropriate business technologies are adopted for the right business reasons.

In general, most client business drivers fall into two main categories. First, change to improve business performance. This may as an example involve offering guidance on how to expand global business operations or conduct process improvements. Second, improving efficiencies, which often translates to reducing the costs of conducting business. This typically involves streamlining business as well as IT costs while maximizing service efficiencies. The magnitude of these drivers has bubbled up and down over the years. For instance, both the dot-com and the 2007 economic experiences were prefaced with optimistic spending followed by stringent cutbacks. Now considering the economic recovery, businesses are promoting cautious spending while investing in established capital using strategies such as outsourcing, business partnering, and there is a notable increase in mergers and acquisitions (M&A) to strengthen business portfolios.

In fact, the economic bubble (although unpleasant at times) attributes in many aspects to innovation. I mean think about it; business today is conducted over the Internet using more cost-effective and efficient capabilities such as AppStore services; the use of social collaboration or "social-ware" is more profound in business decision making; mobile technologies have been around but global growth and consumption patterns continue to expand; and cloud computing—or "cloud" for short—is becoming more prevalent for providing core, not just minor, business competencies.

Cloud in Context

Most businesses have heard the term cloud and understand it to mean a business service model that enables consumption and delivery of business and IT services on a "pay for what you use" basis. This capability is enabled through subscription or flat rate service charges, similar to the rates you pay for mobile use or magazine subscriptions, and consumption-based pricing or metered charges, which are more exact charges or up to the minute. Purchasing services in the cloud allows you to invest in assets that are off-premise as opposed to investing in-house. In general, it is less expensive and more efficient to purchase cloud solutions off-premise than it is to outright buy assets that you may or may not use, or build the capability internally. Private clouds are different in that you own the assets so there may be some up-front costs, but there are tangible benefits due to ready-made solutions, economies of scale, and again consumption-based pricing. That being said, you probably are not surprised that the adoption of cloud makes for a compelling business case. Many companies for instance are concerned that their IT staff has been spread pretty thin over the past years and would benefit from "ready-made" solutions that are available in the cloud. Cloud delivery models, although necessary to understand, are not as interesting as understanding the business innovation and opportunities presented with the adoption of cloud computing.

Why the Strategic Emphasis?

I certainly agree with the benefits of cloud and support the use wholeheartedly, but I also believe that you can get even more out of your cloud investments if you strategically position and ready your company for cloud. To me, and this may have to do with my upbringing in athletics, strategy is your combined vision and playbook. You must have a vision, one that others can imagine and embrace, and you have to execute the right plays to attain your vision. In addition, you must evolve your strategy to grow and remain competitive, especially considering that a cloud adoption strategy today requires market analysis and agility to remain effective tomorrow. To prepare for cloud adoption, you might specifically require the immediate discipline of portfolio management and governance at executive levels so that good decision making and exception handling practices are carried forward into adoption decisions; you may need to strategize business patterns for adoption that include development of a diversified cloud portfolio or stronger business partnerships so that you contain business risk; you might choose to broaden the marketing depth of your CTO so that you, as a company, are more business savvy when it comes to ideation and propelling the use of cloud across your value net; or quite frankly, you might decide to focus on building internal assurances so that members of your highly regulated vertical organization (e.g., healthcare) are trained on compliance procedures and can apply these requirements to guide cloud adoption choices.

Whatever your situation, you need to sharpen your readiness for cloud by developing a strategy that embraces change so that you effectively perform now and in the future. In essence, it is not about the adoption; it is how you strategically plan, grow, execute, and maintain the adoption of cloud in your company. One thing is for certain, and you hear this as you read: There is so much more to cloud than technology.

One way to ready your company for cloud is to incorporate cloud into your enterprise architecture (EA)—your integrated business and IT strategy. To provide some context, there are three dimensions of EA: strategy (which is the focus of this book), management and control, and execution. There are numerous ways to depict an EA, and essentially there are four domains: business architecture, information systems architecture (which are applications and data), technology/infrastructure architecture, and governance. Definitions of each domain are provided in the glossary. As you contemplate your decision to adopt cloud, albeit now or in the future, you should consider each domain and incorporate cloud considerations for two primary reasons. First, the value of cloud continues to generate a compelling business case for small and large companies, and as such it is never too soon to begin preparations; and second when you think about the domains it is important to understand that each can be outsourced in its entirety or in part to cloud and therefore strategic consideration is prudent and will make your transition that much smoother. Suppose you are interested in consuming SaaS (Software-as-a-Service) collaboration services because you feel that developing applications internally is too costly and simply not worth the investment at a given point in time. The question emerges: What are some key business considerations for SaaS adoption in your company? For example, are you prepared to intertwine your SaaS applications with your current business processes and applications, and are others willing and ready to embrace the required changes? The magnitude of adoption of course depends on your business needs, and you learn as you read that sometimes cloud is not the right fit or course corrections are needed to sustain the adoption.

One of the central messages in this book is the need to create an enterprise cloud adoption strategy; one that is reusable and positions you to make sound choices. Figure P.1 illustrates the life cycle of an enterprise cloud adoption strategy that commences with initial planning and concludes with implementation planning ensuring that there is a smooth transition from strategy to project delivery. As you read, you find the topics expounded throughout this book with expressed focus on the cloud adoption life cycle in Chapter 3, "The Life Cycle of Your Enterprise Cloud Adoption Strategy."

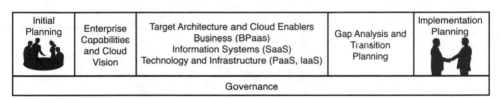

Figure P.1   Life cycle of an enterprise cloud adoption strategy

Yes, This Book Is Applicable to You

Is this book applicable to you if you are a small to mid-market company or perhaps if you do not have an EA? Yes. Consider the following three points. First, the value and expectations of a cloud adoption strategy are described as well as key considerations such augmenting your delivery model with cloud that includes dealing with multisourced environments, risk mitigation, financial considerations, and other strategic imperatives such as roadmap development. All of these are business criteria that must be considered to develop an effective strategy, and such insights are significant for all business models irrespective of the size of your company. Second, special considerations for the small to mid-market company are incorporated into this book. Third, if you have a business strategy and if you have an IT strategy, you have some basic EA fundamentals and you will learn techniques for incorporating cloud so that your organization reaps optimal benefits. So read on and discover how you can ready your company for cloud, and learn how you can enable yourself to make more effective, strategic cloud adoption choices. Finally, if you are wondering how cloud computing can make your business more nimble, differentiate your business, or open new markets the content herein will be invaluable.

Introduction

If you are too tactical (implementation focused) in your cloud adoption pursuits, you run the risk of adopting solutions that temporarily add value with a rate of diminishing returns that is faster than you are able to offset. If your approach is too strategic, you run the risk of developing a strategy that is too high level, one that is difficult to relate to and might not get executed as you intended or your strategy becomes shelfware. What then can you do to guide successful cloud adoption in your company?

Understanding your business classification as well as your competencies (as discussed in Chapter 4, "Identifying Cloud Candidates") is one example consideration that is critical to establishing a value-centric cloud adoption strategy. Knowledge as to where you are as well as your target state can influence cloud adoption decisions. Listed are some common consumer considerations:

1. Small-medium businesses (SMB) might be more interested in Storage-as-a-Service and at a smaller capacity than larger enterprises.
2. Industry verticals, such as healthcare providers, might lean more toward private or community clouds in an effort to meet regulatory stipulations.
3. Large enterprises are more likely to pay for cloud services on account as opposed to credit card purchases.
4. Value added resellers (VAR) add value on top of cloud offerings in the form of customized services. You need to understand the markup and total costs to you as a consumer.
5. Cloud service brokers (CSB) are likely to partner with numerous vendors to generate the best cloud solution for your company. In this book, the expression CSB, systems integrator, and service integrator are used interchangeably and scenarios are elaborated throughout with descriptions in the glossary.

Consider the following business scenario for a mid-market cloud consumer:

The company decided to authorize designated purchases of cloud services using corporate credit cards only. This mid-market company's business requirement therefore was that cloud service providers allow credit card purchases knowing that it is more common for larger companies to purchase solutions using other mechanisms such as purchase orders because of the larger quantities. A key business discussion pertained to credit authorization and more important, billing services. How consumers would be billed for services in a pay per use model, would charges occur daily to credit cards or accrue on a monthly basis, and when would payments get processed? What exactly does pay per use imply with respect to service charges? Another key discussion was how services would be disabled if, for example, usage exceeded an authorized credit limit. In this particular case, the company negotiated the appropriate activation and deactivation of cloud services with the provider with an eye for maintaining outstanding service levels. You learn more about this case study in the epilogue; however, a key message for you to consider is that as you go about planning adoption of cloud in your company, you need to establish enterprise business policies (e.g., purchasing standards for cloud services) as well as establish a governance model that requires appropriate parties to engage in the decision making process at appropriate times.

This book, *Is Your Company Ready for Cloud?*, is a first complete guide to cloud decision making for executives and leaders in both business and technical strategy roles. Using practical experiences with enterprise customers, situational analogies, and vignette style business scenarios, this book contains strategies for readying your organization for cloud adoption and explores cloud business trends and consumption patterns. Included are techniques for selecting cloud products and services, and strategies for driving business value into organizations by planning your adoption through the use and/or extension of enterprise architecture (your integrated business and IT strategy).

This book is not an introduction to cloud computing or EA, but rather illustrates the business value aspects of cloud, offering insights to help you the consumer determine which cloud adoption strategy is the most suitable for your business. If you do not have an EA, this book is applicable as you learn some strategic principles that you can embrace to guide decisions such as data center considerations, operating in multi-sourced environments, intellectual property management, and how to recognize and apply cloud business adoption patterns. Example topics include identification and prioritization of cloud candidates and enablers, techniques for developing an enterprise cloud adoption strategy, business integration, and governance of your adoption for optimal usage of cloud within your company. At times you find contrasts to organizations with and without an EA and the respective cloud adoption experiences.

Cloud-Sourcing and Traditional Sourcing Options

The expression cloud-sourcing is referenced throughout because there are similarities as well as differences in approaches that you must consider. For instance, from a transition planning perspective, if you are accustomed to working with outsourcing vendors, you may be able to leverage those same vendors as cloud providers, which could lead to more favorable contracts along with a smoother transition due to internal acclimation to outsourced services albeit on-premise or off-premise. At the same time, there are differences in cloud-sourcing that for instance require more self-service in the areas of service selection as well as problem ticketing with which you must become accustomed. In essence, you have some advantages to cloud-sourcing if you currently practice traditional sourcing strategies such as outsourcing and managed operations, but there are challenges that you must consider as you prepare your company for a successful cloud experience.

Suggestions for Reading This Book

It is suggested that you read the book from beginning to end, because each chapter builds on the chapter before it, but you can also single out specific chapters to support your circumstances. So read on and let me know what you think, you can contact me at pkisom@mac.com, @pkisom on Twitter, or on my cloud consumer insights blog at https://www.ibm.wm/ developerworks/mydeveloperworks/blogs/CloudConsumerInsights/?lang= en. Kerrie can be reached at klholley@us.ibm.com or on Twitter @kerrieh. Chapter highlights are

- **Chapter 1, "Business Value of a Cloud Adoption Strategy"**: What is the business value of a cloud adoption strategy? In this chapter, ten expectations are described in an effort to emphasize the significance, relevancy, and the impacts of strategy omission.

■ **Chapter 2, "Business Value of Incorporating Cloud into Your EA":**
What value is expected by incorporating cloud into your enterprise architecture? This chapter answers such questions and describes the impacts of
considering both business and technology to guide cloud adoption decisions. You learn of key considerations for organizations that may not have
or practice the discipline of EA and the effectiveness when it comes to
cloud adoption.

■ **Chapter 3, "The Life Cycle of Your Enterprise Cloud Adoption
Strategy":** This chapter describes the life cycle of an enterprise cloud
adoption strategy. You review new additions and/or augmentations to
existing EA work artifacts as applicable from a consumer's perspective.
You review examples and approaches for determining key considerations
that help you recognize and capture cloud-specific business requirements.
And you find specific considerations for organizations that have incorporated service oriented architecture (SOA) into their enterprise.

■ **Chapter 4, "Identifying Cloud Candidates":** How do you go about
deciding the contents of your cloud service portfolio? This chapter provides techniques for identifying cloud candidate components (including
components within larger outsourcing or managed services solutions) as
viable solution alternatives.

■ **Chapter 5, "What About Governance?":** You may have experienced
the outcomes of organizations where governance is strong as well as those
situations where governance is merely paperwork with no compliance.
This chapter provides practical considerations for enabling governance in
an enterprise where cloud is a part of the organizational landscape.
Because cloud solutions often involve outsourcing, this chapter also provides guidance for governing in the presence of outsourcing.

■ **Chapter 6, "Mitigating Risk":** Learn how to recognize and mitigate
cloud adoption risks, including information security breaches, cost overruns, and inadequate operational performance by making explicit mitigations, which are implicit with older alternatives to cloud such as IT
outsourcing, time-sharing, and the use of in-house server farms.

■ **Chapter 7, "Planning the Transition":** This chapter provides transition
planning considerations and example roadmaps for transformation to
cloud with perspectives for the consumer, provider, and integrator. Topics
covered include addressing legacy applications, business process transformation, and outsourcing.

- **Chapter 8, "Financial Considerations":** This chapter provides financial considerations required to build and maintain sponsorship of your cloud business case. This chapter also provides strategies for considering as well as integrating cloud into your EA so that implementation projects leverage the knowledge and guidelines presented.

- **Epilogue, "Thinking Beyond the Race":** This epilogue provides a summary of the book's contents and provides suggestions on how to apply. Forward thinking commentary includes cloud business adoption patterns and trends, and emerging business technologies.

- **Appendix A, "Augmenting Your Delivery Model with Cloud":** While Chapter 2 demonstrates how to incorporate cloud into your EA and Chapter 3 emphasizes development of your enterprise cloud adoption strategy, this appendix provides business considerations for augmenting your delivery model, such as the use of data centers with cloud as well as strategies that you should consider to maintain or even improve your brand.

- **Appendix B, "Cloud Case Studies and Common Questions":** Additional examples and analysis of cloud solution decisions made with and without the use of EA. This section includes some common questions asked about cloud and provides responses, along with case studies for cloud adoption in small and large companies.

- **Appendix C, "More on Cloud Business Trends":** Initial discussions on cloud business trends occur in the epilogue. The topic is continued with a focus on innovation and thoughts pertaining to the future of cloud computing.

Target Audience

The target readers are executives (non-IT as well as IT) of companies who are, or will be, making business process automation and enablement decisions. The roles include C-level executives such as the CIO and CFO; non-IT C-level executives; business architects—technical and non-technical; enterprise architects; business process owners; and line of business (LOB) leaders. In addition, the vignette style and practical case studies are conducive to academics (schools, colleges, and universities). Some example audience types that would be interested in this book are those who make, influence, and/or recommend business enablement decisions including department leaders and delivery teams.

References

Several books were consulted while working on this project. Thank you to each of the authors for your work!

- *100 SOA Questions Asked and Answered* by Kerrie Holley and Ali Arsanjani (Boston, MA: Pearson Education, 2010).
- *Cloud Computing for Business by The Open Group*™ (Zaltbommel, Netherlands: Van Haren Publishing, 2011).
- *Enterprise Architecture as Strategy* by Jeanne W. Ross, Peter Weill, and David C. Robertson (Boston, MA: Harvard Business School Press, 2006).
- *Get Ready for Cloud Computing* by Fred Van der Molen (Zaltbommel, Netherlands: Van Haren Publishing, 2010).
- *Information Systems Project Management* by Mark A. Fuller, Joseph S. Valachich, and Joey F. George (Upper Saddle River, NJ: Pearson Education, 2008).
- *Innovation Nation* by John Kao (New York: Free Press, a division of Simon & Schuster, 2007).
- *The Greening of IT* by John Lamb (Boston, MA: Pearson Education, 2009).
- *The Investment Answer* by Daniel C. Goldie and Gordon S. Murray (New York: Business Plus, 2011).
- *The New Language of Marketing 2.0: How to Use ANGELS to Energize Your Market* by Sandy Carter (Boston, MA: Pearson Education, 2009).

1

Business Value of a Cloud Adoption Strategy

Sharon is a cloud business consultant for a boutique consulting firm. In a conversation with a colleague, Paul, she expressed that one of her clients (Distributors, Incorporated) was intrigued by the possibilities of cloud computing and expressed interest in eliminating all in-house Information Technology (IT) software and hardware capacity in exchange for cloud-sourcing. Paul found the conversation intriguing because his experiences had been with clients using cloud computing to address moving specific workloads, but never offloading all software and hardware to the cloud. Paul did not think this approach was feasible. His rationale was that although support, servers, and services can be offloaded, some core networking and security solutions are required internally to support cloud adoption. Sharon expressed that the CIO of Distributors' survived the economic downturn by effectively controlling expenditures and planned to continue on this course as a major part of the business strategy to maintain profitability.

Sharon and Paul agreed that offloading IT capability to the cloud is a growing reality, as industry analysts predict that by the year 2014, 20 percent of businesses will shift the ownership of IT assets to third parties, causing a decrease in the total amount of IT asset requirements.[1] Sharon and Paul then asked themselves is this how Distributors' should be looking at cloud computing?

Sharon and Paul exchanged client experiences and decided that Distributors, Inc., was looking at cloud adoption too narrowly. The CIO views cloud adoption solely as a way of reducing costs and increasing IT efficiency. However, Sharon and Paul knew that cloud computing could offer a much greater value proposition than cost reduction or expense control. Sharon concluded that a critical success factor for Distributors' is to develop and realize a cloud adoption strategy that has the potential to be the next driver of business innovation by focusing beyond cloud sourcing, where the emphasis is purely on sourcing IT services (e.g., platform, middleware, infrastructure, and applications) from a public cloud.

NOTE

A company's recipe for success in adopting cloud computing entails creating a strategy that explores a multitude of factors: business process as a service, as well as software, platform, and infrastructure as a service. However, these factors are not enough. Examining how cloud provides access to new markets and increases the value proposition of IT are essential elements of a cloud adoption strategy. Socializing a common definition of cloud computing within the enterprise solidifies and communicates an organization's point of view and business objectives for cloud adoption. Each of these subjects is explored later in this chapter.

Ten Expectations of Your Cloud Adoption Strategy

You can expect cloud to become an integral part of your company (if it isn't already) as cloud computing matures (e.g., standards and technologies), associated ecosystems (e.g., BPaaS or open cloud computing) grow, and as more and more companies use cloud as a catalyst and engine for business innovation. If you consider the range of application functions, software and platform services available in the public cloud at a fraction of the cost of traditional IT services, you can expect your business units to continue adoption at an increased pace (without IT approvals, mind you), while at the same time looking to both business and IT stakeholders to participate in the decision process. Your teams, whether directly making cloud purchases or not, can expect to offer insights on how to use cloud to improve business outcomes, they should be prepared and ready to provide insights relative to cloud vendor and solution evaluations, and you should expect that guidance will be given on how to adopt cloud for your company's strategic advantage.

Cloud computing is more than a model for elastic workloads, cost reduction, capital preservation, and improved IT efficiency. Cloud computing is evolving and has the potential to be a major driver of your business innovation, opening up new customer segments and markets. Hence, your cloud adoption strategy should consider additional and potential benefits as part of its target state. Key business and IT stakeholders can accomplish this by collaborating and brainstorming where several key questions are addressed:

- Where can productivity be improved with cloud adoption? For example, can we provide business stakeholders new tools such as process modeling?
- Any opportunities to alleviate the IT queue, to eliminate IT for developing business solutions?
- What opportunities exist for innovation? Such opportunities might exist in leveraging mobile computing, big data, analytics, or the holistic use of all three.
- Any new geography that can be tapped for new opportunities? Perhaps new markets can be examined for localized solutions or new services can be offered.
- Can the workforce be transformed for greater collaboration and productivity?
- Where can we converge business and IT to create faster and greater value?
- Do opportunities for experimentation exist to tap into innovation?

A first step toward understanding the business value of a cloud adoption strategy is to explore the expectations or elements of an effective strategy. The following list outlines ten expectations. As you read through this chapter, you find applicability to both consumers and buyers of cloud services, as well as for providers and sellers of cloud solutions. This list serves as a preliminary table of contents for your cloud adoption strategy. The remaining chapters provide guidance for evolving your strategy and infusing cloud throughout your company using enterprise architecture.

1. Create Your Cloud Vision
2. Identify Cloud Use Cases
3. Drive Business Innovation
4. Define Business Outcomes and Projected ROI
5. Determine Opportunities for Cloud as a Fifth Utility
6. Specify Cloud Ecosystem
7. Determine and Publish Stakeholder Involvement
8. Develop Metrics
9. Define Governance
10. Develop Roadmaps

1. Create Your Cloud Vision

Your cloud adoption strategy sets the direction toward realization of your vision. Although this might sound trivial, coming to terms on a common definition and perspective of cloud where stakeholders agree is essential to have a common language to form a cloud vision. Two similar definitions of cloud are listed below. The first is an enterprise cloud provider's definition perspective, while the second is a published industry point of view:

1. Cloud is the industrialization of delivery for IT services. Cloud is a new consumption and delivery model inspired by consumer Internet services; enabled by service automation, virtualization, and standardization enabling self-service, economies of scale, flexible pricing models, and workload based IT resource provisioning.
2. Cloud computing is a model for enabling convenient, on-demand network access to a shared pool of configurable computing resources (e.g., networks, servers, storage, applications, and services) that can be rapidly provisioned and released with minimal management effort or service provider interaction.[2]

Once you have agreed to a common perspective and definition, a logical next step is to determine your opportunities for increasing business value. Your strategic entry point should be identified, your vision articulated, and a roadmap to incrementally realize the vision put in place.

- Opportunities for differentiation, market share growth, increased revenue, capital preservation, transformation, or improved efficiency should be identified as part of your vision, your cloud position.

- Entry points are where adoption commences pertaining to the identified opportunities ranging from the basic offloading of workload to the greater value of business innovation.

- Your vision is an amalgamation of strategic and tactical goals; use cases that can make a difference today and some in the future. The vision should enable innovation, which may require transformation to reach the end state.

- Your roadmap is a living plan, managed and implemented incrementally, grounded in risk management, and doing the art of what is possible.

It is necessary to realize that cloud computing continues to evolve, which means its definition, use cases, and technologies are evolving. In the opening scenario, Sharon faced a client experience in which the vision was to eliminate all IT assets and services. Through analysis, it became clear that business process sourcing to cloud was in scope and not just offloading of IT assets. It was also clear that the full value proposition of cloud was not well understood, thereby limiting the vision of what is possible for Distributors, Inc. Sharon's challenge was helping Distributors, Inc., understand the value propositions of cloud for its business and how to go about realizing the company vision while helping the client maintain optimal business performance.

Depending on your vision, your entry point for cloud adoption can be vertical where you cloud-source one or more business processes such as order fulfillment; or your entry point can be horizontal where cloud is adopted to provide cross-business unit capability. A good example of a horizontal service is virtual desktops. You can choose an entry point that provides both vertical and horizontal capabilities, where, for instance, the mobility line of business commences use of virtual desktops prior to other business units, and you can have more than one entry point. Your end point outlines where you plan to be at a designated point in time. Your roadmap, which is discussed later in this chapter, reflects the actions required to reach your end point along with a timeline.

Your cloud adoption strategy should reflect your statement of position. A cloud statement of position comprises three elements:

- **Roles:** Address roles of cloud consumer, provider, or hybrid.
- **Service types and deployment models:** Consider types of services (i.e., BPaaS, SaaS, PaaS, or IaaS) and type of deployment (i.e., private, public, hybrid, or community cloud).
- **Sphere of influence:** Clarifies the scope of your adoption strategy and identifies consumption patterns.

Figure 1.1 presents each of these elements, and the following text elaborates further.

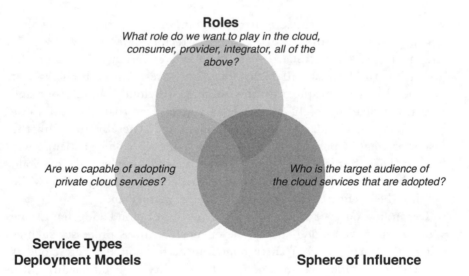

Figure 1.1   Three essentials of a cloud statement of position

The first element of your statement of position describes the roles you will play in the cloud. For instance, does becoming a cloud service provider make sense for your company? Is the role of cloud service consumer more appropriate for your organization? Perhaps you are considering a combined role or would prefer to take on the responsibilities of cloud service integrator.

The second element of your statement of position describes the service types and deployment models appropriate for your company. Valid service types, as described in Table 1.1, are Business Process-as-a-Service (BPaaS), Software-as-a-Service (SaaS), Platform-as-a-Service (PaaS), and Infrastructure-as-a-Service (IaaS). Valid deployment models, as described in Table 1.2, are public, private, hybrid, and community.

Table 1.1 Cloud Service Types

Service Type	Description
Business Process-as-a-Service (BPaaS)	Business process services are any business processes (horizontal or vertical) delivered through the cloud service model to multiple internal or external consumers. Example services are employee benefits management and procurement processes. In BPaaS, the provider is responsible for delivery of the cloud services
Software-as-a-Service (SaaS)	SaaS is generally (but not always) a public cloud offering. These are predefined applications such as customer relationship management (CRM) and enterprise resource planning (ERP). In SaaS, the consumer uses provider-based applications that are available in the cloud and accessible from various client devices. Generally, consumers from multiple organizations share a single application instance, with virtualization technologies employed to segregate customer data and maintain privacy. In SaaS, the consumer does not manage or control the underlying cloud infrastructure with the possible exception of user-specific configurations, such as to set up user profiles or to customize the user experience.
Platform-as-a-Service (PaaS)	PaaS services deliver compute infrastructure plus a predefined middleware stack that is typically structured for developers or advanced IT users. Providers can choose to offer a variety of service products that are configurable by the consumer. Examples include database, Web, or application server software. Configuration and management of these middleware resources are the responsibility of the consumer, but the provider may offer to maintain standard images once they are defined. In PaaS, the consumer does not manage or control the underlying cloud infrastructure, but has control over the deployed applications.

Table 1.1   Cloud Service Types

Service Type	Description
Infrastructure-as-a-Service (IaaS)	IaaS provides cloud service consumers with the ability to rent processing, storage, networks, and other fundamental computing resources where the consumer is able to deploy and run arbitrary software, which can include operating systems and applications.
	IaaS can be delivered in a consumption-based business model, for example, by the instance-hour used or gigabytes transferred; or as a fixed fee for a virtual device with predefined capacity and configurations. Either way, resources are accessed via the network, typically over the Internet.
	In IaaS, the consumer does not manage or control the underlying cloud infrastructure but has control over operating systems, storage, deployed applications, and possibly select networking components, such as firewalls.

Source: IBM Corporation "Defining a framework for cloud adoption: How common ground can help enterprises drive success with cloud computing."

Table 1.2   Cloud Deployment Models

Deployment Model	Description
Private cloud	Both the consumer of cloud services and the provider of those services exist within the same company although services can be managed by a third party. The services are utilized by a single company and the ownership of the cloud assets typically resides within that same company.
Public cloud	The consumer and the provider of cloud services exist in separate enterprises. The ownership of the assets used to deliver cloud services typically remains with the provider.
Hybrid cloud	Combines multiple elements of public and private cloud, including any combination of providers and consumers, and might also contain multiple service types. An example hybrid case study is provided in Appendix B.
Community cloud	Supports a specific community of shared services that support shared interests (e.g., healthcare provider community). Ownership of the cloud assets might be the organizations or a third party and the services can reside on or off premise.

Service types are often referenced as a part of a cloud "stack," as depicted in Figure 1.2, to demonstrate the required level of structure, standards, and the relationships among the service types. Higher layers, such as BPaaS for instance, require more business process structure than PaaS or IaaS. Deploying the underlying IT infrastructure should be unnecessary when you purchase BPaaS services because these service types are typically provided with underlying software, platform, and infrastructure services. Lower layers of the stack, on the other hand are foundational centric services such as compute and storage capacity. These services are typically horizontal which means they require less business process structure since they provide services for numerous initiatives and/or business processes.

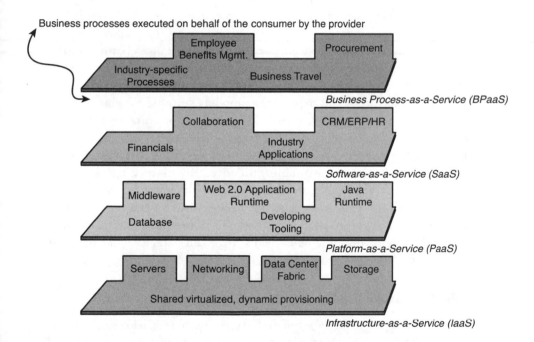

Figure 1.2 The cloud stack

Any of the service types are viable entry points for cloud adoption addressing your specific business requirements. Some of the more common entry points are IaaS and PaaS. This approach can lay a foundation for future adoption of cloud services that are farther up the stack. Each entry point comes with its own set of requirements; for example, BPaaS may require multilanguage support or geographic awareness for business rules. As a consumer, you need to clearly understand and articulate your requirements and usage scenarios prior to partaking in cloud vendor (e.g., SaaS or BPaaS) negotiations. The same is applicable to providers who must understand usage scenarios and workloads to meet service level commitments.

The third element of your statement of position is sphere of influence. The focus is your business users. Consider the role of the cloud service consumer. What are viable consumption patterns, and who are the expected end users of the cloud services that will be adopted? For example, do you want the services to be available to your existing customers, internal employees only, or both? Do cultural or bilingual considerations exist, influencing your decision to invest in cloud or drive selection of cloud providers? For example, the allowance of public clouds for research and experimentation may be suitable while a private cloud is required for searching driver records to address insurance claims. Similar to the requirements as a cloud consumer, cloud service providers need to know the sphere of influence of their service offerings.

Just as service types and deployment models suitable for your organization should be articulated, workloads that are not suitable should be specified. The cloud adoption strategy provides referential and actionable guidance to enterprise stakeholders, and defining patterns in scope and out of scope provides suitable guidance. Regulatory requirements generally dictate acceptable and unacceptable deployment models. For example, in several countries, it is not permissible for data to be transported across geographical boundaries. This regulatory requirement impacts the use of public clouds for exports and international business transactions.

2. Identify Cloud Use Cases

These scenarios present a set of archetypal usage scenarios to illustrate a few of the ways in which cloud computing might be adopted and leveraged for your organization:

- Business process improvement. Is there an opportunity to do any of the following in one or more lines of business or IT:

- Skills improvement in process modeling
- Delivery maturity in lean six sigma, business process re-engineering or other process-centric programs
- Platform provisioning where a BPM Enterprise Platform in the cloud provides lines of business a ready-made platform and solution for business process management
- Standardization of process models for accelerating horizontal and vertical processes within the business
- Transformation of how modeling is done from representing process models as drawings to durable engineering artifacts that can be more readily converted into deployed solutions

- Business intelligence and Big Data. Is there a benefit to business stakeholders for improved decision making, and analytics, in any of these areas:

  - Opportunity for predictive analytics to create models that can foresee customer behavior with analysis of large data sets (structured and unstructured)
  - Analytical infrastructure providing for new classes of analytical algorithms such as scoring engines, risk models, direct marketing models, or any online models
  - Information supply chain where the cloud platform provides data warehousing, integration capabilities, and analysis capabilities for cubes, Big Data, and streams

- Establishing or advancing an innovation center that would benefit from additional computing power, infrastructure, middleware, or platform support. The innovation center could take advantage or leverage any or all of the cloud service types: BPaaS, SaaS, PaaS, or IaaS. The innovation center focuses on exploring new opportunities for business value such as e-commerce, mobile computing, Big Data, social media, or other. Any business line requiring experimentation to explore new market opportunities would leverage an innovation center.

- Development a proof of concept capability used by enterprise architects or development teams to leverage cloud service types (primarily Paas or IaaS) to shorten the time necessary to test drive new technology whether for functional or technical fit (i.e., performance).

- Model-driven development platform using cloud for middleware, infrastructure, and platform where a complete end-to-end life cycle of development tools is provisioned through cloud computing. For example, the

cloud environment could be a multinode, multiproduct software environment, where there are different instances. This environment would support developers using modeling and design tools for more efficient
application development, testing, and management of solutions.

- Cloud provisioning life-cycle platform, which embraces all software configuration management life cycles. Release management would be performed as well as part of this life cycle.

- Cloud services. Cloud-based storage and disaster recovery are examples of
cloud services, while an example enablement candidate is secured access
to storage and disaster recovery services to mitigate business risks.

Your evolving portfolio of use cases (candidate services and enablers)
serves as a baseline for not only adoption but also management of your
internal and external clouds. At a minimum, your portfolio should contain a description of the services, the business purpose, owners, enablement candidates, and vendor-specific requirements.

3. Drive Business Innovation

Business innovation incorporates the process for exploring and considering new ideas such as new business models, collaboration, workforce transformation, and alternative product development approaches,
leveraging new technologies (e.g., Big Data, social media, or mobile
computing), or simply alternatives for how to eliminate IT for business
solution development across your enterprise. At the core of business
innovation is business agility. Your cloud adoption strategy should fuel
innovation by providing techniques and patterns that equip your company and stakeholders to anticipate business challenges, address complexities, and accelerate problem resolution.

Innovation should be a key element of your cloud adoption strategy.
Analyst firm IDC describes the emergence of the intelligent enterprise,
where the convergence of social networking, intelligent devices, ubiquitous broadband, and analytics ushers new opportunities. For some companies, this translates to cloud-based mobile applications tracking
inventory or leveraging social technologies to determine customer sentiment. Big Data represents the flood of new data where predictive or
sophisticated analytics can be used to make better decisions, allowing
retailers or telecommunication carriers, for example, to optimize decision processes such as pricing in response to real-time sales.

You can try out applications and see if they fit your business situation, and you can do this at a fraction of the cost. For instance, numerous wellness plans are available in the cloud that you might offer to employees with usage incentives. Considering the wealth of information and interconnectivity enabled with cloud, your suppliers are instantly notified of product demands so that supplies remain available on demand. Many universities require students to use secured compute servers and dedicated supercomputers that are available in the cloud for assignments as well as to promote social connectivity and team collaborations. Your ability to provision fully configured development and test environments without the expense of buying assets that you may only use for a season allows you to address peak season performance requirements. And as you will read in the case study presented in the Epilogue, "Thinking Beyond the Race," Sta-up International is excited about cloud and has decided to become a reseller of storage as a service and virtual desktops as a service in an effort to increase its international customer base although its traditional business model is communications. This is an example of leveraging cloud to add new products and services that might be considered outside your core competencies.

4. Define Business Outcomes and Projected ROI

Your cloud adoption strategy should be business-centric and contain business cases that add value to your organization. While you might think solely in terms of generating revenue streams or making more money, a senior vice president from IBM responded to that notion in a recent exchange pertaining to the business expectations of cloud, stating that one of her business objectives is to drive cost takeout, in other words keep revenues steady while eliminating costs so that profits increase. Business outcomes of cloud adoption should be described and corresponding ROI projected. Business outcomes must be measurable and developed with key c-suite business stakeholders.

ROI is a financial ratio that indicates the degree of profitability of a business. Simple cloud ROI is the result of calculating projected gains from cloud investments divided by the projected investment costs. The computation is

((total benefit − total cost)/ (total cost) * 100)

For example, if you expect to invest $2,500 in cloud services and support for year 1, and you project earnings of $10,000 after the first year as a result of your investment, then your projected ROI is 300 percent, computed as follows:

(($10,000 – $2,500) / 2500) * 100)) = 300 percent

A positive ROI indicates that your projected gains compare favorably to your projected investment costs. To understand the true value of ROI implications, you must compare your projected ROI with cloud to your projected ROI without cloud. For instance, if without cloud, you project a higher ROI in the first year, you should examine the projected benefits for years 2 and 3 before making a final decision on moving forward with cloud. Appendix B, "Cloud Case Studies and Common Questions," contains example ROI projections for adoption of a private cloud development and test environment and considers the savings in comparison to traditional hardware/software investments.

Examples of business outcomes include expanded market share to become first in the market in retail sales or reduced operational costs by 5%. The ability to quickly expand business operations locally and abroad due to instant, secure access to the information, software, and hardware that without cloud adoption could take months to purchase and deploy versus days is also a business outcome and an example agility improvement. Another example is faster time to market of goods and services, which stems from the improved cycles as a result of instant or near real-time access to cloud solutions such as real-time analytical business process as a service. Predictive business analytical applications are available faster and at a fraction of the cost than it would take to launch a project to conduct requirements analysis, design, development, testing, and deployment. Examination of the total cost of ownership (TCO) of cloud investments helps determine the lifetime costs associated with acquiring and implementing cloud. TCO analysis along with ROI facilitates making prudent cloud investment choices.

Business areas and processes that benefit from cloud-sourcing are essential inputs to TCO and ROI analysis. Strategies are not static but fluid hence continued research of your business and market opportunities is necessary for your strategy to be active and impactful. It is essential that your strategy describes imperatives that can be realized with use cases and supported by measurable business goals. Armed with strategic imperatives where measurable business outcomes take center stage the implementation can be tracked and realized.

Whether you adopt internal or external cloud services, knowledge of your company, customers, and market accelerates sound cloud adoption choices reaping optimal, enduring business benefits and viable ROI projections. A wealth of public knowledge exists on creating sound ROI projections for cloud. Various models exist in the public domain providing an excellent set of models for ROI creation.

The Open Group provides ROI models demonstrating how cloud benefits your company's stakeholders. This is an excellent contribution to the industry that should be reviewed as part of building an ROI model for cloud and for developing cloud adoption metrics. In addition to the models provided by the Open Group your ROI model should factor the following measurements:

- IT queue reduction as business stakeholders no longer require internal IT or system integrators for IT services allowing the business to do more with less
- Preservation of capital for key business imperatives reducing investment dollars when developing and implementing solutions due to asset reuse and availability
- Time to value improvement where a category of projects can now be deployed faster
- Ability to innovate where capital preservation, IT queue reduction, and time to value are all applicable to experiment, prototype, or research new opportunities to create sustained value

5. Determine Opportunities for Cloud as a Fifth Utility

To ensure you are optimizing returns and controlling the level of risk introduced, you should rationalize and determine supplemental actions that support your cloud adoption strategy. This might mean, for instance, as a cloud consumer creating a private cloud provider environment, for the potential use cases identified earlier. Creating such an environment requires billing and metering tools. Determining opportunities for cloud as a fifth utility (others are gas, water, electricity, and miscellaneous utilities, such as trash removal or your telephone bill) means leveraging cloud computing, where applications run over the Internet, SaaS, without having to buy, install, or manage your own servers. You run your company's IT operations simply using a browser and a high-speed Internet connection. Applications (SaaS), middleware (PaaS), servers (IaaS), and network switches all sit in the cloud and are managed by your cloud-computing vendor. The cloud ecosystem continues to evolve requiring continuous awareness of the growing cloud ecosystem by your vendor management. Moving out of the comfort zone of IaaS (a focus of traditional utility-based adoption) and onward to BPaaS and SaaS planning will be required.

Utility computing is often compared to public utilities and the metered accounting and billing mechanisms for electricity, water, and other services rendered. Cloud computing can solely be the fifth utility, providing IT as a service. During the mainframe days, multiple users who were charged for the actual system resources consumed shared a computer. As with cloud, mainframes are centralized, which drive costs down due to economies of scale and increased efficiencies due to the use of a high performing computer and timesharing, which made the mainframe more affordable for both small and large companies.

Utility computing and its corresponding pay-per-use subscription style services and flexible pricing structures should be included as a part of your cloud adoption strategy in an effort to meet your consumption-based goals for consumers. A difference in strategy, however, is that with cloud, you are not limited to IT-focused outsourcing (as is the case with utility computing). Instead, your emphasis is to optimize your business processes, which might very well involve outsourcing all four of the service types described in this chapter.

Grid computing links disparate computers over a network (public, private, or Internet) to form a virtual system that solves problems that have large processing requirements, often by dividing them into smaller ones and carrying out computations simultaneously. Grid or high performance computing (HPC) options should be considered as a part of your overall cloud adoption strategy particularly for those large workloads that require distributed, parallel, and specialized processing. Remember to discuss the risks and alternatives with your stakeholders and of course your cloud provider unless you elect to be the provider and consumer.

Several benefits accrue from leveraging the cloud as a fifth utility. These include eliminating the need for upgrades, dealing with down systems, and war rooms for trying to find or fix infrastructure issues. Just as with any utility the cloud is always on, 24 by 7, which may provide availability improvement and continuous service. The ability to access any application from anywhere is a powerful capability of cloud as the fifth utility. Sites that must be adjusted for spikes because of promotions are advanced as cloud adjusts to the site's performance needs.

Finally, cash flow is improved with a subscription or pay-as-you go model.

6. Specify Cloud Ecosystem

Your cloud adoption strategy should be viewed as a supply chain that delivers computing power, BPM platforms, analytical platforms, development platforms, services and applications such as CRM or ERP, and other services. Like all supply chains its requires governance to address privacy and security, and must be actively managed and optimized for all stakeholders. The supply chain may contain a hybrid of service types and deployment models. Cloud computing will be a driver for increasing business value, where an early Stage 1 of your cloud computing supply chain is to standardize and baseline where opportunities (i.e., cloud use cases) exist for innovation and business improvement. Stage 2 is characterized by its focus on capital preservation, cost reductions, and IT efficiency improvements. Stage 3 stresses innovation, where the business takes advantage of new opportunities that were not as viable without cloud computing. Stage 4 extends cloud computing to partners, suppliers, and the outside world. This indicates that when choosing suppliers great care should be given toward establishing your network of strategic partners, building both short- and long-term relationships, and utilizing your ecosystem in a way that maximizes business growth and stability.

In the past, the notion of the extended enterprise centered on business partner relationships coupled with end-to-end supply chain management. Cloud has, however, brought a different perspective to the concept. The performance of your business is only as good as the performance of your cloud, which as a consumer you may not have total control over. Your cloud adoption strategy describes actions in accordance with your defined enterprise boundaries. For example, it makes sense to express requirements for on- and off-premise visibility into the performance of business critical cloud services. On the other hand, the use of search engines, for example, Google, Yahoo, or Microsoft's® Bing, is noncritical, and therefore monitoring the information flow using worldwide repositories as results are retrieved is simply not necessary.

What is relevant, however, is to know what providers are doing with your data. For instance, besides returning results, you want to understand how companies are using your credentials, such as who are your providers reporting what you search on to and why, and what are your provider's content management policies?[3]

Your choices for cloud solutions must consider interoperability and integration within your existing environment. If, for instance, you are considering cloud services for your payroll needs, what are your intentions for in-house payroll systems and processes so that you do not open the door to fraudulent activities? It is important to consider and plan to eliminate duplicate processing and systems, as certainly you want your company to operate in a consistent manner, adhere to regulatory guidelines, and maintain all required certifications. In addition to performance efficiencies, this approach helps you prevent inappropriate systems use or fraud. Subsequently, your cloud provider's security model must integrate with your existing security framework. Where it doesn't, you should develop compensating controls or document and accept the risk.

You must also be careful to control and maintain a system of record of information, such as customer and billing data. If you do not do this, you will end up with duplicate or excessive data sources that are difficult to maintain and defeat the purpose of your investment in cloud, one of which is simplifying business complexities.

You must consider the integration of cloud and the implications of using cloud within your organization, across business units, across other enterprises, and within the cloud itself. And as a consumer, one of your central objectives should be to leverage cloud to simplify business operations. So while an element of trust is established between consumers and providers, both parties can manage several requirements. For example, explicit service level requirements—policies such as nondisclosures, proactive management of information sources including establishing a single system of record, and more importantly, appropriate and viable service level agreements and operations (SLAs and SLOs).

7. Determine and Publish Stakeholder Involvement

It can be daunting to figure out who should be involved in the development and evolution of your cloud adoption strategy; however, the bottom line is your strategy should not be developed in a silo, given that the information and insights that you need to establish a solid strategy are dispersed throughout your organization. Understanding that this is easier said than done, the more socialization on the relevancy of the adoption to your business, and the more you listen and apply pertinent considerations from enterprise stakeholders including business partners and buyers as well as sellers of your services, the more effective and actionable your strategy becomes.

Consider the article, "Spotlight on the effective organization: the execution trap," published by Harvard Business Review (HBR), in which the author describes a choice-cascade model for strategy evolution. The goal is to empower employees to willingly partake in the process as opposed to operating as "choiceless-doers"[4] of executive decisions. The author encourages bidirectional collaborations as signals that although executives might initiate strategies, they are open to feedback and reconsideration, which leads more readily to adoption. Continuous stakeholder involvement is essential to a successful cloud adoption strategy.

8. Develop Metrics

One way to measure the value of your adoption strategy as well as the value of using cloud in your enterprise is through the use of metrics. This requires understanding your existing environment to assess the implications of cloud decisions. Each metric should be traceable to your business goals and expected benefits so that you are effectively measuring the results, impacts, and business outcomes from cloud adoption.

The following examples provide a goal and corresponding metrics for measuring the impacts of your cloud adoption strategy:

Goal	Metric
Reuse of cloud adoption strategy to avoid cloud silos and cloud clutter	Number of cloud instances
	Reduction in capital expenditures
	Increase in number of customers
Improved customer satisfaction	Improved release cycles for projects due to automation and standardization
	Increased self-service opportunities

Additional metrics for measuring the impacts of cloud adoption can be developed for continuous improvement of your cloud adoption strategy:

- Who is spending what on cloud by measuring the cost of cloud by business unit
- How much does cloud cost as a percentage of line of business revenue
- Cost of cloud by workload
- Number of mobile applications deployed because of cloud
- Number of social media solutions enabled by cloud

- Reduction in IT queue by line of business
- Capital preservation by line of business
- Decrease in software license costs

9. Define Governance

Governance pertains to decision making at the right time by the right business and technical stakeholders where decisions are implemented and remain relevant in changing business conditions. Cloud-specific governance includes stakeholder and decision rights establishment and enablement, such as determining authority figures for procuring solutions and the required level of stakeholder involvement; developing cloud decision making processes, for instance, deciding that internal social media usage is appropriate for collaboration while decisions are finalized through steering committee meetings; and management, which includes establishing and enforcing decommissioning policies for cloud providers.

Cloud silos or cloud clutter where the goals for cloud computing fragment or diffuse intent is a real possibility with any cloud adoption. Implementing a governance strategy provides consistency in data usage, integration, and policy management. Your cloud adoption strategy outlines the enterprise governance model that encompasses cloud. The governance model refines and prioritizes during roadmap creation and implementation. Chapter 5, "What About Governance?," provides an enterprise governance framework and elaborated discussions.

10. Develop Roadmaps

The purpose of the roadmap is to establish the technology investment initiatives and to lay the groundwork for realizing your cloud vision. The roadmap serves as a baseline for reviewing the plan and implementation strategy with the various stakeholders—thereby helping to establish a common cloud adoption strategy for communicating business strategy, technology strategy, and laying a clear path toward accomplishment of future business goals.

Your roadmaps describe the prioritized approach and alternatives for reaching your target state, your vision. The roadmap reflects immediate to three years of activity and includes targeted rates of adoption as well as metrics. The metrics are used to assess continuously the success of the roadmap item and to adjust as necessary. Roadmaps are derived from the entry points with the necessary details to move forward with cloud adoption while maintaining optimal business performance. Your roadmaps are reflective of your current and anticipated business conditions. For instance, if new product development is underway in your organization, it is reasonable to commence your adoption with marketing and sales divisions in anticipation of increased product advertisements and order fulfillment workloads. The archetypal usage scenarios should be codified as actual use cases providing input of actual initiatives or projects in the roadmap.

The emergence of governance maturity models provides an opportunity to further develop a roadmap. For example, most emerging models leverage the Capability Maturity Model Integration (CMMI) process approach, where the goal is to help organizations improve performance. CMMI provides five maturity levels:

- **Level 1:** Initial where processes are unpredictable and poorly controlled
- **Level 2:** Managed characterizes processes are now controlled and managed
- **Level 3:** Defined where proactive management of processes and standards are in place
- **Level 4:** Quantitatively managed where processes are measured
- **Level 5:** Optimized where the focus is on process improvement

In cloud computing, several such models (search "Cloud Maturity Models") have been published that should be reviewed for applicability. Your roadmap may encompass moving toward level 5 of such maturity models, or you may elect to develop your own maturity model. Your roadmap describes how you advance in your defined maturity model. You will learn more on applying CMMI in Chapter 3, "The Life Cycle of Your Enterprise Cloud Adoption Strategy."

Harvesting the Value

An executive once stated, "If I forgot and left my strategy on an airplane and it was retrieved by a competitor, I would not be concerned. Strategy does not work because it's articulated or written down, strategy works if people can implement the strategy." Strategies become paper-weights when there is no viable roadmap and the governance to make the strategy happen. Strategies become nightmares when coupled with expensive and time-consuming transformational and restructuring activities. Your cloud adoption strategy can avoid these pitfalls with a vision grounded in use cases that produce strategic and tactical business outcomes, governance focused on continuous improvement, metrics designed to determine what's working and what's not, and a roadmap that incrementally reaches the vision by creating outcomes that matter to the business. Without a cloud adoption strategy focused on meeting the expectations outlined, you are gambling with the performance of cloud computing making a strategic, positive impact to your business.

Strategic planning and adoption guides decisions pertaining to the inclusion and deliberate omission of cloud and helps realize and measure the benefits that led to initial considerations. Examples are increased profits, faster and more efficient procurement of assets, development of products and services that customers want, optimized ROI, a more agile and elastic capacity to adjust to changing market conditions, easier integration of cloud services, and innovative opportunities to expediently bring competitive products and differentiating solutions to bear.

Summary

Our economic climate forces us to make our companies lean and efficient with a strategic "lookout" for opportunities to do more with less. As we recover from the economic downturn, many of you are expressing the intent to continue on the lean path and are turning to cloud for performance efficiencies, service optimization, and demonstrable financial advantage. This is why it is important to develop a cloud adoption strategy that helps identify where to begin and how to successfully proceed with your journey. Your strategy must encompass candidate scenario enablers along with the actual cloud services, and you must develop roadmaps that drive positive, realistic business outcomes.

Your cloud adoption strategy is a critical success factor for providers who need to be able to respond to your requirements for cloud computing and provide specifics on how they will meet service level agreements. It is prudent to leverage cloud providers and vendors while forming your cloud adoption strategy as they will be integral in its development and implementation.

Cloud adoption strategies should be innovative and actionable; the intention should be on business innovation, increasing business agility, and while dealing with a world of increasing complexity, optimizing your return on investment, and lowering your total cost of ownership to preserve capital. Without a strategy your vision might be compromised and growth and assurance of business value diminished over time due to planning shortfalls and disappointing business results.

This chapter discussed ten expectations of a cloud adoption strategy, including a vision for leveraging and increasing cloud computing value and benefits that can be realized when the expectations are fulfilled. Success depends on the ability to integrate across your value chain (internal and external) and build upon the capabilities provided by others as well as learned expertise. The next two chapters share activities and techniques for developing a cloud adoption strategy and further elaborates Sharon's interchange with Distributors, Inc.

Endnotes

1. Gartner, Inc. By 2012, 20 percent of businesses will own no IT assets. See http://www.gartner.com/it/page.jsp?id=1278413. Appirio, Inc., has reported operating as a serverless enterprise with all applications running on a cloud platform from day 1. See case study at http://www.slideshare.net/appirio/appirio-case-study-serverless-enterprise-march-2010-3494546.

2. National Institute of Standards and Technology, Information Technology Laboratory. See http://mattcegelske.com/wp-content/uploads/2012/03/NIST-SP800-145.pdf.

3. Samson, T., 2010. "Google and Facebook Clash over Data Sharing." Infoworld. November 2010. See http://www.infoworld.com/t/data-security/google-and-facebook-clash-over-data-sharing-833?source=IFWNLE_nlt_blogs_2010-11-10.

4. Martin, R. L. 2010. "Spotlight on the Effective Organization: The Execution Trap." *Harvard Business Review* (July-August, 2010). See http://hbr.org/2010/07/the-execution-trap/ar/1.

2

Business Value of Incorporating Cloud into Your EA

Sharon and her team conducted cloud adoption interviews with C-suite executives as well as business and IT leaders at Distributors, Inc., to further understand their business objectives and requirements. Findings revealed the desire for cloud-sourcing was driven by the lack of in-house resources to deliver products and services to market when needed. Issues pertaining to business and IT performance levels were shared, and high frustration levels were evident among some of the interviewees.

Some of the interviewees displayed confidence that cloud-sourcing was the way to go, but this information was based solely on what they read and from some competitor testimonials. IT leaders were in agreement with cloud adoption because they were stretched thin in their day jobs and would benefit from the help. On the other hand, not all IT leaders agreed that all IT capability would or should be delivered from the cloud.

However, what Sharon found most interesting were insights on why the focus now on cloud, and what some described as new technology architecture. There was a perception that the diverse and complex environment in play at Distributors, Inc., was built because of silo planning and that current IT course and speed do not support Distributors' growth plans nor was it sustainable in the long term.

Business trends were unmistakable: time to market pressures, diverse regulatory environments, and the continuous cost and margin pressures. Several Distributors, Inc., executives commented that new growth must be sustained by entering new markets and countries. Currently, this was a challenge given margin pressures and the cost of putting IT capabilities in those markets.

Sharon and her team made recommendations for Distributors to strategically move forward with cloud. In the process, she shared with the team that cloud should be incorporated into the enterprise architecture (EA) for current and future-state cloud adoption, and why this incorporation would be required to achieve tactical and strategic objectives of cloud computing. She further discussed the business value of such actions as EA advances business and IT strategy through codifying best practices and through its approach to governance—the key organizational construct that ensures your strategic intent is realized through initiatives and projects.

Your Integrated Business and IT Strategy

As EA evolves and becomes focused on business value outcomes[1] through coordinated efforts of business and IT, it is important that cloud is incorporated accelerating time to value. This inclusion is particularly necessary for understanding the impacts of adoption and generating shared value across your enterprise network. With cloud considerations incorporated in EA, several assertions come to life:

- Your cloud adoption strategy becomes business centric and cost efficient.
- Your enterprise increases agility.
- You gain more benefits from enterprise portfolio management.
- Your projects when implemented naturally conform to cloud enterprise standards due to the holistic and federated nature of EA.

The federal government, for instance, applies federated EA[2] (Federal Enterprise Architecture) principles for strategic alignment of initiatives, information, real-time portfolio management, and asset reuse. A financial services company encompasses cloud in its enterprise reference architecture to sustain situational-based card services enablement that includes standardized on-boarding and credit verification services. More details of these case studies and additional examples can be found in

Appendix B, "Cloud Case Studies and Common Questions." These examples demonstrate how the adoption of cloud improves agility and enables increased value across your value networks.

Your EA is an evolving representation of your enterprise strategy and business platform. That is, EA incorporates both the business and IT architecture and specifies the standards necessary for realization. EA should be written and stored in a way that makes it easy for all stakeholders to leverage. Ensuring projects can exploit the architecture standard cloud components requires each part to be described and published in an easy-to-use, easy-to-find catalog style and format. Incorporating cloud considerations (public, private, and hybrid) and other aspects adds value by strengthening your business agility.

Business agility is the collective capabilities and constructs allowing a business to continuously transform to achieve its business outcomes, be predictive, flexible, responsive, and launch business initiatives in times of change and uncertainty. EA with cloud incorporated provides a catalogue of these capabilities. The ability of a business to continuously adapt rapidly, effectively, and cost efficiently in response to changes in the business environment is business agility, and EA increases the opportunity for such. Adoption of cloud enables organizations to nimbly adjust to and take advantage of emerging opportunities. For example, the use of cloud can reveal opportunities that support the dynamic means in which you conduct business (today, it's Internet and desktop productivity for your employees and lines of business, and tomorrow, it might be that you run entire business operations from smart phones).

The perception of some prominent stakeholders is that EA is an IT responsibility that exists solely to serve the IT community. However, such adoption patterns fail to take advantage of the value of EA. EA must include both business aspects of the enterprise as well as underlying IT and operational strategies. In fact, the way your business processes are managed can be a differentiator for you in the marketplace in terms of agility, growth and industry perception; and internally in terms of performance optimization and speed. The transformational impacts of cloud on your business (not just IT) warrant enterprise consideration and thus EA inclusion.

EA should be a living and evolving construct embodying business and IT strategic and tactical ends. Considering this context, EA is defined throughout this book as your integrated business and IT strategy, which considers and directly influences your operational model. Cloud is incorporated within your EA to drive business and IT alignment and adoption; and to ensure consideration of internal and external enterprise ecosystems with the adoption. Some expected outcomes are business value endurance, enhanced ROI (return on investment), service optimization, and stronger business performance. A primary value proposition of EA is driving portfolio planning in a strategic context and directing change toward common enterprise goals. This is a primary reason why cloud should be incorporated into your EA, so that the right changes relative to readying your organization for cloud are determined and enacted in the right way.

Figure 2.1 depicts EA with cloud incorporated. When cloud is incorporated into your EA, you naturally form an enterprise cloud adoption

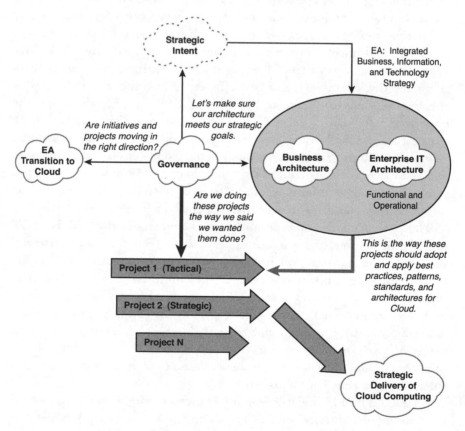

Figure 2.1   EA enables your integrated business and IT strategy where Cloud Computing is incorporated to form your enterprise cloud adoption strategy.

strategy. Identifying viable projects that help realize your cloud adoption requires a good set of *models*, capable of portraying the overall "as is" and "to be" architectural landscape. EA provides these models for your cloud adoption strategy.

Chapter 3, "The Life Cycle of Your Enterprise Cloud Adoption Strategy," elaborates on this topic with demonstrable examples on how to incorporate cloud into your EA, and you find various viewpoints on how to illustrate the core EA domains (business architecture, information systems architecture, technology/infrastructure architecture, and governance) with embedded cloud considerations. Each of these domains supports respective cloud adoption entry points as discussed in Chapter 1, "Business Value of a Cloud Adoption Strategy," enabling you to determine the best, holistic strategy for your business.

For organizations that might not have an EA or don't effectively use an EA, an upcoming section, "What If You Do Not Use EA?," elaborates, with business scenarios, why EA should become visible and actionable in your organization. The business benefits of embracing EA, for effective enterprise cloud adoption, is described using examples.

Business Benefits of the Convergence

What are the impacts of your converged business, IT, and cloud strategy? Convergence allows you to exploit all the benefits of cloud: consumption based pricing models, speedy builds and delivery of products and services, on-demand provisioning and decommissioning of what you need when you need it with impacts that positively affect your enterprise core capabilities and beyond.

A primary benefit of convergence is business *agility*. Incorporating cloud within EA enables you to better predict and respond to market changes and environmental pressures rapidly and with optimal effectiveness, which drives organizational agility that extends beyond technology. Critical to measuring the effectiveness of convergence is the use of the following:

- **Key agility indicators (KAIs):** How well your business can adapt to change. KAI measures how well your company is sensing and able to respond to the market fluctuations. Example KAIs are time to collaborate across your enterprise network, your speed to adapt to a merger or an acquisition prior to its occurrence, and time to reflect market demands into your enterprise strategy.

- **Key performance indicators (KPIs):** How well you are performing business as usual. KPIs measure your business based on performance or an occurrence of an event. Example KPIs are rate of cloud adoption and percent of business processes eliminated.

As Figure 2.2 illustrates, increased business agility, which is an outcome of the convergence, has a positive impact on your business's performance.

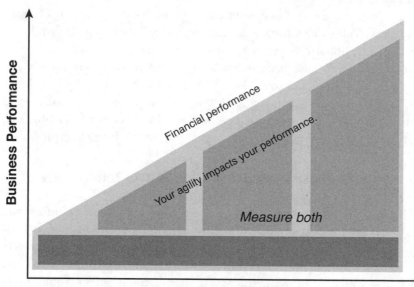

Figure 2.2   Business agility positively impacts business performance.

A *second* benefit of convergence is federation. Investing in cloud that serves a single department or sits idle is a waste of resources. Federation facilitates leveraging the cloud to a wider set of stakeholders within the enterprise. Experiences show that federation should not be an after-thought but a keen part of your enterprise strategy. Think about the business complexities and adoption possibilities such as on-premise; off-premise; security; all, part, or none of your business sourced from cloud; varying service-types; and more, and the enterprise interoperability requirements to support varying cloud scenarios.

Figure 2.3 illustrates how federation can be applied to optimize adoption of departmental approved clouds. In the example, you as a consumer request services from your private cloud (Cloud A) that applies your EA standards and regulatory requirements to collaborate with other approved public or private clouds to address your business requirements. Federation, in this example, is about enterprise clouds seamlessly and legally using other clouds to meet service level commitments. Legality is important because the federated pattern takes into account enterprise regulatory requirements and governmental restrictions. Two significant benefits of applying federation are no additional asset investment expenses and no additional sign on efforts, both due to the shared services aspects of federation.

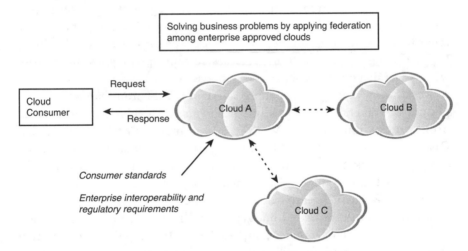

Figure 2.3 Federation example

Many organizations begin EA at a divisional and propagate processes and assets across divisions while respecting autonomy and specialized departmental requirements. This concept is known as federation, where each division retains autonomy while at the same time standardized practices are introduced and applied in the organization. On a financial services engagement, for instance, executive sponsors expressed specific requirements to commence definition of EA, first as a model for the Asset Management division, followed with strategic planning, reuse, and governance across other organizations. With cloud embedded in EA, the natural application of federation contributes to greater rewards and sustained use of cloud investments.

For organizations that are early adopters of cloud, the best practices that you apply and the experiences that you gain should be incorporated into your EA so that other business divisions and tactical initiatives apply the same best practices.

In the early stages of cloud adoption, it is natural to consider Infrastructure-as-a-Service (IaaS) or Platform-as-a-Service (PaaS) as an entry point. Because these are infrastructure related, you might consider sole reliance on IT teams to determine your cloud opportunities, or you might bypass IT as a whole and empower business units to purchase solutions that are readily available. The problem with this model, and this happens quite often, is the omission of integrated stakeholder perspectives and thus the omission of an integrated cloud strategy. So regardless of your role, you need to consider the perspectives of business, IT, and potential users of these services so that optimized value is realized as you make cloud adoption decisions.

Recall from the chapter-opening scenario that Sharon listened to complaints of stakeholders regarding performance levels that resulted in high frustration levels. Well, a prominent problem was that Distributors' business and IT teams operated in isolation and did not coordinate work efforts. This behavior resulted in IT solutions that the business did not want and solutions that were delivered too late. In addition, the business units did not set clear or realistic expectations, primarily due to misaligned budgeting and planning processes between the two teams. This is an example of organizational behaviors that should not be carried forward with cloud adoption.

Instead, a *third* benefit of convergence, improved collaborations, should transpire. Sharon brought this issue to the team's attention and offered ways to improve collaborations using basic EA principles. EA governance and business architecture (BA) helps you identify the required coordination and tools necessary for achieving cross-collaborative business solutions, while adding tangible business value.

Executives generally view enterprise architects as front-line contacts and a conduit for translating business needs into IT needs. They trust the advice of enterprise architects to guide them with thought leadership and best practices. This means your EA practitioners need to be well informed and able to discuss advantages and disadvantages of cloud in the context of business enablement and transformation. At the same time, decision makers look to your EA as a foundation for cloud enablement and a baseline for making strategic adoption decisions. If enterprise architect resources are ill-equipped, or unavailable, decision makers might turn to less reliable sources for guidance, which simply does not lead to positive outcomes. Accordingly, a *fourth* benefit of convergence is sustained trust and emerging reliance on EA resources for cloud purposes. Consider the following:

- Consumers rely on EA for simplicity in cloud adoption, which involves interoperability with existing enterprise initiatives and standardization (e.g., self-service catalogs or integration with existing IT—front, middle, and back office—solutions and services). Simplicity in this context means your ability to make more informed decisions is easier due to readily available information that is represented through EA, while enabling faster fulfillment of service requests.

- Providers rely on EA for enablement requirements such as the network, storage, and relative assets so that cloud services perform. An added capability, such as ubiquitous access to your cloud, enables consumers to use their technology of choice from any location at any given time and thus adds to your value as a service provider. At the same time, performance of your network (which is generally taken for granted) can negatively impact your credibility if consumers perceive slowness or bottlenecks.

- Systems integrators rely on EA for an understanding of business core competencies and cross-agency or line of business collaboration—they use these inputs to help customers choose business processes and associated workloads that are suitable for cloud.

Figure 2.4 illustrates some scenarios that must be considered when determining whether cloud is appropriate for your company. Reading from the top left to right, the consumer leverages a storefront to purchase cloud solutions from a marketplace. Business support services (BSS) are components put in place by providers so that you can order cloud services. Some examples are the service offering catalog or as illustrated in the marketplace, your dashboard profile and entitlements, pricing and rating of services, accounting and billing of services per the terms and conditions, and offering management. The BSS are the components that you, the consumer, see and directly interface with.

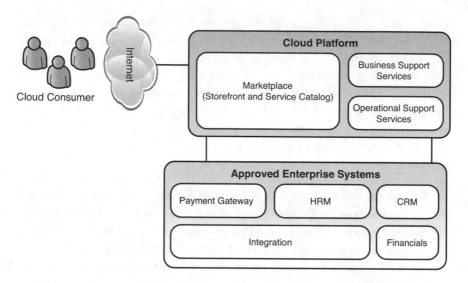

Figure 2.4   Leverage EA to guide cloud integration decisions

Operational support services (OSS) are required to run the cloud environment; these components actually carry out your specific service requests. While the component details are seamless to you, some core capabilities are service provisioning, monitoring and event management, automation, virtualization, image management, incident management, and capacity/performance management. Your EA should contain a list of company approved service offerings and providers. Your EA should provide guidelines for cloud vendor selection as well as BSS/OSS considerations.

Your backend systems are significant when it comes to cloud consumption. As discussed in the previous chapter, it is important that should you choose to leverage the cloud for key processes that you avoid duplicate systems and processes, and maintain a single system of record of data. In the example, the consumers' enterprise standard is to use a predetermined payment gateway to process online payments while accounts are managed using the Financials system that, in this case, addresses billing and subscriber reconciliations. Your EA should be a reference point for you to understand approved enterprise systems and all official systems of record. This information helps you understand the key integrations so that your decision to adopt cloud is holistically thought through and the impacts of adoption are understood from a companywide point of view.

Again, returning to the specifics in the chapter-opening case study, Sharon evaluated the core competencies of the division in scope, and based on ROI and risk analysis along with her understanding of business goals, drivers, key processes, and pain points—all attributes of BA—she produced a prioritized list of cloud enablement and service candidates. At the top of the list were marketing and advertising and a Human Resource Information System (HRIS) in which she proposed vendor evaluations as part of the requirements for BPaaS and SaaS enablement. Key vendor assessment areas include financial viability, product strategy, industry-specific compensation management, and pricing for services. Key functional assessment areas include campaign management, performance management, and key HR and payroll processes. Interestingly enough, IaaS and PaaS opportunities were identified, but Sharon did not isolate these as suggested entry points.

In a nutshell, your EA should be leveraged to influence your cloud investments along with any usage and integration decisions. When you can think about EA and cloud in the same breath with coordinated processes and resources, then you have an EA that can execute at the speed of business. This is why an investment in EA is prudent—to equip and enable your business with the right technologies and resources at the right time.

Developing Your Enterprise Cloud Adoption Strategy

Keeping in mind that EA is your integrated business and IT strategy, you can leverage the EA methodology to prepare and validate your cloud adoption strategy, as depicted in Figure 2.5. The EA method is applied to form your enterprise cloud adoption strategy. This leads to a *fifth* benefit of convergence, which is optimized ROI and total cost of ownership (TCO), where a significant portion of this optimization is attributed to strategic asset development and reuse. Recall the expectations of your cloud adoption strategy were described in Chapter 1 with elaborations on both ROI and TCO.

The following is a list of steps (or phases) for defining and evolving EA with cloud incorporated. The section demonstrates a prescriptive technique to prepare and validate your cloud adoption strategy. You use EA to identify and prioritize cloud enablement and service candidates, establish an adoption roadmap, and conduct governance of the cloud implementation and adoption. As you read on, it is important to note that the method is cyclical, iterative, and agile in nature for continuous improvement and that each phase builds upon capabilities and lessons learned from the previous phases. For your reference, Table 2.1 succeeds the method discussion with a listing of the ten expectations discussed in Chapter 1 and a mapping to an EA methodology.

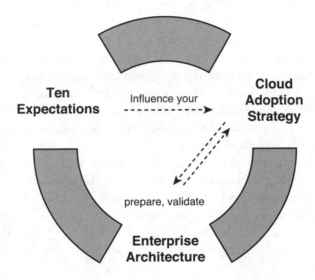

Figure 2.5   Leverage EA to prepare and validate your enterprise cloud adoption strategy

1. **Conduct initial planning:** Conduct initial planning of the engagement, determine stakeholder requirements, and determine your delivery approach. This phase is often referenced as the homework phase. During this phase, you plan activities that enable you to determine your cloud adoption goals and objectives.

2. **Understand your current enterprise capabilities and establish your vision:** Conduct evaluations of the business and IT (including operational) landscape. Include company resources (people, process, information, and technology) and the capabilities required for establishing your cloud vision.

   Here is where you determine your cloud position as a company.

3. **Baseline and define your future state business architecture:** Using a prescriptive approach, capture the following items so that it is clear which relationships create value for the business and to ensure that an appropriate level of traceability exists for managing change as your company transforms and grows:[3]

- Your goals
- Your business mission and objectives
- Key business functions
- Key business interactions and interrelationships with partners, vendors, and external entities
- Business assets and other resources available to support business operations; business operations, standards and guidelines
- Business process models
- Key performance and agility indicators relative to the various business processes
- Business information model, which is the key information required to run your scope of business

Here is where commencement of cloud enablement and service candidates occurs, integrating with your business architecture (BA). In this phase, your governance approach is also determined and outlined. Business Process-as-a-Services (BPaaS) enablement is a focus area, and it is expected that BA will influence cloud adoption decisions in the other domains.

4. **Baseline and define your future state application architecture and data architecture:** Derive which information systems are relevant to your company, and what those systems need to do; determine the required applications and the major types of information sources, content, and high level relationships.

   Here is where commencement of your cloud enablement and service candidates occurs and integrates with your information systems architecture. Software-as-a-Service (SaaS) enablement is a focus area, and it is expected that associated application and data requirements will influence cloud adoption decisions in downstream domains.

5. **Baseline and define your future state technology and infrastructure architectures:** Map application and information requirements from the previous step into a set of software, middleware, and hardware building blocks.

   Here is where commencement of your cloud enablement and service candidates occurs and integrates with your technology and infrastructure architecture. PaaS and IaaS enablement are general focus areas and cloud-specific decisions should be traceable to steps 3 and 4 to help drive business value.

6. **Conduct strategic gap analysis and transition planning:** Derived from a compilation of the findings collected during steps 2 through 5, conduct strategic gap analysis and prepare transition plans for evolving to your target state. Gaps include identification of key building blocks, such as the need to re-train staff to support the identified cloud business opportunities.

   Here is where your enterprise cloud adoption roadmaps are formed.

7. **Conduct implementation planning:** Using inputs from the prior steps, prepare implementation plans to ensure that activities are coordinated and prioritized.

   Here is where your cloud implementation plans are developed and projects initiated.

8. **Govern the implementation:** Govern the EA and ensure that projects are implemented to the standards and per the strategic roadmap. Determine how change is to be managed and include methodologies and tools.

   While governance is an ongoing activity, here is where governance of your cloud implementation commences.

Table 2.1   Checklist: Strategy Expectations and EA Mapping

Expectations	EA Methodology
Create your cloud vision.	Conduct initial planning.
	Understand your current enterprise capabilities.
	Establish your vision.
Identify cloud use cases.	Baseline and define your future state business architecture.
	Baseline and define your future state information systems architecture.
	Baseline and define your future state infrastructure architecture.
	Govern the implementation.
Drive business innovation.	Define your future state business architecture.
	Govern the implementation.
Define business outcomes and projected ROI.	Conduct initial planning.
	Understand your current enterprise capabilities and establish your vision.
	Govern the implementation.

Table 2.1 Checklist: Strategy Expectations and EA Mapping

Expectations	EA Methodology
Determine opportunities for cloud as a fifth utility.	Baseline and define your future state business architecture.
	Baseline and define your future state information systems architectures.
	Baseline and define your future state infrastructure architecture.
	Govern the implementation.
Specify cloud eco system.	Conduct strategic gap analysis and transition planning.
	Conduct implementation planning.
Determine and publish stakeholder involvement.	Understand your current enterprise capabilities and establish your vision.
	Govern the implementation.
Develop metrics.	Define your future state business architecture.
	Govern the implementation.
Define governance.	Govern the implementation.
Develop roadmaps.	Conduct strategic gap analysis and transition planning.
	Conduct implementation planning.

NOTE

The EA methodology described in this section is derived using the TOGAF framework as a baseline with modifications added to support cloud adoption. TOGAF is an industry standard architecture framework that might be used freely by any organization that wants to develop an information systems architecture for use within that organization.[4]

What If You Do Not Use EA?

In practice, it is unlikely that you do not have an EA because it is your integrated business and IT strategy, but it is likely that the discipline of EA is not practiced at all or it is practiced insufficiently. Referencing Figure 2.5, recall the terms prepare and validate. The diagram implies that although not required, EA is recommended to validate that you meet the ten expectations, but more importantly to ensure preparation and development of an actionable enterprise cloud adoption strategy.

The scenarios in the following sections demonstrate the three business benefits of embracing EA principles to develop your strategy:

- Effective business transformation
- Reducing costs and redundancies
- Developing or refining your enterprise cloud adoption strategy

Scenario 1: Effective Business Transformation

Distributors, Inc., required assurance that public cloud adoption would transform business operations without causing downtimes. This assurance was in direct response to executive support of using cloud services to improve product delivery cycles and to apply widespread adoption—beyond immediate departmental needs. Though Distributors did not have an EA (per se), Sharon worked closely with the vice president of business process transformation and the recently hired enterprise architect applying business architecture (BA) concepts and governance to gain an understanding of goals and drivers, key corporate events, and categorizations of differentiating and rudimentary processes. This approach enabled her to determine opportunities to improve business operations with cloud-sourcing. Together, they formed a visual depiction of the EA with an emphasis on BA as an immediate starting point and for future reference for others to use to guide cloud decision making.

Sharon addressed each of the ten expectations including initial formation and prioritization of cloud enablement and service candidates, and the team developed a three-year enterprise cloud adoption roadmap. Significant benefits were the opportunity to offload rudimentary workloads to cloud, a shift of IT resources to focus on more strategic and business critical tasks, improved governance and coordination of budget and planning activities across business and IT, and refinements to existing governance processes to include cloud as well as other enterprise recommendations.

Scenario 2: Reducing Costs and Redundancies

A South African cell phone company experienced test and development environment resource availability issues, poor scheduling processes for sharing resources, and a significant amount of test server waste due to poor enterprise governance and management. The company experienced a situation where every project request for test and development resources was easily approved and virtualized capacity went unreleased once development-testing initiatives were completed.

Building and maintaining the enterprise environments that now incorporate cloud involved a multitude of tasks that required involvement and coordination across various teams. The team embraced EA governance and management to overcome the obstacles generated from a complex, hybrid IT landscape with issues that included an over proliferation of cloud environments and an architecture review board that needed to actively engage in cloud adoption, procurement, and exception processes.

In this case study, the financial benefits were projected over a five-year timeframe to be $1.9 M, breakeven (BE) in 8 months, net present value (NPV) of $1.9M, and a total return on investment (ROI) of 316 percent. You can find more on this case study in Appendix B.

Scenario 3: Validating and Forming Your Enterprise Cloud Adoption Strategy

Provider A (a private cloud provider in financial services) reviewed the ten expectations of a cloud adoption strategy and conducted a formal assessment to address each for an organization. Provider A created the adoption strategy referencing an industry provided EA methodology that contained steps similar to those described in this chapter as a checkpoint and for validation of the completeness of the strategy. Provider A ultimately formed an enterprise cloud adoption strategy, executed the strategy, and continues evolution today.

While this initiative was an infrastructure focus at the start, the strong business collaboration and interdependencies excited the business units in a manner that they actively engaged and are planning use of the cloud solutions to accelerate their business models. In addition, IT organizational improvements surfaced and were implemented as a result of cross-divisional teaming that include centralizing a decentralized IT organization.

Summary

When you think about cloud, you may likely presume that you don't need an EA, thinking that you will outsource all of your business needs to someone else. In reality, you need your EA for overall business continuity whether you consider cloud-sourcing as a small or large percentage of your operations. In fact, your EA is more critical the more you leverage system integrators and third parties for your delivery of IT services. EA provides both the standards and guidelines for third parties to operate while providing you with the framework for bringing back in-house at selected times those services or capabilities that provide better return if sourced in-house.

Your integrated business and IT strategy ensures that your business will perform by first and foremost enabling your company for cloud consumption and second, focusing your company on choosing the right strategy, projects, and business solutions for the business outcomes that make a difference. From an adoption perspective, you can use EA to identify and prioritize enablement candidates and cloud services, establish an adoption roadmap, and conduct governance of the adoption in your organization. The following list summarizes the value statements of incorporating cloud into your EA as discussed in this chapter:

- Business agility which directly attributes to performance optimization
- Federation
- Increased collaboration
- Sustained and emerging EA capabilities
- Optimized cloud ROI and TCO
- Integrated business transformation
- Reduced costs and redundancies
- Enterprise cloud adoption strategy

Discussed were correlations between organizations with an EA, well-defined or not, and techniques for meeting the ten strategic expectations of a cloud adoption strategy (from Chapter 1). Included also is a section specifically for those who may not have or use EA, or feel as though your EA is inadequately applied in your organization. To help clarify some of the benefits of embracing EA principles in your cloud adoption, three business scenarios were provided—one of which is Distributors, Inc. Although the use of EA principles is optional, the scenarios share benefits of applying some key principles to prepare or refine your strategy for cloud adoption so that you reap optimal benefits.

While this chapter focused on the business value of incorporating cloud into your EA, the next chapter introduces you to the life cycle of an enterprise cloud adoption strategy, sharing practical guidance and some applied experiences on how to augment your EA with cloud considerations. You will also find discussions relative to the applicability of service oriented architecture (SOA) and the implications to your plans for cloud adoption.

Endnotes

1. Allega, Phillip et al. 2010. "Predicts 2011: Enterprise Architecture Shifting Focus to Business Value Outcomes." See http://www.gartner.com/DisplayDocument?doc_cd=208671.

2. According to the Department of Defense Enterprise Architecture Federation Strategy, the foundation for net-centric operations is to give users the ability to access the information and applications where and when needed. The key enabler is the DoD GIG, which will move from Net-Centric concepts to Net-Centric reality. See http://www.eng.auburn.edu/csse/classes/comp7700/resources/GIG_Architecture.doc.

3. Harishankar, R. et al. 2010. "Actionable Business Architecture." This whitepaper articulates the evolutionary aspects of BA and its contributions toward business transformation. See ftp://public.dhe.ibm.com/common/ssi/ecm/en/gbw03113usen/GBW03113USEN.PDF.

4. TOGAF is an industry standard architecture framework that may be used freely by any organization that wants to develop an information systems architecture for use within that organization. See http://www.opengroup.org/togaf/.

3

The Life Cycle of Your Enterprise Cloud Adoption Strategy

In the previous chapters, you learned about the business value of developing a cloud adoption strategy and the value of incorporating cloud into your enterprise architecture (EA). You also learned some EA principles that you can embrace to help you determine and develop the appropriate strategy for your company. Armed with an understanding of the value of enterprise architecture for cloud adoption, you are ready for this chapter, which describes the life cycle of your enterprise cloud adoption strategy, an outcome of integrating cloud into your EA. You use the life cycle as your foundation for strategically planning your cloud adoption as well as to evolve your EA to include cloud specific goals, cloud standards, best practices, and project guidance on cloud usage. The focus is "how and what to" incorporate to ready your company for success along your cloud adoption journey. In this chapter:

- You review supporting cloud adoption activities and learn key work artifacts—points of view for documenting details such as your organization's
  readiness for cloud adoption and models for capturing your cloud service
  portfolio. These work artifacts can be leveraged with cloud providers for
  requirements specificity, and they should be added to your EA so that
  your business goals are realized through active governance and management using EA.

■ You discover approaches and techniques for determining key considerations that help you recognize and capture cloud business opportunities so that you can develop the optimum strategy for cloud adoption in your enterprise.

■ You learn considerations for strategy development relevant to organizations that have incorporated service oriented architecture (SOA).

The life cycle is comprised of six phases, as illustrated in Figure 3.1:

1. Initial Planning
2. Enterprise Capabilities and Cloud Vision
3. Target Architecture and Cloud Enablers
4. Gap Analysis and Transition Planning
5. Implementation Planning
6. Governance

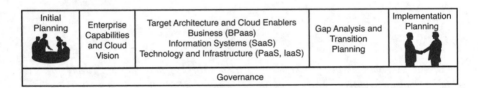

Figure 3.1   Strategically plan and position your company for successful cloud adoption.

The following sections examine each phase of the cloud adoption life cycle in greater detail.

Initial Planning

The initial planning phase involves exploration of your business to establish the context for enterprise cloud adoption and produce the initial, high level plan. You should review the existing case studies, such as those depicted in Appendix B, "Cloud Case Studies and Common Questions," to justify development and execution of your strategy.

In addition to business and IT executives, you should assign an enterprise architect with cloud business strategy and governance experiences as this leadership facilitates the process now and in subsequent phases. Requests for Information and Proposals (RFIs/RFPs) are submitted for budget, planning, preliminary return on investment (ROI) analysis, and vendor selection criteria are determined. Security considerations are incorporated throughout each phase as is governance.

NOTE

At this point, you are focused on determining and developing the appropriate cloud adoption strategy so vendors with synergistic strategies, adoption, and governance experiences are selected.

Key activities in the initial planning include

- **Determine business context:** Your business context helps stakeholders understand the purpose, goals and expected business outcomes for cloud adoption. Adoption of cloud computing must be treated as a strategic choice not a technology or outsourcing choice. Cloud is a huge change in how you acquire and use technology and how you interact and support your employees and your customers.

  Envision new opportunities, new markets, and where cloud computing accelerates the strategic direction of your company.

  Envision an IT infrastructure capable of supporting a rapidly changing business model—one in which IT is not a queue or bottleneck for new business capability.

  Envision a computing architecture in which platform or systems no longer constrain business agility—one in which business solutions could be composed rapidly and deployed on demand to any authorized user on any system, anywhere in the world.

  This is your vision for a powerful new computing architecture. This vision is not about building castles in the sky but rather about a target state for your new computing environment fueled by cloud computing.

- **Describe the business environment, boundaries, and targeted beneficiaries of your strategy:** This is where you get more specific using scenarios and or use cases to describe what will be possible, what will be different, what future business capabilities will be made possible with cloud computing.

  You examine the benefits of cloud adoption and these benefits translate to scenarios, which accelerate realizing strategic imperatives.

You work with key stakeholders to identify, detail, and prioritize use cases for cloud adoption. These use cases are specific and detailed such that all stakeholders see the value proposition of cloud adoption.

- **Determine required stakeholders:** Some lines of business or some business processes will gain greater value of cloud adoption than others. Adoption may create dependencies between stakeholders and processes. Hence, key stakeholders must be understood and identified by key initiatives for cloud adoption. Stakeholders can make or break the success of cloud adoption in terms of their willingness to sponsor the transformation required in organizational changes, governance, vendor partnerships, and possibly technology adoption. Stakeholder influence must be considered along with their ability to motivate and navigate their key influencers.

- **Explore cloud case studies:** Gaining visibility into what other companies have experienced as value, risks, and lessons learned from cloud adoption is essential. This requires working with analyst companies, technology vendors, and system integrators to understand the art of what is possible with cloud. Grounded in the context of actual successes of other companies' business results with cloud adoption.

- **Establish your approach for developing your strategy:** Making a determination of how the strategy will be developed and realized is essential. Strategy without implementation is worthless as it's the implementation of the strategy that creates business results. Developing a strategy armed with an actionable roadmap or plan is a requirement.

  Determining whether facilitated workshops, blogging or social collaboration, or all of the above will be used to solicit input and feedback for strategy development is required. This is where identifying the key stakeholders makes a difference because interviews with each will be required to define the approach as well as defining the strategy.

  Publishing your high level plan and a clear set of expectations for moving onward to the next phases of the life cycle is necessary.

- **Establish vendor selection criteria:** Understanding your partners necessary to realize your cloud adoption strategy defines key elements of your eco system for cloud adoption. Determining where gaps lie in your current cloud capabilities that are necessary to reach your vision makes it possible to radically improve and implement your cloud strategy. The vendor selection criterion becomes a tool for selecting and maintaining the necessary vendor and partner mix.

- **Secure executive sponsorship:** Identifying and gaining commitment from the necessary executives are fundamental to successful cloud adoption. Executive sponsors must possess authority to make binding decisions and the willingness to exercise this authority. Hence, executive sponsors must be cultivated.

Key work artifacts resulting from the initial planning include

- Business context, which describes the future for your organization in adopting cloud—for example, new business models enabled or new capabilities made possible.
- High level plan, which is more than a Gantt chart. It should consist of a plan of projects along with the expected business outcome to be realized, the project owner, metrics for gauging the success of the project, dependencies and risks that must be managed.

Enterprise Capabilities and Cloud Vision

It is essential that you understand your enterprise goals and objectives. You need this information so that you establish a realistic cloud adoption strategy, and just as with EA you want alignment between your enterprise vision and your strategic vision for cloud adoption so that activities and outcomes add value to your organization. Specifically, you want to understand your enterprise goals and objectives in the following areas:

- New capabilities that the business needs to bring to the market in the next 12 months
- Services or applications currently constrained due to time to market needs
- Opportunities to preserve capital or avoidance of operating expense
- Requirements or needs to provide ubiquitous access to consumers, customers, or devices
- Needs for improved scalability

Factoring in your understanding of enterprise goals and needs into the formation of your cloud vision provides the business context to make cloud computing transformational for your business. That is, the business use of technology changes as technology related business risk is identified and managed; and IT queues get eliminated as a barrier for creating new business capabilities.

All of this requires you to plan for governing your cloud adoption strategy as it ensures appropriate development with proper controls for progression with business continuity, and upon execution governs implementations so that cloud projects are in alignment with your strategy. The introduction of any new technology or technology paradigm shift creates pressure on the organization. Previously, enterprise architecture may have evolved solely to address internal provided technology solutions, and now it extends to address unique aspects of cloud computing in improving agility, enabling new business models, or simply preserving capital investments.

Questions such as the following must be answered during this phase of the life cycle:

- Is your business and IT aligned? If not, can cloud computing facilitate this convergence between business and IT?

- Do your applications and IT architecture support your changing market needs?

- Is your IT environment inflexible?

- How does your cloud adoption strategy support strategic imperatives—that is, your company's vision?

- How is your company performing today—that is, what's not working that would make a difference in business performance?

- Does cloud computing make your processes more effective and more efficient?

- What cloud business adoption patterns are suitable for your company?

- Who is accountable for making cloud adoption decisions?

- What is your organizational readiness capacity for cloud adoption?

- How will you ensure that your cloud adoption strategy is realized?

While you might have started preparation of your business case in the previous step, it is most likely that stakeholders require additional information to sustain initial approvals. In this second phase, you focus on understanding your overarching ability to undertake or extend business operations to support private, public, hybrid, and/or community clouds. Approaches for obtaining information include conducting visioning workshops and capability assessments. Pilots and/or proofs of concepts are optional, but highly recommended.

NOTE

It is important to recognize that a proof of concept (PoC) is not intended to be a production deliverable. It is generally applied to validate or demonstrate a capability such as a new technology or product feature. A pilot, on the other hand, is usually intended as an early production deliverable and requires change control and requirements management. Experiences show that projects can quickly get out of control when the two are inappropriately applied. For instance, your PoC becomes a production deliverable and you are soon required to manage defects although that was not the original intention, or there is no change control applied to the pilot and it therefore becomes dormant. Be sure to explicitly specify your desired outcomes (i.e., success criteria) and then plan your PoCs and pilots accordingly.

Key activities in the enterprise capabilities and cloud vision include

- **Develop your cloud decision model:** Developing the cloud decision model is described in Chapter 4, "Identifying Cloud Candidates." This model provides the use cases for cloud adoption based on strategic goals of the business. This model is essential to understand the future state made possible for your enterprise with cloud adoption. This decision model is grounded in the reality of what is possible coupled with the optimism of a future state.

- **Develop your cloud business case and ROI inputs:** The business case and corresponding return on investment (ROI) model should look at a comprehensive cloud adoption versus ad hoc adoption. It's not easy to do ROI analysis as most companies use intuition or guesswork. You might also easily spend months or a year doing ROI analysis necessary for business case development. Using the following approach can help:

1. Create a benefit value tree where when selecting benefits (such as those described in Chapter 1, "Business Value of a Cloud Adoption Strategy") you distill the value drivers for cloud adoption such as capital preservation, increased time to market, new business opportunities, workforce transformation, accelerated time to market, and so on. Scenarios or use cases should be created for each value proposition..

2. Identify the applicable cost scenario for each use case.

3. Calculate the initial, simple return.

4. Assess and select the cost scenario for the second and subsequent implementations.

5. Keeping the benefits constant, calculate the returns for the second and subsequent implementations.

- **Assess your enterprise's cloud adoption maturity level:** Understanding shortfalls between your target state, your cloud vision, and the current state is essential for successful planning and realization of your cloud adoption strategy. Using the traditional CMMI (Capability Maturity Model Integration) thinking, organizations can easily determine whether they are in the formative stages or optimized stages of cloud adoption maturity. Figure 3.2 depicts this model. This determines what level of assistance is required to move faster or whether the current pace is sufficient. You should plan for improvements and incorporate this input into your roadmap as a natural outcome of this assessment.

- **Conduct vendor selections:** A vendor selection process is necessary to select the partners and vendors for enablement of your cloud adoption strategy. A team should be assembled with a vested interest in the cloud selection process. The first task that the vendor selection team needs to accomplish is to define, in writing, the service, capability, and features required from a partner. This gets further elaborated into a defined set of business and technical needs or requirements. Also, define the vendor requirements. Finally, publish your document to the areas relevant to this vendor selection process and seek both internal stakeholders and vendor inputs. Now you are ready to select vendors.

- **Determine areas to assess to fully understand your capabilities to succeed with cloud adoption:** Figure 3.3 illustrates the cloud capability assessment areas. Customer and market insights provide clarity on the art of what is possible and how other companies are both innovating and differentiating themselves with cloud computing. Areas where business innovation can occur must be assessed and understood. Are your EA and/or SOA capability where it needs to be for the cloud adoption strategy to be successful? Assessing yourself in these areas provides a baseline for improvement and successful realization of your cloud adoption strategy.

- **Outline your enterprise governance strategy:** Governance will be mandatory for achieving the goals of your cloud adoption strategy. This includes defining roles and responsibilities for stakeholders essential to cloud adoption.

  Your EA governance processes should be utilized, as EA will be a critical success factor in accelerating cloud adoption. Your governance should include a governing body that can create and manage the following aspects of a cloud computing environment:

  - Policies
  - Procedures
  - Organizational effectiveness
  - Accountability and reporting
  - Communications
  - Standards adaptation

- **Secure executive endorsements:** Making sure key executive stakeholders and the executive sponsor are onboard and committed is another critical success factor of your cloud adoption strategy. Establishing steering committees or other mechanism for reporting and regular, timely communication is required.

Key work artifacts resulting from the enterprise capabilities and cloud vision phase include

- Cloud Vision, which has a vision statement. Examples of vision statements include
  - The enterprise cloud adoption strategy is the playbook for cloud adoption at our company. We will use cloud computing to drive revenue growth of 50 billion by 2017 and promote our business theme "Win, Drive, and Innovate through the use of smarter business technologies."
    Motivation: Business value is maximized through consistent and effective adoption of cloud solutions.

- We will adopt strategies that expand business efficiencies by enabling our enterprise to operate more effectively during constantly changing business conditions, with ready access to global markets while delivering enterprise-grade performance and cross-border compliance.
- Sample table of contents for your published vision document:
  - Chapter 1: Introduction—Cloud Computing for Our Enterprise. This chapter introduces cloud computing, identifies the document intended audience, and explains the purpose, scope, and organization of the document.
  - Chapter 2: Context for a Computing Paradigm. This chapter takes a first look from an industrywide perspective at how cloud computing can help remove IT roadblocks and permit a powerful new approach to creating value and realizing strategy.
  - Chapter 3: Cloud Concepts and Principles. This chapter provides a canonical view of cloud computing—what it is, how it's constructed, and how it works; and its value propositions.
  - Chapter 4: Usage Scenarios. This chapter presents a set of business archetypal usage scenarios to illustrate ways in which cloud adoption can be leveraged for competitive advantage and differentiation.
  - Chapter 5: Cloud Vision. This chapter is specific to what you want to accomplish by leveraging cloud computing. It describes what is different, new business models or markets made viable. The benefits and value propositions made possible are also described along with any business motivators.
  - Chapter 6: Reference Architecture. This chapter describes the cloud reference architecture to be leveraged as inputs or created as an output of your enterprise cloud adoption strategy.

- Chapter 7: Vendor Eco System. This chapter describes the universe of vendors for helping with the realization of cloud computing.
- Cloud Business Adoption Patterns describe the relevance of the patterns described in Table 3.1 to the business situation at hand. Each pattern to be adopted should address the key questions identified in the decision analyses. The answers should find themselves in your published vision document for cloud computing.
- Business Case provides the benefits, value propositions and ROI for cloud adoption.
- Governance Model addresses the unique characteristics of governing and managing cloud adoption. The model should focus on decision rights and accountability and include processes, policies, roles, responsibilities, metrics, and organizational change suggestions and procedures needed for successful cloud adoption.
- Transition Plan describes the initiatives and projects necessary for successful realization of the vision. For each project or initiative there should be a corresponding description that includes project objectives, expected business outcomes ownership dependencies, and resources required.

NOTE

The Cloud Vision document is essential to motivating stakeholders and stating clearly how you expect the value propositions for cloud computing to materialize. You can derive aspects of the vision document by conducting a cloud adoption maturity assessment. Your Cloud Vision document may be necessary for final executive endorsements and to firm detailed plans.

Table 3.1   Cloud Business Adoption Patterns

Business Adoption Patterns	Decision Analyses
Allocation	How will cloud service types get distributed within your company or a specific business unit? In other words, what percentage of cloud-sourcing will be Business Process-as-a-Service (BPaaS), Software-as-a-Service (SaaS), Platform-as-a-Service (PaaS), Infrastructure-as-a-Service (IaaS), or other emerging service types?
Broker	Should you leverage a third-party company (e.g., a cloud consultant or service integrator) to make cloud adoption decisions or suggest recommendations for you?
Bundling	Is your preference to buy bundled offerings such as SaaS that is packaged with additional cloud solutions and/or services?
Diversification	What cloud service types and deployment models make the most sense for your company?
Federation	Is it feasible to standardize the use of multiple clouds to collaborate to solve your business challenges without your explicit request prior to each occurrence?
Rebalancing	Will you govern and manage your cloud portfolio such that the benefits balance with solution alternatives and update your portfolio accordingly? For example, shift from IaaS (bottom up) to more BPaaS (top down) or rebalance cloud-sourcing and outsourcing for greater business impacts and to stir innovation.
Resell	Are you interested in reselling cloud services that you buy? And if so, how will you manage profitability?
Self-Service	Should direct interactions with cloud providers be permitted for making cloud purchases, and if so, how and for which stakeholders?
Sourcing	Should you invest in-house, outsource, or cloud-source business solutions?
Trade	How will you handle unused assets due to cloud adoption? Will you sell the assets, repurpose in your organization, trade (e.g., rent out use of assets* or spot trade)?

*The value of the sale of the assets occurs immediately as opposed to future trades, where value is realized at a later point in time.

Approved cloud business patterns are an integral part of your enterprise cloud adoption strategy.

Business pattern usage can vary per business unit.

The successful adoption of cloud computing increases with organizations having effective enterprise architecture practices. Organizations without effective EA practices can start with the transition to cloud computing. Maturity models have come under criticism and praise, but nonetheless such models provide a tool for performing gap analysis when adopting new architectures or computing models.

Figure 3.2 illustrates common enterprise capability measures that are derived from the Capability Maturity Model Integration (CMMI).[1] The model is frequently used for EA capability assessments. By applying the cloud-specific considerations discussed in the next section, you can use this maturity model to determine your cloud adoption capability and develop an actionable, comprehensive strategy suitable for your business.

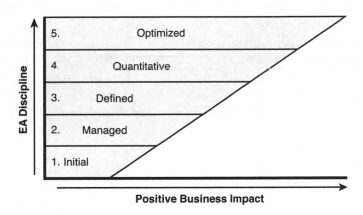

Figure 3.2 Enterprise cloud adoption—Capability Maturity Model

1. **Initial:** EA program is not well-defined and most likely generated solely by and for IT. Projects tend to run over budget and success is nonrepeatable. Company has exploratory or project-specific cloud adoption capability.
2. **Managed:** EA program is forming. There is some manageability and repeatability across departments; however, project compliance in the organization is unpredictable and usually reactionary in nature. Company has departmental and business unit cloud adoption capability.

3. **Defined:** EA program is well-defined, governed, and managed across the organization enabling and generating measurable business outcomes and companywide standards. Project compliance and executive accountability are the norm. IT collaboration is critical to achieving business agility and performance objectives. Company has enterprisewide cloud adoption capability.

4. **Quantitative:** EA program is both qualitatively and quantitatively managed. Quantitative objectives are based on the needs of the customer, end users, and the organization. EA process and performance are managed from strategy throughout project implementations. Company has capability to sense and respond to market demands—a differentiating capability. Company has complex cloud adoption capability that encompasses collaborative partnering and innovation with business partners.

5. **Optimized:** EA program is advanced and continuously improved to support current and emerging business models. Analysis of project data identifies shortfalls or gaps in performance and process improvements. Company has complex cloud adoption capability that encompasses on-demand, dynamic business partnering and innovation.

In theory, the more the discipline of EA is applied throughout your company (whether small, midsized, or large), the greater the opportunity for positive business impacts and a sustainable cloud adoption strategy. For instance, organizations that operate in silos have a lower EA maturity level[2] and are more likely to have a lower capacity for cloud adoption (levels 1 or 2) and smaller business impacts, while enterprise wide capacity is reflected at levels 3 and above signaling business and IT alignment of cloud undertakings along with governance and management that optimizes the adoption across the entire value network (levels 4 and 5), indicating sustained and larger business impacts.

During this phase of the life cycle, you determine areas to assess to fully understand your capabilities to succeed with cloud adoption. The information collected helps derive your target state as well as what is required to get you to your desired state. Figure 3.3 suggests assessment areas.

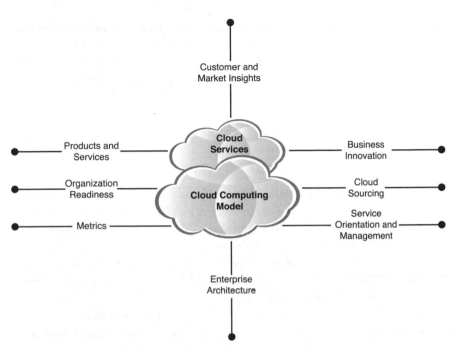

Figure 3.3 Enterprise cloud capability assessment areas

The enterprise cloud capability assessment areas provide the mechanism to make informed decisions in your cloud adoption. Such assessments ensure a common understanding of your organization's experiences and business capabilities so that you make informed business decisions. A description of the enterprise cloud capability assessment areas follows:

- Customer and Market Insights are evaluated to determine your capability to anticipate and respond to demands. This assessment intends to uncover whether your organization actively seeks to understand market trends and directions that impact your business and enterprise. Does your organization proactively seek external viewpoints to improve? Keeping a pulse on trends and directions allows your organization to choose its proper path of innovator/leader, fast follower, or an organization that only pursues paths with historical proven track records.

- Business Innovation is evaluated to determine your innovative talent and practicing skills base. This is essentially an ideation capability and is influenced by your business networks and your ability to partner to create and explore new ideas. Also explored is your process for determining high-value ideas and transforming them into business solutions.

NOTE

The relationship between UPS and Toshiba provides an example of partnering for business innovation. When someone sends in a Toshiba laptop for repair, the UPS company is actually responsible for the repairs although this is not a UPS core business competency. The arrangement stemmed from a business relationship where UPS was warehousing the laptops while Toshiba had repair locations across the U.S. The agreement was that Toshiba repair technicians would become a part of UPS. UPS would thereby cut the mean-time-to-repair (MTTR) cycles by reducing the need to redistribute laptops to Toshiba locations across the U.S. for repair. The agreement reportedly saved in transportation and inventory overhead, and reduced Toshiba's carbon footprint.[3] Your enterprise capabilities and cloud vision should seek to identify partnering to innovate.

- Cloud Sourcing experiences are evaluated to determine your skills and experiences using external providers to source solutions. This includes traditional sourcing experiences such as service level agreement (SLA) creation, contract management, and transfer of services to and from service providers. The objective is to learn from what works and what does not work in your culture in working with vendors and partners.
- Service Orientation and Management are assessed to determine your familiarity and capability to operate in a service-oriented capacity. Are you using services and SOA thinking to improve the effectiveness of your business and IT?
- Enterprise Architecture assessments of your practices include integrated business and information technology architecture and capability. The key components assessed are business architecture, information systems architecture, infrastructure architecture, and governance.
- Metrics must be identified to enable continuous improvement. Metrics provide a measurable attainable goal and can be used to improve the

adoption approach. The objective is to understand what metrics have
been captured in your company to-date and the experience and confidence levels in the organization with measurement programs.

- Organization Readiness assesses your culture and organization readiness
  for adoption of cloud. Purchasing patterns are examined to determine
  whether there is a culture of objective based decision making in purchases and procuring of services.

- Products and Services are assessed to determine your core competencies
  and for tracking delivery of products and services.

Target Architecture and Cloud Enablers

This phase is a reminder that whether you are pursuing cloud adoption now or anticipate adoption in the future, it is a good idea to update
your architecture to include cloud considerations. For example, what are
your business principles for cloud adoption? Such principles represent
durable statements of direction and guide adoption decisions when the
principles have been vetted with the proper stakeholders. How should
you govern in a single or multisource environment, and what are your
standards for conducting business in virtualized environments? Other
examples of cloud considerations are to understand the targeted consumers of your cloud services, their locations, and your potential for new
business. The answers to these types of questions form the basis for a stable foundation (your architecture) that all business units can reference
and leverage for creating sustained value. It frees your teams to focus on
more business critical initiatives such as innovation and developing
practices to effectively manage cloud service providers, bringing competitive advantages to your organization. If a solid foundation is not in
place, extra work might be required to plug in adopted solutions, which
most likely will cause inefficiencies in your cloud adoption.

You are encouraged to select cloud solutions that are business driven.
Focus on business processes that might be enhanced with cloud computing, innovated, augmented, or newly formed due to cloud. Your business
drivers and processes are reflected in your business architecture (BA).
Regardless of your target entry point (SaaS, IaaS, and others), your BA
can influence architectural decisions in each of the respective domains to
enable any selected entry point, and it helps you determine requirements

for your cloud providers. If, for instance, your targeted business markets (reflected in your BA) are of international scale, you should team with your business and technical teams first, followed by potential providers to ensure that your networks can handle the added capacity in a secure manner and that potential cloud solutions are compliant with regional and corporate regulations.

The following sections provide recommended conceptual considerations and updates to your EA to promote enterprise cloud adoption readiness and consistency in adoption throughout your company. Three areas are explored for updates in your enterprise architecture:

- Business Architecture and BPaaS
- Information Systems and SaaS
- Technology & Architecture and PaaS and IaaS

NOTE

High level requirements are depicted in each of the following discussion topics. These requirements influence cloud adoption decisions and are inputs into service and operational level agreements generated during the implementation phases. In addition, the requirements can represent organizational change (people, process, information, and technology).

Business Architecture (BA) and Business-Process-as-a-Service (BPaaS)

Now that you understand your business capabilities, and have established a vision for cloud adoption in your organization, the next step is to establish your target BA. This includes your core competencies and strategic business priorities, as discussed previously, where you leverage this information to determine key business events, processes, and opportunities for cloud sourcing. In essence, your BA is a visual, comprehensive representation of your company's business strategy. It contains all the information discussed and is a cloud enabler. Figure 3.4 illustrates a high level, one page view of a BA. There are minor augmentations to BA when it comes to cloud consumers; however, the role of the business architect and the use of BA can significantly influence your cloud adoption decisions.

Consider that you decide to use a provider's platform to support your SaaS solutions. In this situation, you still need to ensure that the appropriate stakeholders (generally reflected in your BA) are able to consume the appropriate services. You also need to ensure that there is an information taxonomy and business information model (described later) that is shared and understood by your organization and can be discussed with your provider so that, for instance, a Sales ID that is used on premise means and is applied as a Sales ID in your cloud environment.

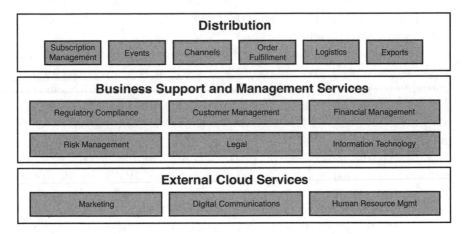

Figure 3.4   Target business architecture (excerpts)

NOTE

A business's information taxonomy represents a division of a subject into ordered groups or categories along with the logical relationships between them. The understanding of the information an enterprise uses is expressed in a business information model.

If the decision is to adopt one or more on-premise private clouds, understanding your business events and processes (which are elements of your BA) is required so that you know your elasticity needs as volumes are expected to peak as well as hit low points. You are required to communicate these business requirements to your providers (in-house in this situation) so that they can ensure that the solutions are interoperable, but also to adequately plan to meet your service capacity requirements such as when they can expect and plan automated ramp-ups of server and storage capacity.

Your BA contains information such as business events, stakeholders, business rules, geographical locations, and policies. For example a business policy for key business processes is that there is zero tolerance for provider inaccessibility and system downtime. These influence your cloud business requirements and adoption decisions. You should utilize your BA as a first point of reference in guiding your cloud adoption decisions regardless of expressed entry points. You should review your BA, frequently, with key stakeholders so that it continuously evolves as your business priorities evolve.

In this phase, you establish mechanisms for displaying your BA and cloud opportunities, and you incorporate decision considerations for outsourcing business processes in entirety or in part to cloud. This information is captured and reflected as a part of your integrated business and IT strategy as guidance for cloud implementation planning and development initiatives.

Key activities relative to this phase of cloud adoption, target architecture and cloud enablers, business architecture and BPaaS include updating your BA:

- **Document your business competencies:** Review and document your business competencies: abilities, skills, proficiencies, experience, and expertise. That is, essential capabilities necessary for the success of your business.

- **Identify core business processes and events:** Document business operational locations, business interactions, and actors.

  Document the relationship interactions between organizations and business functions across the enterprise using a Business Interaction Matrix. This helps illuminate the value chain across organizational boundaries.

  The Business Interaction Matrix shows several key entities and relationships: business services rendered by business function and/or organization, dependencies, and business service relationships.

- **Capture BPaaS business requirements:** Understand which applications and supporting processes can be replaced with a shift to a vendor-provided application platform. This requires an understanding of what information can be shared and lives in the cloud and business processes that can operate in the cloud.

- **Review and document business agility indicators:** Documenting the agility indicators for a process is necessary in making the decision on BPaaS. For example, what is the degree of customization required? How often do regulatory changes occur? What is the impact of loss, data security, or non-compliance? Answering these questions helps define the flexibility (i.e., agility) needs of a given function or process.

- **Capture your financial strategy:** This entails defining acceptable BPaaS pricing models for your stakeholders.

NOTE

Consumability[4] is an example high level cloud business requirements category that focuses on end user experiences. You need to ensure that consumability is not overlooked when making decisions on cloud enablement. Your work artifacts for capturing requirements should include consumability by addressing ease of use and integration needs. You should have standardized business requirements work artifacts of which consumability should be added as a category.

Key work artifacts relative to cloud adoption, target architecture and cloud enablers, business architecture and BPaaS, include updating your business architecture with

- Business Interaction Matrix defining a meta-model of key business entities and their relationships; functional domains, business services, business services rendered by functional domains, organizational boundaries, and the dependencies. Developing this matrix helps in understanding the value chain where aspects will be BPaaS cloud candidates.

- BPaaS Cloud Adoption Principles reflecting durable statements of direction when adopting BPaaS. Such principles are vetted with key stakeholders and are used to refine requirements so that they satisfy satisfy the principles or suitability of vendor/partner solutions. Principles should pass a simple test of "so what." That is, if the principle does not have impact or cause some debate it may not be a durable statement of IT direction. The intent of principle development is to avoid statements that everyone would agree to; that is, statements that do not cause transformation or change are not as valuable or impactful as those that do force change toward strategic goals. Some example cloud adoption principles are listed in Table 3.2.

- Business requirements for BPaaS, which might address the types of applications or business processes suitable for BPaaS. Types of applications might be grouped into processes that are not differentiated; vertical applications that are self-contained crossing few organizational boundaries; standardized process models; or applications with few if any real-time connectivity requirements. Business information that must be included is also addressed. Use cases for BPaaS candidates are created along with corresponding user profiles.

- Agility Metrics, which inventory by process or functional area and gauges the relevance and necessity of BPaaS. Those gauges could include number of dynamic business rules, degree of customization, geographical variations, compliance, or security.

Table 3.2 Example Cloud Adoption Principles

Principles	Description
1	Cloud adoption for BPaaS will be used to reinvent business processes while providing rapid delivery of new services realized without boundaries.
2	Ownership models will be established as cloud portfolios will be governed and managed by business and IT owners.
3	Workloads will be optimized with cloud adoption to preserve capital by driving greater efficiency and performance.
4	Standardized processes that require rapid deployment of new infrastructure or platform must adopt cloud computing.
5	Cloud adoption must comply with regulatory and corporate policies.
6	Applications with unacceptable high costs will be migrated to a cloud support model.
7	Providers with cloud computing solutions must employ open standards and promote business interoperability.
8	Information that will reside in the cloud must be documented in an Information Model with governing characteristics such as information accountability.
9	Cloud exit strategy must exist for each cloud adoption addressing data segregation, data privacy, and data security.

As illustrated in Figure 3.4, Distribution and Business Support and Management Services represent core business competencies where three known cloud solutions exist for Marketing, Digital Communications, and Human Resource Management. This diagram is elaborated in the next chapter when discussing how to identify cloud candidates. Although cloud services are illustrated in the example BA artifact, you should identify a formal structure for capturing your cloud services portfolio. This portfolio serves as a baseline not only for adoption but also for management of internal and external clouds. You can use the following as a cloud services portfolio template to gain consensus within your organization:

- Cloud service name, which provides a unique identity for each cloud service in your portfolio.
- Description of the service enables consumers to understand the capabilities rendered by the service.
- Business purpose describes the expected outcomes when using the cloud service.
- Service type of BPaaS, SaaS, PaaS, or IaaS.
- Deployment model of private, public, hybrid, or community cloud.
- Owners who have responsibility for granting access and ensuring the continued viability of the cloud service.
- Required enablers describing prerequisites for consumers necessary to leverage or use the cloud service.
- Traceability (optional) shows the business process or component that is being replaced or augmented with cloud if that is the case; this is useful for portfolio management.
- Hierarchy (optional) depicts relationships of the cloud to other clouds; this is useful for workflow orchestration and in composite cloud situations.
- Vendor-specific requirements capturing capabilities enabled by the cloud vendor necessary for the service.
- Industry, which shows whether the cloud is associated with a specific industry.

NOTE

An industry vertical cloud, such as life sciences or healthcare, is often governed by a set of industry regulations. One such example is the Federal Drug Administration (FDA), where an example qualification requirement of providers is verification that the cloud is installed and performs as intended throughout all anticipated operating ranges. In such cases, provisioning and decommissioning differ from a horizontal cloud where, since the services are intended for multiple markets or industries, latitude is given to providers to deploy clouds to your consumer specifications and without compliance to industry-specific regulations.

Information Systems and SaaS

When it comes to EA, information systems (IS) comprises two architectural aspects: Information Architecture (IA), which can be summed up as your enterprise's data, structure, and standards for enablement and adoption; and the Application Architecture, representing your enterprise's applications, structure, and standards for adoption and enablement.

SaaS adoption can augment or replace your IS in part or in its entirety, and therefore just as business considerations were discussed earlier, this section discusses information and application considerations for cloud adoption, which relates to SaaS, as sourcing and enablement options must be evaluated.

Information Architecture (IA)

Integration of your business and information systems is required to ensure ongoing value of SaaS investments. With the inception of cloud, boundaries for information ownership and accountability can become blurred, and easy access to SaaS services, although convenient, introduces quick yet inadequately planned adoptions that can result in short-term fixes and an abundance of SaaS solutions that are difficult to manage. A key to success, therefore, is understanding your information and recognizing when it makes sense to source information from cloud.

Figure 3.5 presents a summarized list of some information management and governance considerations that augment traditional IA, which in itself is an enabler of cloud. Each high level requirement, information assurance, information integration, information security, and governance of information, influences cloud adoption decisions and must be considered both in the context of your company's BA and upon the auspices of enabling growth and/or enhancing profitability through deliberate analysis of costs, savings, risks, and rewards.

Figure 3.5   Cloud considerations for SaaS (information and applications)

The following questions help solidify the context of your IA requirements and, at the same time, should be leveraged to stimulate conversations with providers to further refine your requirements and to make selections as to suitable providers. Chapter 6, "Mitigating Risk," provides additional details. Resolve to answer each of the following questions to solidify your understanding of the requirements for information architecture in cloud adoption:

1. Information assurance
   - What information is required to run your business?
   - Can cloud effectively manage your global stream of information?
   - Will the adoption of cloud reduce your sales team's data quality problems?
   - What are the implications if your provider becomes unavailable or gets acquired by another company?
   - What mechanisms are required to prevent the adoption of cloud from forcing you into counterproductive situations such as you cannot access your own information, or you are forced to continue working with a provider once your contract ends?
   - What are your cloud backup, retention, and recovery requirements?

2. Information integration
   - How will information seamlessly integrate across cloud and your company?
   - How well will cloud based information models integrate with corporate information models?
   - What patterns are appropriate, self-service, broker, federation, others?

3. Information security
   - What are financial implications of information security in the cloud or lack thereof?
   - What are necessary changes (organization, procedures, and policies) to ensure domestic and global regulatory compliance?
   - What information is qualified to enter into the cloud?
   - How will information security breaches get resolved?
   - Is information restricted to company employees only (single tenancy) or are multiple companies allowed to view and use information provided in the cloud (multi-tenancy)?

4. Governance of information
   - Who will make decisions relative to cloud adoption and how will your company communicate, enforce, and address exceptions?
   - What are business policies for on- and off-boarding to and from the cloud?
   - Who are information stewards and what are the responsibilities?
   - How will you determine what information goes into the cloud?
   - Who will own information that resides in the cloud?
   - What are required information management and governance tools?
   - What is the chain of custody for information in the cloud?
   - Given a lack of regulatory or legal guidelines to address data privacy, how will you ensure local governments or bodies don't have access to personal information in the cloud?

Key activities relative to this phase of cloud adoption, target architecture, and cloud enablers, include updating your IA:

- **Create or Update your Business Information Model (BIM):** The BIM contains information to be consumed or shared in the cloud. As your company adopts cloud you are still accountable for your data but may no longer be responsible for it. BIM helps in deciding what data should reside in the cloud. Such a model contains a framework that outlines how your company will gather and use information for SaaS adoption and usage. Data segregation and data security responsibilities should also be defined.

- **Review and update cloud adoption principles.** Table 3.2 describes a set of principles that can be updated to address principles necessary for IA and SaaS.

- **Document high level information requirements:** Requirements in areas of service levels, security, privacy, and other operational needs must be captured to ensure they are fulfilled with cloud adoption.

- **Enhance governance to address information in the cloud:** Information governance must be enhanced to address cloud adoption: data traceability, managing entitlements and identities for authorized users, data retention policies, data separation, and chain of custody for information are examples.

Key artifacts created in this phase of cloud adoption, target architecture and cloud enablers, for Information Architecture include

- Business Information Model (BIM) defining your taxonomy, where taxonomy provides a view and structure of your information model. It provides a conceptual framework for organizing content so it can easily be identified and located. Taxonomies are typically hierarchical, multilevel, and show the relationships between concepts of the information model. Table 3.3 lists key characteristics and the process for generating a BIM. Levels 0 and 1 provide the highest level of specificity; these levels are conceptual in nature and appropriate for strategic planning of information required for your cloud adoption. Levels 2 and 3 provide lower level specifications and are most appropriate for project-specific cloud solution planning where development of logical and physical data models are most appropriate. Continuity of business alignment is maintained throughout each level.

- Cloud Adoption Principles for Information Architecture—SaaS must be identified and vetted with key stakeholders to guide and prioritize requirements or cloud adoption decisions. The intent of principle development is to define statements of directions that serve to break ties or guide choices when making decisions about the BIM or SaaS. These principles become part of a single set of Cloud Adoption Principles.

- Business requirements for Information Architecture—SaaS can be compiled using the answers to the questionnaires listed earlier in this chapter. Information as a service requirements should be identified.

- Information Governance and Management Strategy addresses the characteristics of governing and managing the BIM in the context of cloud computing. It should address processes, policies, roles, responsibilities, metrics and organizational change suggestions, and procedures that are not represented in your existing IT or EA governance.

Table 3.3 Enterprise Business Information Model Characteristics

Level	Specificity	Description
0	Conceptual	Presents a high level view of information subject areas important to the business and establishes a foundation from which information designs can progress. Analysis at this level is required to determine and specify which information is needed and appropriate for cloud-sourcing.
1	Conceptual	Depicts a high level statement of the main entities comprising the business subject areas defined in Level 0. Analysis at this level is key to determining and specifying information appropriate for cloud-sourcing.
2	Logical	Depicts a detailed statement of the entities comprising the business subject areas in Level 0 per further elaboration of the concepts and entities presented in Level 1. Logical models should contain cloud-sourced solutions.
3	Physical data	Depicts the physical realization of the logical model (Level 2). Physical models should contain cloud-sourced solutions.

BIM is derived from BA and represents information intended to be consumed or shared in the cloud.

A subject area reflects a major classification of information valuable to the enterprise per its business context.

Application Architecture (AA)

Your company will pursue SaaS not met by your capability to extend business functionality, address new markets, create business outcomes faster, or simply to bring solutions to market faster. The benefits of rapid ROI, reduced up-front investments, global availability, and the ability to increase efficiency of your IT budget make SaaS an appropriate course of action.

It is also possible that you will streamline and preserve in-house applications in an effort to optimize return on legacy investments. EA helps as it provides a comprehensive view of your applications, dependencies, and the underlying architecture where, in most cases, your application portfolio is an integrated landscape of in-house, outsourced and cloud-sourced solutions.

You need to understand and manage your application portfolio, cloud included, and one way to do this is to assign ownership and accountability from both the business and IT organizations. This comprehensive view of your applications equips you to make informed and justifiable decisions relative to SaaS adoption and enabling technologies. Similar to IA and as is depicted in Figure 3.5, four cloud considerations must be explored in the context of cloud adoption:

- Application assurance
- Application integration
- Application security
- Governance of applications

Consider the scenario where regulatory stipulations inhibit sharing of specific company information in public clouds. In this scenario, your IA provides directives and requirements to reflect that some information will be sourced from SaaS while proprietary company information must remain internal. Your AA provides directives and requirements that reflect the need for standardization and strategic direction as to appropriate SaaS purchases, as well as federated security patterns to prevent end users from signing on to multiple systems to view reports for which they have no authorization. This scenario emphasizes the need for an integrated internal, external, and business aligned information systems architecture to enable cloud computing in a manner that drives value and sustainable business outcomes.

Key activities relative to this phase of cloud adoption, target architecture and cloud enablers, include updating your AA:

- **Create and/or Update the Application Architecture aspects in your EA:** Application types or categories that are suitable for SaaS adoption should be identified. New applications that can be satisfied through a SaaS model should be reflected by stating when specific qualities are met.

Those aspects could include shorter deployment time, compliance to service levels not otherwise achieved in-house, ability to eliminate costs, and ubiquitous access.

- **Review and update cloud adoption principles:** Table 3.2 describes a set of principles that can be updated to address principles necessary for AA and SaaS.

- **Document high level SaaS requirements:** Service and operation levels should be captured and understood when adopting SaaS. Determining whether application architecture documentation will be maintained representing the various layers of the architecture may be a SaaS requirement. Understanding APIs available to pull and push data may be a requirement. Service level agreement requirements must also be defined.

- **Enhance governance to address SaaS:** Access to applications should be tracked with audit trails in SaaS models. Secured access to data centers and application level intrusion detection are of the utmost importance. Change management, portfolio management, repositories, retention, and accountability for recovery are some key governance aspects that must be addressed with SaaS.

Key artifacts created in this phase of cloud adoption, target architecture, and cloud enablers, for Application Architecture include

- Business requirements for Application Architecture—SaaS should be identified addressing a variety of issues described as follows. AA questionnaires can also be used to capture requirements.
    - Service level agreements: Requirements, escalation if not fulfilled, and of course the types of SLAs (e.g., availability and performance)
    - Integration capabilities describing types of application programming interfaces (APIs) that are available for pushing and pulling data
    - Standards that would be leveraged
    - Security model describing identity management, authentication, and authorization options
    - Exit strategy

- Cloud Adoption Principles for Application Architecture—SaaS must be identified and vetted with key stakeholders to guide and prioritize requirements or cloud adoption decisions. The intent of principle development is to define statements of directions that serve to break ties or guide choices when making decisions about the types of workloads suitable for SaaS. These principles can become part of a single set of principles as is depicted in Table 3.2.

- Applications-as-a-Service questionnaires should be developed to aid in the principle development and the requirements capture. The IA questionnaire can be used as a template.

- Application Governance and Management Strategy addresses the characteristics of governing and managing the application architecture, SaaS, in the context of cloud computing. It addresses governance issues not currently represented in your existing EA governance. Cloud candidates should surface as an output of the governance activities where specific workload types or application types might be most suitable for SaaS.

Technology and Infrastructure, PaaS and IaaS

A significant advantage of cloud computing is your ability to free up IT staff to work on strategic initiatives while nondifferentiating workloads are outsourced to cloud. This is effective whether you choose public or private cloud settings. In fact, according to a recent Computerworld report, a primary reason for NASA's cloud adoption is to get out of the business of running data centers and focus on its core competencies, which are space exploration.[5] The same is applicable to technology and infrastructure architecture (TA), meaning you can expect your IT software and hardware expenditures to decline considering that cloud-sourced services have better pricing and chargeback features, and you can expect your data centers to shrink in size and energy consumption due to reduced capacity and optimized usage of existing assets such as servers. With this in mind, your strategy should encompass considerations for leveraging alternative, more cost efficient data centers.

According to The Corporate Executive Board Company,[6] there is overall acceptance of private clouds in the industry, with the adoption of public clouds increasing as a natural progression and due to the maturity of public cloud capabilities. Figure 3.6 shares excerpts of a consumer's data center, the home of technology and infrastructure architecture. The example illustrates requirements for Developer (PaaS) and Storage (IaaS) clouds, and is a reminder that although sourced from a provider, these services are ultimately the responsibility of the consumer. This requires service level agreements and integrated service management—both topics are discussed in depth in Chapter 6.

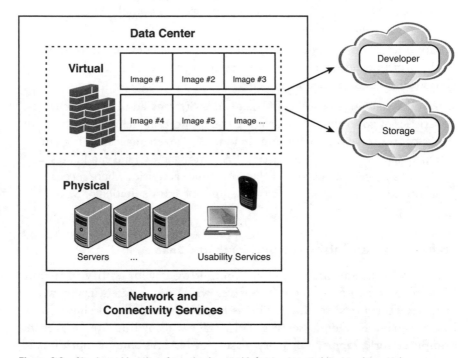

Figure 3.6   Cloud considerations for technology and infrastructure architecture (excerpts)

NOTE

Keep in mind that at this phase of the life cycle you are not focused on implementation details, so from an SLA perspective you provide strategic guidelines, such as who should be involved in contract negotiations, techniques for SLA creation, and you provide SLA mitigation considerations. As you transition to implementation planning and know which cloud services are suitable for your specific situation, you provide project-specific guidance.

Following are core technology and infrastructure components relative to private cloud adoption that you should consider:

- **Capacity:** Organizations should be careful that adequate capacity (e.g., servers, storage, licenses) is on-hand to support cloud consumption while controlling hardware and software spend.

- **Cloud Computing Management Platform (CCMP):**[7] Consult with your providers regarding their cloud computing management platform. CCMP defines the operational and business support services commonly needed for delivering and managing any cloud service. This specific capability augments traditional EA and SOA environments and is applicable for public and private cloud adoption.

- **Networks:** Be aware that operating your cloud from central data centers and over the WAN can add to latency and degrade cloud performance.

- **Virtualization:** For manageability, you should standardize on a core set of virtual images and a common cloud platform.

Referencing Figure 3.6, should your company have a desire to offload IT workloads to a public cloud, you can eliminate a significant portion of your physical assets (as depicted) with the exception of usability and network/connectivity services since these components are required for both cloud consumption and enablement.

NOTE

Figures 3.4 and 3.6 are deliberate and recommended to discuss strategic cloud opportunities and explore the implications of decisions, such as the scenario just described. Detailed designs will evolve as solution architecture and cloud-specific projects emerge.

Key activities relative to this phase of cloud adoption, target architecture and cloud enablers, include updating your Technology and Infrastructure relative to PaaS and IaaS:

- **Review and update cloud adoption principles:** Table 3.2 describes a set of principles that can be updated to address principles necessary for PaaS and IaaS. For example, a principle could state that "an exist strategy must be defined when adopting PaaS and IaaS."

- **PaaS and IaaS Requirements:** Review and document technology and infrastructure requirements. Include reliability, availability, and service-ability (RAS) service and operational levels.

- **Update your data center strategy:** A data center strategy addresses capacity and cost capabilities necessary for an efficient operation of a data center. Incorporating data center best practices that include cloud adoption must be included in the strategy.

Key artifacts created in this phase of cloud adoption, target architecture and cloud enablers, Technology and Infrastructure relative to PaaS and IaaS:

- Cloud Adoption Principles for Technology and Infrastructure—PaaS and IaaS must be identified and vetted with key stakeholders to guide and prioritize requirements or cloud adoption decisions. The intent of principle development is to define statements of directions that serve to break ties or guide choices when making decisions about operational concerns. These PaaS and IaaS principles become part of a single set of Cloud Adoption Principles. PaaS and IaaS questionnaires can be developed to aid in the principle development.

- Technology and Infrastructure Governance and Management Strategy addresses the characteristics of governing and managing the adoption of PaaS and IaaS.

- PaaS and IaaS requirements should be documented, which include cloud candidates for PaaS and IaaS.

Gap Analysis and Transition Planning

You have commenced formulating the contents of your strategic roadmap in prior phases, and at this gap analysis and transition planning stage (phase 4), your focus is on reviewing, prioritizing, and finalizing the contents of your roadmap to prepare your organization for cloud adoption.

Gap analysis helps compare your company's actual performance with its potential. Gap analysis provides a foundation for measuring investment of time, money, and human resources required to execute your enterprise cloud adoption strategy and is often referenced as shortfall analysis. Two common shortfalls when it comes to strategic planning for cloud adoption are ongoing training of others on how to apply the cloud adoption strategy and the principles therein across the enterprise and educating stakeholders on conducting requirements and change management in cloud settings. You will find in the scenarios and case studies that many organizations were mindful to conduct training of team members so that they could effectively maintain the cloud adoption. However, a common omission is managing change and integrating requirements management processes for cloud solutions. Both activities are required transition and implementation planning activities.

Transition plans are the required actions to prepare you for change. Inputs into your transition plans are prioritized shortfalls identified during gap analysis as well as information learned from subsequent phase analysis. As with all the other phases, one of the outcomes of your cloud adoption strategy is deciding who should be involved in developing your transition plans. The format of transition plans varies; however, Chapter 7, "Planning the Transition," provides some examples and discusses the subject in more depth.

Key activities relative to this phase of cloud adoption, Gap Analysis and Transition Planning:

- **Perform a gap analysis:** Assessing what you do well and where improvements can be made is essential to a successful cloud adoption. Table 3.4 provides an example of the results of an assessment.
- **Understand change management needs:** Sustained success with cloud is essential to achieving benefits. Often this requires an understanding of whether organizational changes are needed, education for key stakeholders, or training materials. Often, organizations must seek outside advice to develop change management recommendations and corresponding actions.
- **Develop your Enterprise Cloud Adoption Roadmap:** The roadmap provides an actionable, living plan for how to make your cloud adoption strategy come to life. Risks must be identified and corresponding actions taken in the plan to address.

Key artifacts created in this phase of cloud adoption, Gap Analysis and Transition Planning, include

- Change Management Plan, which addresses how people, the organization, moves from its current state to the future cloud adoption state.
- Enterprise Cloud Adoption Roadmap, which describes the initiatives and projects necessary for achieving the described benefits of cloud adoption for your enterprise.
- Transition Planning Report, which covers several items:
    - Updated business case.
    - Candidate cloud portfolio and sourcing models. The sourcing models indicate your cloud-sourcing and other sourcing recommendations, an example is illustrated in Figure 3.7.
    - Cloud vendor selection criteria.
    - Change Management plan.
- Enterprise Cloud Adoption Roadmap.
- Technology and Infrastructure Governance and Management Strategy addresses the characteristics of governing and managing.

Table 3.4 Information Stewardship Gaps and Recommendations for Successful Cloud Adoption

Summary of Gaps	Recommendations
Lack of consistent, coherent, and coordinated governance with span of control across the organization. Lack of governance at the executive level.	Establish global governance board with information stewards. Realign groups to streamline governance with span of control that includes cloud.
Lack of global data quality methodology, policies, communication procedures, metadata, etc.	Establish and enforce global data quality methodology, policies, metadata, etc.
Lack of enforcement of data quality and procedures to address issues. Poor control of data sources. Cloud adoption will exacerbate this problem.	Set and enforce data quality controls and measures, improve and certify quality and integrity of data and management prior to commencement cloud adoption initiatives. Publish guidelines for appropriate use of cloud.
Lack of coordination between governance bodies and regulatory/audit compliance processes.	Ensure alignment of common processes through formalized communication channels and/or shared membership. Add cloud business and technology expertise to the governing body.

An enterprise governance structure with common methodologies and procedures is lacking; enterprise information practice is immature; governance boards at the executive level do not exist.

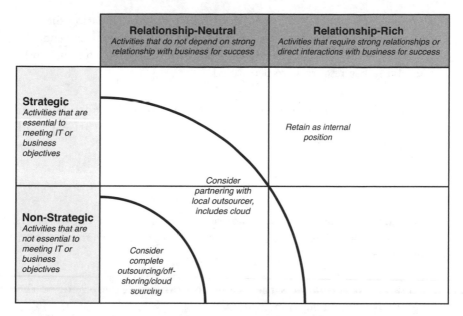

	Relationship-Neutral *Activities that do not depend on strong relationship with business for success*	Relationship-Rich *Activities that require strong relationships or direct interactions with business for success*
Strategic *Activities that are essential to meeting IT or business objectives*		*Retain as internal position*
Non-Strategic *Activities that are not essential to meeting IT or business objectives*	*Consider partnering with local outsourcer, includes cloud* *Consider complete outsourcing/off-shoring/cloud sourcing*	

Figure 3.7   Sourcing model template to be completed prior to commencing implementation phase (Source: 2011, The Corporate Executive Board Company, slightly adjusted based on project experiences)

Implementation Planning

Implementation planning is the final phase. It is derived from the strategic, prioritized roadmap and is project-specific. Implementation arrangements are made with providers in this phase and contracts signed to commence work efforts. Chapter 7 provides detailed discussions on both transition and implementation planning with practical examples.

Key activities relative to this phase of cloud adoption, Implementation Planning, include

- **Define SLAs and select vendors:** Defining SLAs and selecting vendors is a key activity to realize the roadmap. Preparing cloud procurement plans is performed. Reviewing requirements from prior phases is a key input for the SLAs. Cloud provider selection occurs as a final task.
- **Develop integration requirements:** Understanding dependencies and integration needs as you adopt cloud becomes an input into the planning process.

- **Refine your Enterprise Cloud Adoption Roadmap:** Updating the Enterprise Cloud Adoption Roadmap occurs based on the actual vendors and SLAs agreed upon. Updating the plan with reasonable timelines and identifying key resources are performed.

The key work artifacts relative to this phase of cloud adoption, Implementation Planning, is the updated/refined Enterprise Cloud Adoption Roadmap.

Governance

Three areas of governance are addressed in this book, expressly in Chapter 5, "What About Governance?," and each incorporates cloud considerations:

1. **Strategic direction:** Sets the vision and directs development of the enterprise cloud adoption strategy.
2. **Management and control:** Develops and manages execution of the enterprise cloud adoption strategy; drives and makes updates to EA.
3. **Execute:** Implements the enterprise cloud adoption strategy and communicates experiences and lessons learned.

Key activities relative to this phase of cloud adoption, governance, include

- **Develop the governance framework:** Establishing stakeholder decision rights and authority in terms of cloud purchasing and vendor selection is performed. The communications plans are addressed in this framework. The cloud decision model described in Chapter 4 will be used.
- **Create a cloud reference architecture:** Updating EA to include a cloud reference architecture provides guidance to executives, key stakeholders, or lines of business as to what's available for cloud adoption in the enterprise.
- **Refine your Enterprise Cloud Adoption Roadmap:** Updating the Enterprise Cloud Adoption Roadmap occurs based on the actual vendors and SLAs agreed upon. Updating the plan with reasonable timelines and identifying key resources is performed.

The key work artifacts relative to this phase of cloud adoption, Implementation Planning, are

- Governance Framework provides the model for implementing governance for cloud adoption.
- Cloud Reference Architecture, which becomes part of the Enterprise Architecture. This reference architecture provides the guidance and direction necessary for teams to successfully adopt cloud in your enterprise.
- Enterprise Cloud Adoption Roadmap that describes the initiatives and projects necessary for achieving success with cloud adoption.

The Significance of Service Oriented Architecture (SOA)

If you have incorporated service oriented architecture (SOA) into your EA program, you are much farther along when it comes to developing and implementing your enterprise cloud adoption strategy. As you have seen in this chapter, aspects of EA such as applications or infrastructure can be sourced in part or in their entirety from cloud in a shared services (public or private) capacity. If you are familiar with the architectural style of SOA, you know that shared services are a central theme while the uniqueness of cloud is the dynamic ability to expand and contract resources on demand to fulfill shared service requests and meet your business needs.

Some basic attributes of SOA are embedded in cloud that you should consider when developing your enterprise cloud adoption strategy:

1. Understand your business processes and use this information to guide identification of service candidates. You will follow the same or similar principles to identify cloud candidates. This topic is discussed in Chapter 4.
2. Reuse and share services across your value net as much as possible in an effort to reduce costs and optimize return on investments. The same applies to cloud although sharing is between larger and often unknown audiences, particularly in the case of public cloud consumption.
3. Establish appropriate business patterns. Some examples are the extended enterprise, which can be applied to reflect your company's representation of a hybrid of internal and external cloud solutions;

and self-service patterns, which reflect your company's on-demand cloud adoption position.

4. Capture your service management requirements. With cloud, the concept of service management can have even more impact than with SOA if you consider that you can source core business capabilities from the cloud, and often SLAs, along with strong portfolio management, are the only indicators that you might have relative to delivery assurance.

   A key point of contemplation when it comes to service management requirements development and negotiations is the criticality of the services that you are cloud-sourcing and the business impacts should your provider get acquired by another company or if services suddenly become inaccessible.

5. Determine whether a cloud center of competency is needed in your organization. Centers of competency provide resources with deeper skill levels in a subject area. These resources are generally sought to validate cloud provider capabilities and help determine the business needs and opportunities for cloud. Some focused skill sets are contract negotiations, product architecture and branding (re-branding is gaining increasing momentum in the marketplace), cloud subject matter expertise, and the ability to manage cloud providers.

Standards

Standards are significant since proper use can drive interoperability and a smoother integration of cloud solutions within existing or target environments. Some standards are specific to your organization, such as your billing or integration standards, some are open and commonly used across industries, and others are specific to cloud providers.

While cloud standards are maturing, it is common to find consumers that insist on cloud capability that can be exposed through Web Services or application programming interfaces (APIs) using industry protocols such as representational state services (REST) or simple object access (REST) or simple object access protocol protocol (SOAP) so that consumers are not bound to a specific provider. Many consumers, for instance, have standards that require exposure of cloud services through their in-house portal. Your flexibility to add new services to your portfolio irrespective of providers, as well as to remove cloud services in a simplistic, self-service manner is enabled by selecting cloud providers that use open industry standards in addition to ensuring that your in-house teams apply similar concepts.

Following is a summarized list of standards that you should consider for cloud adoption—these standards are applicable to each of the life cycle phases. You will refine this for your specific company needs:

- Corporate policies and standards such as purchasing, chargeback, and budgetary guidelines.

- Industry-specific and/or regulatory standards such as the U.S. Patriot Act and the influence of this standard as to where and how your applications and data will be stored in the cloud. Some international companies, for instance, are concerned about information residing in U.S. data centers because the Patriot Act allows the government to monitor data.

- Standards that enable clouds to consume other clouds with identity management, such as identify federation.

- Standards that promote front-office, back-office, and companywide cloud integration, such as SOA and open APIs.

- Standards that promote simplified, cost affordable movement of applications and data into and out of the cloud, such as open transport protocols.

- Standards that drive security and privacy of your assets, such as audits and assurances, so that once you provision cloud services (for example, virtual machines) your assets are protected, including from your originating provider.

- Service level agreement and operational (SLA/SLO) standards.

- Standards that drive cloud portability so that you can use one provider's platform today and another's tomorrow such as Open Virtualization Format (OVF).

Summary

Following a life cycle of your enterprise cloud adoption strategy ensures investments in cloud are meaningful and positively impact your organization. This chapter described the life cycle and provided some practical examples of how to realize the life cycle. The chapter also highlighted the significance of augmenting traditional EA (your integrated business and IT strategy) with cloud considerations. If you do not incorporate cloud into your EA, your cloud adoption principles, policies, and procedures will become nonstandardized, which will add to a complex, inflexible environment, and issues with a rogue, cluttered, inconsistent cloud adoption might surface. Worse, the benefits of cloud computing will not be fulfilled.

EA encourages you to make holistic cloud adoption decisions that examine both horizontal—across business units—as well as vertical—business process specific—considerations so that you make informed cloud business decisions. EA domains are examined for relevancy and to guide effective integration and enablement of cloud. A high level mapping of cloud delivery models and EA is provided in more detail than in the previous chapter to demonstrate the interconnectivity of EA and cloud. Business domain defines the processes and standards by which your business operates. The information systems perspective defines and classifies data (structured and unstructured), applications, and the standards that your organization requires for adoption and enablement of business solutions. The technology/infrastructure domain defines the hardware, software, and networking requirements. Examination of each is required to determine best-fit cloud opportunities and ensure development of a sustainable enterprise cloud adoption strategy.

Leverage enterprise architects who drive consistency when it comes to cloud activities and in the development and use of business, technical, and security strategies. In addition to your cloud architects and subject matter experts, leverage the skills of business architects. Business and enterprise architects are accustomed to taking advisory roles and guiding business technology adoption and usage decisions. If you have adopted SOA, you are accustomed to applying cloud adoption principles, such as shared services and reliance on service providers for business capability. You most likely experienced best practices and lessons learned that you carry forward into your cloud adoption strategy, such as balancing legacy and sourced solutions. You appreciate that cloud is a complementary consumption and delivery model to SOA, which is not a delivery model but rather an architectural style or solution pattern.

Cloud standards bodies are emerging so instead of providing a comprehensive list of organizations, incorporated in this chapter are some key areas of standardization that you might consider as a cloud consumer and expect from your providers. Examples are portability and interoperability. Following are some standards organizations or consortiums that you may find useful to add to your strategy where in the majority of cases you will consult with your providers on relevance and feasibility. You will modify this list to align with your organizational needs:

- **Cloud Standards Customer Council (CSCC):** An end user advocacy group dedicated to accelerating cloud's successful adoption, and drilling down into the standards, security and interoperability issues surrounding the transition to the cloud. A focus is prioritizing key interoperability issues such as cloud management, reference architecture, hybrid clouds, as well as security and compliance issues.[8]
- **Distributed Management Task Force (DMTF):** DMTF's cloud efforts are focused on standardizing interactions between cloud environments by developing specifications that deliver architectural semantics and implementation details to achieve interoperable cloud management between service providers and their consumers and developers.[9]
- **National Institute of Standards and Technology (NIST):** NIST is a nonregulatory federal agency within the U.S. Department of Commerce. NIST's mission is to promote U.S. innovation and industrial competitiveness by advancing measurement science, standards, and technology in ways that enhance economic security and improve our quality of life.[10]
- **The Open Group (cloud work group):** The Open Group is a vendor-neutral and technology-neutral international consortium, whose vision of boundaryless information flow enables access to integrated information, within and among enterprises, based on open standards and global interoperability. The cloud work group focuses specifically on the development and application of open cloud standards.[11]
- **TM Forum:** TM Forum is a global industry association focused on simplifying the complexity of running a service provider's business; the Cloud Services Initiative (CSI) recognizes that as buyers start to look at using cloud services there are a number of barriers to adoption. The primary objective of CSI, one of many initiatives, is to help industries overcome these barriers and assist in the growth of a vibrant commercial marketplace for cloud based services.[12]

Application of the enterprise cloud adoption life cycle, as outlined in this chapter, helps determine the best fit cloud solutions and enablers along with alternatives for your company. In the next chapter, you learn techniques for identifying cloud candidates. In addition, you learn why Sharon made specific recommendations for cloud adoption and beyond for Distributors, Inc.

Endnotes

1. CMMI Overview—generally used as a baseline for maturity models. See http://www.sei.cmu.edu/cmmi/.

2. EA maturity models and cloud maturity models are fairly popular, but we could not find a converged model for development of an effective Cloud Adoption Strategy. This chapter highlights the convergence maturity model.

3. Colvin, Geoff. 2011. Fortune Investors Guide. "C-Suite Strategies; The UPS Green Dream, Interview with Senior VP Bob Stoffel." A response to inquiries pertaining to operating beyond UPS core business competencies (see p. 49 http://www.amazon.com/Fortune-Magazine-December-2010-162/dp/B004GVIJ4I).

4. Consumability is a necessity for all cloud service types, regardless of whether the adoption is public or private. It is a business requirement that should always be considered when planning cloud adoption.

5. See Computerworld article by Patrick Thibodeau, November 2010, "NASA Wants Its Data Up in the Clouds."

6. See http://www.executiveboard.com/information-technology/infrastructure-executive-council/index.html.

7. "IBM Cloud Computing Reference Architecture," specifically, the Cloud Computing Management Platform. See http://www.infoq.com/news/2011/03/IBM-Cloud-Reference-Architecture.

8. Cloud Standards Customer Council. See http://www.cloud-council.org/about-us.htm.

9. DMTF. See http://www.dmtf.org/standards/cloud.

10. NIST. See http://www.nist.gov/public_affairs/general_information.cfm.

11. The Open Group. See http://www.opengroup.org/.

12. TM Forum. See http://www.tmforum.org/EnablingCloudServices/8006/home.html.

4

Identifying Cloud Candidates

The integrated business and IT leadership team along with Sharon, the cloud business consultant, agreed to focus on strategic business objectives and address challenges facing advancement of Distributors, Inc., business strategy as an approach to how cloud adoption could advance their company. This approach could eventually lead to new business models for Distributors, Inc., new markets for selling their products, workforce transformation for their sales force, or simply offloading significant portions of IT workloads, the original business require-ment. Sharon's objective is to ensure that she helps create business outcomes that matter for Distributors, Inc., by targeting strategic business imperatives. She noticed business agility is often mentioned as part of the strategy as Distributors, Inc., dealt with globalization and an increasing uncertainty in their industry.

The business competencies and initial focus areas are product development and distribution, particularly order fulfillment where business performance was reported as good, and customer management where business performance was reported as on the decline. One indicator of declining business performance was the poor quality of information disseminated to individuals in recognition of purchases that they did not make. Examples include special promotions, e-mail campaigns, and other digital communications.

Sharon learned that Distributors utilizes SaaS in both product development and distribution areas, but no one really understood the process for managing application portfolios and vendor relationships. Sharon was not surprised to find that spreadsheets were utilized to record changes in customer information—a convenient yet costly business practice due to inefficiency in manual processes, the rate of errors, and information integrity issues.

Using the company's business architecture, which was composed with the help of the enterprise architect, Sharon provided a visual depiction of cloud candidates as circled in Figure 4.1.

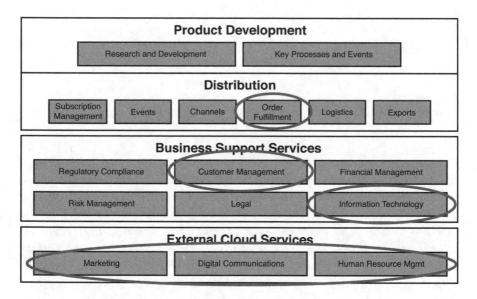

Figure 4.1   Distributors, Inc., candidate cloud services and enablers

Your Cloud Decision Model

How do you go about identifying opportunities for cloud adoption? Several approaches are available. One approach is to apply top-down analysis, where you rely on your business architecture to guide cloud investment considerations. The following sections examine both top-down and bottom-up analysis approaches. Both approaches can use a cloud discovery workshop, which is also illustrated.

Top-Down Analysis

A top-down approach is applied when you are not clear on how to proceed determining how cloud will fit in your organization or you want to drive the decision based on business process needs. This approach guides Business Process-as-a-Service (BPaaS) and Software-as-a-Service (SaaS) solutions that will also influence technology and infrastructure related cloud- and non-cloud-based decisions. During this process, the focus is not on assessing cloud solutions in the marketplace or providers; instead, the focus is on how cloud adoption advances your business strategy and fulfills business requirements.

Four steps are involved in top-down analysis, as illustrated in Figure 4.2 and described in the following sections.

Steps: Cloud candidate identification	
1	Business Vision and Strategy
2	Business Competencies/Components
(3)	Decision Parameters
4	Prioritization

◯ Technology Focused (Bottom Up) Entry Point

Figure 4.2 Steps for identifying cloud candidate services

Step 1—Understand Your Company's Business Vision and Strategy

The strategy may center on becoming number one in a market, capturing a new market, or simply increasing earning per share. Translating market opportunities into new customers might be the goal. Or the vision might be to be known for game-changing products and innovations. The key is to look for strategic targets as a result of the strategy or vision. Understanding your company's business vision and strategy requires understanding the following:

- Vision and/or mission in the form of mission or vision statements or goals
- Strategic directives, the imperatives described or stated by c-suite executives

- Strategic targets, whether they be quantitative and/or qualitative goals
- Product and marketing strategy
- Activities and actions in the form of strategic projects or a roadmap

Armed with this understanding, you will see opportunities for leveraging cloud computing emerge. Opportunities that are transformational, that fuel innovation, or that move your company from incremental change to business outcomes that make a difference should be sought and explored for cloud adoption.

Step 2—Know Your Business Competencies and Components

Understand your business competencies and your performance in each competency. Examples of business competencies are depicted in Figure 4.1: product development, distribution, and business support services. Business competencies are a grouping of business components, a categorization. Competencies refer to capabilities, abilities, skills, proficiencies, and expertise for a defined category such as distribution. Competencies are defined as large business areas with characteristic skills and capabilities, for example, product development or supply chain.

Business components are part of an enterprise that has the potential or ability to operate independently. This means the business component has enough of its own resources and/or business services supplied from the outside to be able to produce its own outcomes. Examples in Figure 4.1 are order fulfillment or customer management.

For each business component the goal is to determine whether this component is a differentiated or nondifferentiated component. Nondifferentiated components become easy targets for cloud adoption where sourcing through the cloud might be the preferred option. Differentiated components provide a unique competitive advantage for the company, and cloud adoption must therefore fuel innovation in that component.

Step 3—Understand Sourcing Options (Decision Parameters)

Understanding the sourcing options for the business component helps in making strategic cost-reduction opportunities by accelerating the right sourcing decisions. For example, a business component like product development might be an internal capability but not best of breed so partnering might offer significant improvements, perhaps with BPaaS or SaaS. Utility components are ripe for PaaS or IaaS as they might operate on specific service level agreements and variable pricing. Other components might be strategic, where the business sees its future and where the business strives for best in class performance. Others might invest in cloud as a platform for ideation and innovation purposes. Examples could be the use of Big Data with cloud as the enabling capability through SaaS, Paas, or IaaS.

With a business outcomes approach and a value-oriented mindset, you need to determine whether an entire competency or key business services should be considered for cloud-sourcing. Decision parameters are value-centric as explained in the following list:

- **Business demand:** There is a business need for considering cloud adoption. You may be experiencing business growth or you have projected functional demands where cloud-sourcing appears to be a better alternative for you to remain operable and/or competitive. You may be experiencing pain points such as invalid dissemination of information to customers as was the case with Distributors, Inc. Whatever the case, your business needs help you identify the scope and impact of the cloud opportunity, for example, an entire business unit/competency or business processes, while the remaining parameters influence your decisions relative to candidate choices and investment viability.

- **Constraints:** Constraints control the extent of cloud adoption or prevent cloud-sourcing altogether. Example constraints are as follows:

- **Security and compliance:** The adoption of cloud must be in compliance with security and regulatory requirements. Highly regulated environments generally (but not always) influence private cloud consumption patterns.

- **Information sensitivity:** Information sensitivity and intellectual property requirements can influence your decision toward private cloud consumption.

- **Business infrastructure restrictions:** You may have legacy assets or special business processing requirements that simply cannot be replaced with cloud consumption, or your data is frankly "too big" to deploy into a cloud environment without causing adverse impacts on performance. While this is not the norm, it is a growing reality.

- **Extensibility:** There is high probability that the adoption will extend across other business units, which simplifies your asset portfolio, reduces redundancies through reuse, and enables your business platform with agility and manageability.

- **Financial advantage:** Total cost of ownership (TCO) and return on investment (ROI) in cloud adoption is commonly better than traditional IT investments and outsourcing; there are demonstrable profitability indicators with the adoption of cloud.

- **Internal capacity:** You are experiencing internal capacity issues, for example, employee turnover and shortfalls that require business technology augmentation.

- **Outsourced or managed services:** There are outsourcing and/or managed services potential, an indicator of an opportunity for, at a minimum, private cloud adoption. With cloud, the adoption process is faster, contracts are generally shorter, and there are self-service, menu style choices that offset traditional software licensing and other expenditures.

  It is feasible to partner with IT outsourcing service providers as they move toward augmenting existing capabilities with cloud.[1] If your providers have not discussed this option with you, you should initiate the conversation. If you are working with an in-house managed service provider, you have greater control of whether to offload capabilities to cloud. Teaming with outsourced and managed service providers makes a good deal of sense considering that you have pre-established business relationships and as long as any new services and innovations add value and no downtimes to current operations (steps 1 to 4).

- **Strategic advantage:** The opportunity is a business differentiator for you with respect to end user services, it improves business operations, and/or it adds innovative market capability; the enablement required to support the adoption is marginal compared to anticipated rewards.

- **Other:** This parameter is optional and reserved for special business considerations. Some examples are industry-specific, such as advancement of remote healthcare and safety, or smarter city values such as traffic and energy efficiencies, which might be of particular interest to you if for instance you are in an overly populated city.

Step 4—Prioritize Your Cloud Candidates

You prioritize cloud candidates based on the importance of adoption to your business. Enablers must be taken into consideration when prioritizing candidate cloud services. Enablers are components required to support the adoption of cloud services that you are considering. An example enablement candidate is governance and in the Distributors scenario an example is Information Technology (IT).

There is no calculation to determine priority; however, each parameter is weighed according to your level of importance and based on the business impacts. Your prioritized candidates become a part of your roadmap, which is discussed in Chapter 7, "Planning the Transition."

Bottom-Up Analysis

A bottom-up approach occurs when buying decisions are IT focused and the solution has immediate impacts on your technology and infrastructure in the form of Infrastructure-as-a-Service (IaaS) or Platform-as-a-Service (PaaS). Consider the following: The IT department expresses performance-related issues with current technologies and is interested in cloud to improve service levels, commencing with IT infrastructure, the bottom of the cloud "stack" as was described in Chapter 1, "Business Value of a Cloud Adoption Strategy." Referencing Figure 4.2, the candidate identification process starts at step 3 where decision parameters are applied. Recall the example from the previous chapter in which Figure 3.6 illustrated both storage and development cloud service candidates along with usability services and network connectivity as enablers.

A difference in this bottom-up approach compared to top-down is that you evaluate your technology domains first to determine cloud opportunities. Again, since you are focused on business technologies, the cloud opportunities must add value and therefore must be traceable to your BA—a common oversight in many cloud adoption pursuits today. Here are some situations where bottom-up analysis might be applied for public and private cloud scenarios:

- Organization has little or no IT staff so you leverage externally provided cloud services to streamline IT asset purchases, configuration, and management expenditures.
- Data center is nearing physical capacity so you reach out to cloud providers for augmented networking and data center efficiencies.
- Leverage cloud for mission critical services, such as high performance computing, business intelligence, Big Data, application/Web hosting, integration, disaster recovery, storage and retrieval, or security services that are unavailable in-house.
- Leverage cloud as a platform for IT research and innovation.
- Reseller of cloud services looking to start with IT services as your early entry point into the marketplace.

- Aging or legacy environment can be replaced with cloud solutions with minimized risk and managed change to current operations.

- Take advantage of cloud virtualization principles for development, testing, and collaboration so that you can keep up with rapid, technology-agnostic change cases.

Cloud Discovery Workshop

Both top-down and bottom-up analysis might benefit from doing a discovery workshop with key business and IT stakeholders, armed with an understanding of the business vision and strategy, to uncover cloud adoption opportunities. This workshop is described in Figure 4.3.

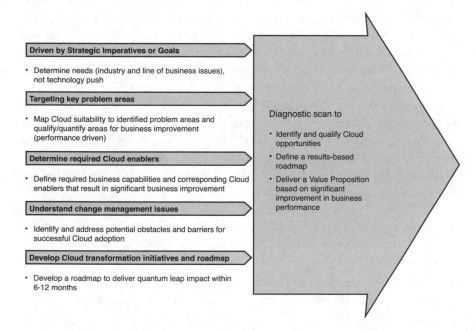

Figure 4.3   Cloud discovery workshop

A cloud discovery workshop can be used to structure a business-oriented session to qualify the most suitable cloud entry points and value proposition for a business competency or business component. The discovery workshop focuses on gaining a common understanding about cloud value proposition for business and IT where the focus is on motivation. Next suitability is determined as to whether, based on business value drivers, opportunities exist to apply cloud thinking. When a possible fit is determined, entry points are discussed to determine initial steps for creating value. Next readiness is understood so that appropriate change management activities can be undertaken. Finally the value case is described with a focus on creating a roadmap where the value case could be any of the following:

- Increase visibility on process execution status and related business object through better integration, activity monitoring, and so on
- Reduce unwanted variety, enforce policy compliance, and closely audit execution
- Cut structural costs to work within new levels of granularity and better quality—process variation support
- Hide internal complexity to simplify business operations and unwanted side effects (ease of doing changes)
- Reduce transaction costs to enable new interaction channels (sales and supplier side)
- Increase ability to be more robust against supply and demand variability
- Innovate business model for entering new value nets
- Lower transaction costs and simplify business boundaries to open up new sourcing options for production and products

The goal of the workshop is to result in cloud adoption opportunities that deliver a quantum leap within 6–12 months for business outcomes that realize the vision and strategy. Relevant key performance indicators are identified with a corresponding cloud solution that becomes part of the roadmap all enabled by cloud capabilities mapped to strategy goals.

Business Scenario: Cloud Decision Analysis for Distributors, Inc.

Considering the good performance of the order fulfillment, one might ask "why consider cloud-sourcing or cloud adoption as an enabler for that business area? Why not just leave well enough alone and focus on customer management where performance was reported as problematic?"

That is like asking Apple, "Why don't you stop building new products, especially after experiencing global success in sales and innovation with the releases of the iPod"—that seems so long ago—"and as of late the iPad and iCloud?" Well that is unlikely, but what is notable about the company's strategy is its ability to market to everyday consumers and gain strong corporate adoption of solutions not directly but through those very same consumers.

In Distributors' case, the team actively pursued enterprise-class order fulfillment functionality that would support anticipated business growth due to new product offerings soon to be introduced to the market. The required functionality and services presented a compelling business case for cloud adoption in comparison to traditional "packaged" solutions.

Sharon saw additional advantages of cloud adoption that would benefit the global sales team. The idea was that a cloud-based order fulfillment system that is accessible over the Internet would prevent downtimes that normally arise when Distributors' internal network becomes geographically inaccessible. In such cases, information is collected on local devices and spreadsheets to be uploaded once systems become accessible. This approach presented challenges to technology teams responsible for maintaining what they expressed as "senseless data repositories."

So, while current financial and service performance was good, there were uncertainties of the current environment's business and technical capacity to keep pace with emerging product offerings and the company's global strategy.

Customer management is a business service area that was notably degrading in performance due to poor in-house customer service and support. The impacts were lost customers, declining sales, wasted spend, and not so positive press. The entire customer management competency was categorized as eligible for business process outsourcing (BPO) using traditional paradigms; the team soon agreed that it was advantageous to consider business process outsourcing to cloud (BPaaS), which by default included offloading IT associated workloads.

Several SaaS solutions were already in use for marketing, digital communications, and human resource management (HRM). The concern was redundancy and again unnecessary spending. For example, one of the marketing providers printed brochures and was paid a premium price for such services, and the CIO questioned the value of such services. Sharon and her team proposed to streamline the amount of SaaS applications to a common business solution where feasibly possible. Portfolio management and improved processes for cloud purchases were highly recommended, and instead of paying premium dollar for print services, the team suggested a focus on green business where such efficiencies would become a part of the company brand. Limited HRM capability was provided by a SaaS provider on a trial basis; since the team was pleased with initial performance Sharon proposed adoption of the provider's HRIS (Human Resource Information System) cloud.

By default, this top-down approach enabled the team to identify opportunities to offload business and IT workloads in a structured and cohesive manner with manageable business risks and continuity. Furthermore, just as the BA was reviewed for candidate BPO opportunities, technical architectural components were reviewed to determine business impacts and associated candidates. This approach is more strategically focused and value centric than Distributors' original, emotional suggestions, which were to offload IT workloads only and without analysis or conducting the proper due diligence.

As mentioned, portfolio management was an issue, but there was also an issue with misaligned business and IT budgets. The net effect and pain point was either ad-hoc reprioritization of IT initiatives to support unplanned business needs or projects were waitlisted causing high frustration levels for all teams involved. This course correction was essential for a successful transition to cloud and required governance for continued operations once new processes were introduced. Figure 4.4 provides a visual illustration of the proposed change, which was to move away from silo to integrated business principles. The left represents the current state where decisions were top down and technology and infrastructure teams were not allowed to collaborate with end users. On the right is the proposed change where decisions would be made collectively and business and technology teams are empowered to collaborate with end users. The infrastructure team would also operate as a service organization as opposed to current mannerisms, which were unresponsive to technology team requests and lacked accountability for poor performance since the technology teams faced the business when issues that were infrastructure related emerged.

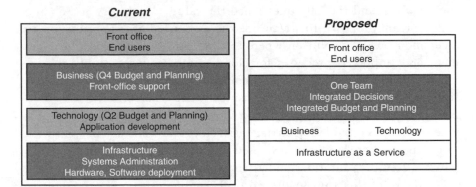

Figure 4.4 Proposed course correction for effective transition to cloud

Summary

This chapter described techniques for identifying cloud candidates as viable solution alternatives and the significance of creating a cloud decision model as an essential element of your enterprise cloud adoption strategy. You were introduced to top-down and bottom-up approaches to identifying cloud candidates and enablers that were supported with real business scenarios and experiences, and considerations for integrating cloud with managed services and traditional outsourcing were discussed.

Often, you might experience situations where business and IT teams are misaligned, but as in the case study depicted, there can be issues in alignment of IT teams and project accountability. In the Distributors case study, which is supported by Figure 4.4, the technology and infrastructure teams operated in silos. In fact, the technology team was frequently blamed by the business units for issues that were infrastructure team-related. The decision to move to cloud was a viable choice, but development of an enterprise cloud adoption strategy encourages stakeholders to look broader and deeper into enablement requirements such as transition planning and governance. In this case, the proposal encompassed recommendations for the infrastructure team to operate as a service organization and provide Infrastructure-as-a-Service, as depicted on the lower right of Figure 4.4. This approach would rectify poor business behaviors and influence more collaborative, proactive decision making between the technology and infrastructure teams with appropriate levels of accountability when it comes to addressing business problems. The approach also supports the company's cloud adoption strategy. Both transition planning and governance are discussed in upcoming chapters.

You might also hear the expression or an expressed desire for teams to look "up" the stack when considering cloud adoption. This is usually due to an emphasis on quick wins or solving immediate pain points without enough emphasis on business process optimization and efficiencies that can have more impact on the organization. Up the stack is therefore where priority is placed on business processes (BPaaS or SaaS) while "down" the stack is when the priority is placed on infrastructure (IaaS or PaaS). Both are suitable when applied in the right context and when you consider your enterprise architecture as was discussed in this chapter.

You can apply the techniques discussed in this chapter to all aspects of cloud decision-making, including application and information sourcing as a strategic and precursory activity to cloud provider selection.

Endnote

1. From TPI Research, "TPI Index: Global Outsourcing Market Not Yet Bouncing Back." See http://www.prnewswire.com/news-releases/tpi-index-global-outsourcing-market-not-yet-bouncing-back-98834619.html.

5

What About Governance?

This chapter describes some business essentials for enabling governance in an enterprise where cloud is a part of the organizational landscape. Included are new and expanded responsibilities; some guiding principles that should be considered when integrating cloud into your enterprise using enterprise architecture principles as a foundation, practical considerations for developing your enterprise cloud governance framework, strategies for governing in the presence of outsourcing, and evolving paradigms such as governing cloud service brokers and organizational innovation. A key outcome of this chapter is insights and added capabilities for communicating the business value of developing and governing your enterprise cloud adoption strategy.

Governance Is Essential for Cloud

Governance is critical to the success of your cloud adoption strategy. You have to think about external forces and the business value that your adoption will bring to your enterprise, and you have to ensure that your adoption fits within your existing environment (business processes, applications, information, infrastructure, standards, and interfaces). Governance is the difference between a successful and sustained adoption where benefits become realized contrasted to a fragmented implementation where cloud adoption makes minimal impact to your strategy and business outcomes.

Example governance considerations include the following:

- Determining how decisions are made relative to cloud adoption, for example, your current review process for business technology adoption should be updated to include cloud and the appropriate subject matter experts
- Determining who in the business owns cloud solutions and ensuring that ownership responsibilities are adequately defined
- Determining who will authorize release of funds for cloud investments
- Authorizing final decision-makers relative to cloud adoption
- Establishing accountability and policies for changing cloud business decisions

This chapter provides practical considerations for enabling governance in an enterprise where cloud is a part of the organizational landscape. Because cloud solutions often involve outsourcing, this chapter also provides guidance for governing in the presence of outsourcing.

Governance can be perceived as an extra (and sometimes unnecessary), but skipping this step often results in poor decision making or none at all, which can lead to wasted time and effort along with unacceptable qualities of service. Essentially, without governance your cloud projects can turn into a mess before they ever get started simply because no one is aware of your strategy or of the necessary roles, responsibilities, or authority levels required for a successful transition to cloud. You probably have experienced situations where no one knows what to do or stakeholders are reluctant to make decisions because they feel that decisions will get overwritten. These are all indicators of little or no enterprise governance.

In their book *Enterprise Architecture as Strategy*, Ross et al. describe IT governance as "specifying the decision rights and accountability framework to encourage desirable behavior in the use of IT."[1] You can apply that same principle to EA governance as "specifying the decision rights and accountability framework to encourage desirable behavior in the use of EA." Now take that definition a step further and apply to this book where governance is "specifying the decision rights and accountability framework to encourage desirable behavior in the use of EA for effective adoption of cloud computing."

Management is the execution of governance and that management by itself is not governance. So while governance is about deriving decision rights, making decisions, and establishing accountability, management is the action or execution of the decision. Both are required and are more effective when integrated.

An Enterprise Cloud Governance Framework

A critical success factor of governance is to not only manage the impacts of cloud on the business (described in previous chapters), but you must also govern the use of cloud. If you have defined your EA, you most likely have defined how it will be governed, for example, through the use of a governance framework where accountability controls are established to ensure appropriate adoption and use of your EA. If that is the case, your next step is to incorporate cloud governance considerations as illustrated in Figure 5.1.

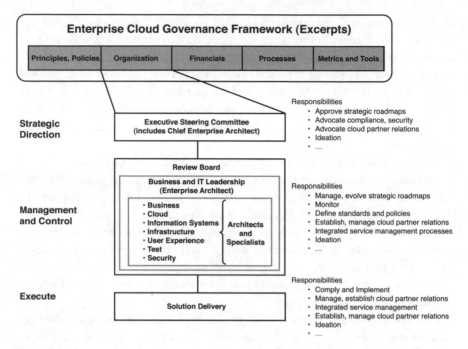

Figure 5.1 Excerpts of an enterprise cloud governance framework. Ideation is added as recognition that innovation is fueled by all stakeholders irrespective of their positions within a company.

If you have not developed a governance framework, you can reference Figure 5.1 as a starting point since some cloud-specific considerations are incorporated. In either case, you should expand and build out the framework to support your enterprise cloud adoption strategy. Here are five core framework components:

- Principles and policies
- Organization
- Financials
- Processes
- Metrics and tools

Principles and Policies

Principles and policies are your business rules and laws for cloud adoption. A principle is a statement of belief that serves as a foundation for establishing decision making policies, while a policy defines the underlying rules that an organization has to use when making cloud adoption decisions. Policies are normally defined at the strategy level. Some examples are decisions relative to cloud provider selection—for example, who is on and off limits, contract restrictions, required service management processes, and specification of enterprise applications and data that are suitable for placement in the cloud. Policies prescribe management direction to guide your organization in meeting its stated business needs and objectives, to ensure the business conforms to prescribed legislation, to demonstrate management commitment, and to clearly define responsibilities. For example, you might have a policy around data encryption or data separation that must be true for private, public, hybrid, and community clouds.

Policies are normally defined at an overall strategy level and can be related to a specific area, for example, security policies or management policies. In many instances, policies reflect the law and givens, which must be adhered to—this is especially true in the case of security and privacy policies. Guidelines may also exist that are general statements of direction, a desired future state that is not necessarily mandated. Guideline statements are similar in content to principle statements but without the associated motivation and benefit statements. Your governance model needs to reflect the mix of principles, policies, and guidelines for IT services whether provided by your internal data center or private/public cloud. Cloud governance requires management of policies given the complex relationships between user groups, cloud providers, and consumers.

Organizational Structure

Organizational structure depicts the leadership and key roles, responsibilities, and levels of accountability that must exist for effective decision making relative to your cloud adoption. An example is establishment of an executive steering committee (ESC) that authorizes and approves cloud purchases and an architecture review board (ARB) that determines the effectiveness of integrating cloud into your environment. These teams are critical toward building, executing, and integrating cloud into your enterprise.

Governance is particularly useful when day-to-day operations are pressing because of the temptation to simply get the job done—whatever it takes—and the adoption of cloud does not remove these tendencies. In a properly governed environment, however, the right decisions are made, clearly communicated, and readily adaptable to both strategic and tactical situations.

A few roles and responsibilities mentioned in the diagram are worth elaborating on as there are additions to traditional EA responsibilities with the adoption of cloud, while Appendix A, "Augmenting Your Delivery Model with Cloud," provides more information on cloud actors and their specific roles and responsibilities. Ideation is discussed in the upcoming section, "Governing Innovation."

The chief enterprise architect must be able to communicate with the most senior executives the value of cloud and the advantages of developing and executing your strategy without going into the intricacies of infrastructure and cloud implementation details. You can expect that senior executives are looking for more than the typical responses such as cloud will allow you to stand up an environment faster than your enterprise IT organization. They are looking for the value and impacts of cloud adoption on the business, and they are looking for opportunities to positively impact the bottom line for an extended period of time.

This responsibility is significant for both small and large enterprises that, for instance, might be interested in expanding their market share, or they might be on the verge of adoption but are wavering because of publicized outage experiences. Your chief enterprise architect might in turn suggest innovative strategies such as the use of aggregated cloud provider partnering to ensure that should a primary provider's service become unavailable, partner services are executed so that service levels and your end user experiences remain in tact.

If you are an enterprise architect, it is highly recommended that you obtain cloud business skills at a minimum and be able to guide decisions. You will be faced with situations such as service management asking about the guidelines for commissioning and decommissioning cloud environments in your organization. Traditionally, this would not be the case; however, because there is a potential to offload key dimensions of your EA to cloud—for example, you can offload a significant majority of your infrastructure components and services—you need the skills to drive the right business decisions that ensure interoperability across your organization and the various lines of business.

The cloud architect was added to the ARB. The skills and talents of this role from a business and technology perspective should not be overlooked. As the South African case study demonstrates in Appendix B,

"Cloud Case Studies and Common Questions," a significant problem was over provisioning cloud environments, which caused more harm than good (the client was initially unable to reap the full benefits of their cloud undertakings due to excess maintenance of virtual environments). The role of the cloud architect can help standardize virtualization strategies and related business efficiencies.

Included is the user experience architect, which is a crucial role for determining the appropriate service interfaces to be presented to end users and consumers of cloud services. Many consumers, for example, require their own portal to remain the entry point for cloud consumption, which implies that provider services are accessible through the use of application programming interfaces (APIs) or Web services. The review board should also include a test and security architect, and both must be adapted to support enterprise integration of cloud solutions through development of test strategies and establishment of adequate processes, procedures, and tools that help validate that any proposals for cloud adoption are secured so that risks for vulnerabilities are mitigated.

NOTE

Security is not a check mark but rather a fundamental part of your enterprise cloud adoption strategy. The sooner we become aware of and start considering security requirements in cloud decision making the less likely projects will experience costly downstream project or vendor related issues once the move to cloud commences. Often, the perception is that addressing security should occur during technical solution discussions, and that the conversation should be led solely by the security team. During a recent life sciences project, the exploration workshop was comprised of business and technology executives and line of business leaders who willingly discussed business security objectives as they contemplated the use of public clouds for fixed content such as e-mail attachments along with backup and recovery of medical image data.

Some organizations have formed a Cloud Center of Competency (CoC) that is comprised of resources with deep cloud business and technology skills. This might not be required for organizations that are purely interested in public cloud consumption. But if private "on-premise" cloud consumption is a part of your strategy, then deeper skills are required. You should also expect that a CoC or similar organization exists within your cloud provider's domain and consider this a part of your provider selection criteria in areas such as product viability.

Significant responsibilities at the strategic level are listed and include the following:

- Approve strategic roadmaps.
- Advocate compliance and security.
- Advocate cloud partner relationships.

The executive steering committee company approves and contributes to development of strategic roadmaps ensuring that budget and funding activities are given priority and that roadmaps are aligned with the over-arching vision of the company. In fact, the more engaged executive sponsorship is during development of your enterprise cloud adoption strategy (typically conducted by a dedicated strategy team) the better, since a key outcome is a strategic cloud roadmap, and because the same stakeholders that comprise your strategy team might very well become members of your executive steering committee.

As depicted, the executive steering committee is an advocate and speaker regarding the necessity of compliance with industry regulations as well as corporate policies, and they speak to the validity of establishing partner relationships in advance leveraging their networks to facilitate the process. Each of the responsibilities described is critical and should not be omitted given the direct impacts on service excellence.

The responsibilities at the management and control layer, particularly of the architecture review board include

- Managing/evolving and defining strategic roadmaps.
- Monitoring compliance.
- Defining standards and policies.
- Establishing and managing cloud partner relations—which traditionally resided at the execution (the next layer) of EA—requires focus prior to execution.
- Integrating service management processes.

The architecture review board is comprised of business and IT leadership and encompasses architects and subject experts or specialists.

Working closely with both steering committees and solution delivery teams, the review board manages and controls cloud adoption within the organization ensuring that your enterprise cloud adoption strategy evolves and remains relevant as your business climate evolves. For instance, if you commenced your cloud adoption journey as a consumer of Software-as-a-Service (SaaS) solutions and you evolve your business to become a value added reseller (VAR) of SaaS services, your enterprise cloud adoption strategy must reflect this vision and the path for reaching your desired state.

The board sets corporate standards, and they are aware of industry standards and the necessary steps for compliance. The team also manages, communicates, and might establish cloud partner relationships in an effort to influence downstream selection of cloud providers for effective cloud solution delivery. Another key responsibility is to establish integrated service management processes, for example, change and release management procedures for adopting and integrating cloud solutions across your company.

The solution delivery team is responsible for executing your enterprise cloud adoption strategy and applying the standards on specific projects. The communication flow is both downstream for specific projects and upstream as feedback to the review board and the executive steering committee typically in the form of practical experiences and lessons learned. Executive steering committee responsibilities include ensuring that projects:

- Comply and implement.
- Manage and establish cloud partner relations.
- Integrate service management policies and principles.

Delivery experiences, where best practices are captured as part of your EA, keep your enterprise cloud adoption strategy viable and relevant as they comply and implement standards, policies, and principles on cloud projects. The team is ultimately responsible for cloud provider selection and managing relationships for the good of the projects they support. The team might establish cloud partner relationships leveraging suggested partners from the ESC and review board, and they integrate and implement service management policies and principles across provider channels for delivery excellence.

Financials

Financial governance is incorporated into the framework and should not be new to traditional EA governance frameworks. Financial governance is a key influencer of cloud adoption and business technologies as a whole. It involves financial stewardship, development of funding models, financial management, and establishment of acceptable business cases for cloud investments.

Financial management may appear less complex for cloud due to the pay per use pricing model and also due to the bundling of services, which at a minimum reduces the amount of contracts that your organization is required to manage, but be prepared for a hybrid environment of traditional and cloud based services and contracts—at least initially. How will cloud services be governed, for instance, so that you manage renewals and only continue subscriptions that add value to the business?

Revenues generated due to the benefits of cloud adoption are an example financial area that should be governed. Considering that the transition to cloud helps organizations improve services to customers (and business units in the case of private adoption) through, for example, faster time to value and reduced costs since support staff is streamlined or no longer required to manage issues with client downloads and server access issues, your cloud adoption strategy might involve budgeting for and reallocating earned revenues for strategic and related corporate imperatives such as the establishment of executive training programs that enable employees to more effectively oversee and govern cloud service providers. Financial governance, in this example, ensures that your monetary objectives are identified and carried forward through stakeholder accountability, budget allocations, auditing of financial activities, tracking of earned revenues and expenditures, and appropriation of funds that are associated with cloud adoption.

It is important to measure the financial viability and impacts of your adoption choices on your organization from both a short- and long-term perspective. This subject is covered further in Chapter 8, "Financial Considerations."

Processes

Governance of the cloud environment forces you to make concrete requirements as to what governance procedures your cloud provider must have in place, or define a collaborative governance process where you peek into their environment to see if processes are executed appropriately. The most effective governance model for you, the consumer, is going to be collaborative governance since you are interested in consuming the cloud versus day to day running of the cloud—which is the responsibility of the provider....With respect to governing your EA with the inception of cloud...management processes may change but your decision framework, which is what governance is all about, should be neutral to sourcing.

Claus Jensen, Senior Technical Staff Member, IBM

Governance processes fall within four main categories, as listed here and illustrated in Figure 5.2:

- Management
- Vitality
- Compliance
- Communication

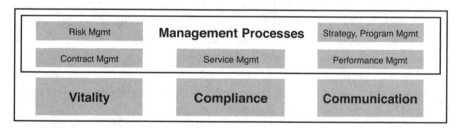

Figure 5.2 Management processes

Management processes ensure executive involvement and oversight of your cloud adoption strategy and execution. Risk management is not a new addition to governance processes, but it is emphasized as a focus point when considering cloud adoption and should be addressed as early as possible during strategy development and considered throughout every phase of your enterprise cloud adoption life cycle. Additions to management processes are establishing responsibility and contract accountability; service management requires more integrated principles (to be discussed in Chapter 6, "Mitigating Risk"). Then, there is performance management. Some key questions that stakeholders will address relative to performance management are

- Where are the opportunities to improve your business performance?
- Where should you allocate IT resources to support your enterprise cloud adoption strategy?
- Which non differentiating activities should be considered for cloud-sourcing?
- When is it appropriate to cloud-source your core business applications?
- Who will update your EA so that cloud adoption and enablement patterns are standardized?

Each of the identified processes can be more difficult to establish and maintain in a cloud setting because you have no real visibility into provider operations, and as such joint development of contracts, service level agreements (SLAs), explicit service requirements such as identifying when and how you want to be notified when an SLA is in jeopardy in addition to business controls are of the essence and will mitigate business risk.

Vitality processes ensure that your adoption strategy is maintained and communicated as your organization evolves and new business and IT components are incorporated into your EA. An example vitality process is standards definition. Standards are specifications that are authoritative and valuable. Standards are what your organization perceives as valuable and chooses to adhere to in an effort to facilitate business performance. As mentioned in the previous section, "Organizational Structure," the execution of your enterprise cloud adoption strategy by your SD team is an example measurement of its vitality.

Compliance processes define a structured approach to review and approve cloud adoption decisions. These processes include formal reviews at key control points prior to and during project implementations. The ability and convenience of expensing IT capability monthly using a cloud business model might allow a business unit to bring in new technology without giving the IT staff and other leaders the opportunity to vet solutions for reuse or to make sure any candidate cloud choices comply with your enterprise security standards and policies for governing information.

Another example compliance process is exception handling and appeals. Exception handling is crucial in the management of risk and complexity as well as the tracking of cloud and other business technologies. Regulatory and industry-specific compliance policies and processes must be addressed sooner rather than later in your decision cycle such as the implications of data privacy on your decision to adopt public, private, and/or hybrid clouds. Your enterprise cloud adoption strategy should contain compliance processes for your common business scenarios and serve as a reference point for those seeking direction on compliance procedures.

Good exception handling is a necessity for ensuring that your strategy is flexible and valuable if applied appropriately. It does not change with the introduction of cloud in the enterprise; however, it is recommended that cloud subject matter experts are a part of the exception and appeals process so that requests are interpreted appropriately. Caution should be taken to approve exceptions that are justifiable so that the exception handling process does not get misused and requests approved by default whereby the process loses its value. The exception handling process is usually initiated by a project manager making a request for an exception.

Communication processes ensure that all stakeholders stay informed about your enterprise cloud adoption strategy.

Metrics and Tools

Metrics and tools enable you to effectively govern, manage, and monitor the performance of local and extended environments that now incorporate cloud; this is an essential component in your governance framework. Metrics ensure that the processes are being properly controlled and are delivering the desired results.

At a minimum, your metrics must have strong correlation with desired goals, be collectable in a consistent manner, and be collected without much overhead. You should include factors for selecting metrics such as frequency of data collection, frequency of reporting, recipients of the metrics, and tools.

Example tools (which are not limited to metrics) are those that support information collection (e.g., cloud portfolio and application inventory), metrics databases, and dashboards that include enablement of self-service entrance to and exit from the cloud with traceability, online training, billing and metering, application development (if applicable you will decide whether you want to invest in-house or cloud-source), quality assurance (QA) and testing, benchmarking, and communication tools. Cloud consumers need assurance that security and privacy policies are consistently applied; therefore, processes and tools are needed to monitor and report compliance or violation of security or privacy policies in remote clouds. Your governance framework will identify the appropriate sets of tools for managing cloud data and environments internal and external to your organization.

TIP

While we recommend each of the types of tools mentioned, I have found that the most commonly overlooked items are the QA and testing tools, particularly on the consumer's side because of the black box approach to cloud adoption. In addition to metrics, test strategy examples, QA guidelines, and suggestions for testing tools are highly recommended as a part of your enterprise cloud adoption strategy to validate your metrics and to govern the adoption of viable cloud solutions and integrated service management.

Key to your metrics and monitoring capability is the use of performance dashboards that allow you to anticipate as well as monitor progression of your organization. For example: What percentage of your organization is leveraging your learning effectiveness system that is powered by cloud for executive leadership advancement? Once learning initiatives are completed, are your leaders performing better, the same, or worse on the job? Considering this same example and more specific to your enterprise cloud adoption strategy, you can more effectively anticipate who will and should be able to use both your performance dashboard and your learning effectiveness systems if they are consumable in the cloud.

Establishing Ownership

Considering that enterprises are becoming more complex due to a mixture of in-house and externally provided services that must be governed and managed, it is important to discuss ownership and some associated impediments. In this context, ownership refers to accountability for the successful adoption and governance of your enterprise where cloud is a part of the solution strategy. The following are three key elements:

■ **Executive ownership:** Too often, executive sponsors are counted on for financial support alone. While financial backing is expected, expressed ownership and supportive actions are just as critical and expected from all sponsors and stakeholders. This includes development of project management staff so that they learn to manage cloud projects more effectively and active participation in workshops, interviews, and information exchanges that drive cloud decisions. Keep in mind that when employees and customers see this executive endorsement, they are more subject to adhere to any organizational changes introduced as a result of adoption.

NOTE

Here are some experienced issues related to executive ownership that you should consider and hopefully resolve as a part of your enterprise cloud adoption strategy, and certainly before commencement of cloud purchases:

■ Executives are inaccessible and appear to support initiatives in name only.
■ Executives need to balance time accordingly for low-value items and high-value projects and prioritization.
■ Decisions are not made in decision forums such as steering committee meetings.
■ The outward demonstration of favored initiatives regardless of the value.

■ **Business unit ownership:** Business owners are typically line of business leaders accountable for the business outcomes of the services and management of the portfolios. They are an integral part of the cloud selection, ownership of the cloud portfolio, and service level requirements determination and agreement processes. Business leaders should work closely with IT leaders to make cloud adoption decisions. This, of course, means decision processes require flexibility and business agility so that innovation and feedback loops are welcomed. Contract management is expected and usually owned by business units but requires technical leadership.

- **Information Technology (IT) ownership:** Addresses operations of the
  services and required interfaces with cloud providers. IT teams play an
  integral part in establishing cloud adoption and integration requirements
  and provide practical guidance in the establishment of service level
  requirements. IT co-owns adopted cloud solutions and services along
  with business units, and they may very well own or co-own the responsibility of governing cloud solution providers.

Governing in the Presence of Outsourcing

Because it is possible that you or your cloud provider might incorporate traditional outsourcing or out-tasking to fulfill service level agreements, it is pertinent to discuss the notion of governance in the presence
of outsourcing.

Outsourcing is the process of subcontracting to a third party where
the relationship or partnership is strategic and generally of a longer
duration than out-tasking. Out-tasking occurs for small scale tasks and
for shorter durations. Because of the task centricity, resource pools are
used to address business needs that are sourced from various providers,
whereas with outsourcing you have a common provider. Cloud-sourcing
consists of both outsourcing and out-tasking workloads to cloud for
automated, transactional-based services, whereas with outsourcing and
out-tasking, automation might not be a part of the equation and therefore efforts remain manual.

If you have outsourced some of your operations and you now choose to
cloud-source others, be mindful that in the traditional outsourced setting you will have more access to people, services are usually not shared
by other customers (e.g., multi-tenancy), and, in many cases, customized
outcomes are easier to accommodate because you own the resources that
are performing the services. That is not the same as in a cloud-sourced
situation where services are digitized and environments are shared with
other customers. You do not own the resources conducting the services
for you (private clouds are an exception), and there is less opportunity to
customize due to standardized offerings. Here are some key messages
relative to governing in the presence of outsourcing:

- Protect proprietary information (including information shared with you
  by outsourced providers, such as their rates, key business processes, and

work artifacts) and ensure that intellectual property rights and clauses are established that clearly specify who owns any project outcomes.

- Do not expect the same types of contracts (outsourcing contracts are generally fixed while cloud contracts are typically variable).

- Outsourced services might require more vendor contact through the use of call centers, for example, whereas cloud providers are likely to be anonymous with more self-service capabilities.

- In an outsourced setting, you own your assets although you might temporarily transfer ownership of your data center, for instance, to your provider, whereas with cloud, you subscribe to and rent assets and at a said period of time you determine whether to renew or discontinue use of the rented assets. Both occurrences (owned and borrowed asset models) must be governed accordingly.

- Know whether your provider is using outsourcing or out-tasking services and factor this in during the selection process. For instance, if your provider uses global resources and that is unacceptable due to regulatory requirements, you should execute your rights to either move on to another provider or if your provider can accommodate your conditions—for example, they will source staff from a designated country and citizenship—then you should explicitly stipulate your requirements and your expectations regarding accountability and noncompliance.

- As with outsourcing, governance of provider relationships in addition to contracts are important, and complacency in this area can be costly for organizations. Consider the following Virginia business scenario and implications: a massive $2 billion computer upgrade outsourcing arrangement was reported as so troubled that core government services were disrupted yet there were concerns that canceling the contract early could cost the state as much as $400 million and leave no one to manage its computer systems.
  The report cited that a prison was left without inbound phone service for hours; the Virginia State Police lost Internet access for more than three days; and computers in DMV offices crashed. It was cited that a "convoluted" governance structure that involved the use of an independent board led to confusion and a need for clarity as to who governed vendor relationships, who had legal accountability for deliverables and service outcomes, what should have happened when a service agreement was not met, and who spoke on behalf of state agencies to the outsourcer.[2]

Governing Cloud Service Brokers

You read about governing the inception of cloud in your organization and the significance of governing your enterprise cloud adoption strategy. In the upcoming Chapter 6, you will review an example checklist for selecting cloud providers in an effort to reduce business risks associated with inadequate provider selection and adverse impacts such as lost customers and top-line revenue declines. As a part of your enterprise cloud adoption strategy, you might consider when and where the role of the cloud service broker (CSB) is applicable. Stakeholders might, for instance, require assistance in determining the best fit cloud solutions, or you might seek guidance on how to optimize the value of any previous or planned cloud investments. Considering your needs and the vast array of cloud services that are available and continue to emerge, the use of CSBs might be appropriate and beneficial to your cause.

CSBs are trusted advisors that act on your behalf and as an intermediary with originating cloud service providers. Although the responsibilities can be carried out by your internal staff (and systems), CSBs, are typically third-party consultants whose responsibilities are to manage a network of providers on behalf of your organization. When selecting CSBs, you should choose those that are capable and credible when it comes to end-to-end integration of selected services with existing enterprise business processes, systems, data, and security in multi-sourced situations. This means that your CSB is able to link the various types of providers together so that business performance remains solid and any issues are resolved efficiently and without service disruption. As the opening case study pointed out, if you do not clearly define the roles and responsibilities of your broker (or agent) with adequate governance that includes performance checks and balances, you might experience undesirable and unexpected consequences.

Clearly defined expectations are essential to an effective governance program and your ability to measure your CSB's performance. Listed are some key decision categories and example expectations that you should include as a part of your CSB evaluation and selection process:

- Decide the business purpose for introducing CSBs into your organization. Ask yourself what the business need is and what the CSB offers to meet your business need that you might not be able to effectively provide for yourself. A trigger for many organizations that leverage CSBs is management of multisourced IT business models where solutions are sourced from cloud, outsourced providers, and other venues. An experienced CSB will simplify the management complexities of multiple service providers, and they can provide a single point of contact and accountability. If you do not have clarity as to the business purpose, how can you effectively govern and manage your CSB's performance?

- Determine how you want to leverage CSBs and what specific services they will provide. You might for instance require them to provide and maintain a common catalog of applications or services from independent service providers (ISVs) to ease the shopping experience of your end users, and to save time and effort on your part in storefront management and cloud service aggregation.

NOTE

We have experienced the interlock of CSBs and ISV SaaS services with both small and large enterprises, particularly in the telecommunications industry. In such situations it is common for CSBs to pass on SLAs for the cloud services it receives from ISVs to clients. Most ISVs provide SLAs of 99.9 percent, some 99.5 percent, and some may not provide SLAs at all; therefore, it is important that you govern and manage all expectations of your providers and your CSBs specific to cloud delivery and SLAs.

Here are some additional examples of how to explicitly quantify and set expectations of your CSBs: You decide to leverage your CSBs to interview and offer suggestions for cloud provider selection or you decide that the sole purpose of your CSB is to design, develop, and orchestrate the integration of on-premise systems and off-premise cloud solutions. In addition to communicating your expectations, you appoint a governing body that oversees the relationship, monitors CSB performance, and promptly addresses deviations so that business impacts are marginalized.

- Determine what decision rights and levels of authority you want to place in your CSBs hands considering that their primary responsibility is to act as a proxy on your behalf for a scope of work and for a predetermined period of time. For instance your CSB can interview and communicate with potential cloud service providers on behalf of your organization, and they can recommend selection of providers with an understanding that the actual adoption decisions are to be made by you and your team.

■ Establish viable pricing strategies for CSB services and be sure to specify that the pricing model depends on the role and responsibilities of selected CSBs. As an example, if your CSB is to operate as a partner and its responsibility is to ensure that your cloud investments are profitable, you might create a consumption based plan where CSBs receive a percentage of the profits that are directly tied to your cloud investments. This example pricing strategy encourages and rewards your CSBs as they partner with you to grow your business. You might apply similar pricing strategies for CSBs that operate as an aggregator of services from numerous providers. Your governing responsibility is to ensure that there is stakeholder accountability for developing and enforcing viable pricing strategies for your company. You will learn of other pricing strategies and techniques as you read upcoming chapters.

■ As mentioned in earlier chapters, companies are creating storefronts or what can be described as "AppStores" where services are distributed through a marketplace for a controlled service portfolio offering and more significantly an efficiently managed end-user browsing and shopping experience. Since the concept of governing AppStores might be applicable to you, here are six (6) key considerations:

1. Ensure that the best fit applications are provided through your AppStore. Success criteria should be quality (since you ultimately are endorsing the applications) and value-add to your organization through internal and external users.

2. Ensure that your AppStore continuously evolves so that appropriate solutions are offered to your customers. Application of business analytics and sentiment analysis can be an invaluable tool for capturing marketing insights and operational metrics. If you are working with business partners or ISVs, they should provide such capability so that the right products are presented to the right groups of customers.

3. Unlike some AppStores where applications are restricted to a specific device type, your AppStore should be accessible from anywhere and contain solutions that are consumable through Web interfaces so that you simplify your end-user's shopping experience.

4. Your AppStore capability needs to respond to inquiries and reported problems with service excellence. You should continuously govern this process. Metrics such as recurring revenues, expenses, and client satisfaction are key to your AppStore use and its sustainability.

5. Establish a product distribution strategy and billing model with a focus on how you will integrate the AppStore into your existing distribution processes. Govern how fast and efficient it is to integrate new and upgraded services into your AppStore with corrective alternatives.

6. Ensure that you market the customer experience and business capability versus marketing cloud. Market the customer experience such as a quick purchasing and billing processes. Market the business capability such as accelerated time to delivery of goods and services. Key to governance is tracking and managing the cost of doing business, the time it takes to integrate new services, and the rate of customer growth.

You can find more on the subject of AppStores in Appendix C, "More on Cloud Business Trends."

Governing Innovation

Technology, to be sure, is only a part of America's innovation story, but it is a critical one.

John Kao, Innovation Nation

Executives are taking advantage of cloud adoption for competitive and strategic advantages such as business model diversification and emergence into new and existing markets with the rapid introduction of products and/or services that stem from improved, cloud enabled business processes. Cloud ideation should therefore be encouraged and invited from business as well as IT stakeholders of all ranks within your organization and your partner channels.

At the core of governing innovation is propelling (not stifling) ideas and actions forward that drive value internal and external to your organization. However, all too often governance within enterprises is perceived as a set of rules and bylaws that have been established by a select body of individuals that might not welcome creativity or the associated changes unless the ideas are initiated by that same body of governors. That being said, here are some questions for you:

- Have you asked your employees and business partners for their ideas on how to take advantage of cloud to drive enterprise innovation?

- As ideas come forward, who listens and how are decisions made as to submitter responses?

- If no ideas emerge, have you asked yourself why, and are you effectively addressing the matter?

- Who is accountable and what are criteria for approving and evolving ideas from concepts to business innovations?

- Who decides which rewards are appropriate?

Google is one of numerous companies known for innovation. Google has a reputation for inviting and listening to ideas brought forward under the auspices that any employee can come up with the next breakthrough. Most notable is the "20 percent time"[3] rule where employees are allowed to work on what they're really passionate about for 20 percent of the time to spark new business innovations. A good example of a business outcome is the company's response to the Japan tsunami that reportedly prompted many "Googlers" to devote their "20-percent time" to crafting Digital Age tools for handling the crisis.[4]

Cloud-based mobile applications are recent innovations offered by numerous companies that are gaining momentum. These applications can scale beyond the capabilities of most smart phones because you are no longer bound to the processing and storage capacity of mobile devices. IBM's business process simulator CityOne[5] is another example innovation powered by the convergence of gaming, social media, and cloud.

When it comes to governing innovation you need to establish a constructive measurement system so that you reward appropriately. While this may vary per organization, the following are some measurements that can be weighted and rewarded based on the value system that has been established for your organization:

- **Strategic impact:** There are value centric business impacts such as new or improved business processes.

- **Financial impact:** There are bottom line impacts that include cost takeouts and improved earnings potential at a local and global scale.

- **Asset reusability:** There is demonstrable reuse potential across your company and clients.

- **Client satisfaction:** Both internal and external clients will benefit from the innovation.
- **Collaboration:** The innovation was developed in a collaborative, co-creative manner.
- **Image:** The innovation adds favorably to your company's reputation.

The following business scenario was derived from practical experiences. The scenario furthers some of the governance topics covered in this chapter and shares some lessons learned from the experience.

Business Scenario: Innovation and Cloud Provider Company

Innovation Inc., was new to the cloud experience. The company had a little more than 50,000 employees with a business strategy as simple as to be known in the market as a cloud consumer, while the strategic vision was to become a cloud provider in the future. The CEO of Innovation often expressed to stakeholders that the reputation and experiences that the company would gain as a cloud consumer would add to Innovation's potential for success as a cloud provider. The goal was to start small and outsource infrastructure components to cloud, followed by platform and some applications. Innovation hired a Cloud Provider Company whom they had conducted business with for years in a consulting and traditional outsourcing capacity. The agreement was that the Cloud Provider Company would provide consulting services initially and then become a cloud service provider or broker depending on the outcomes of the initial assignment and decisions that were made regarding cloud adoption.

The CIO at Innovation (David) met with the CIO (Sandy) and the enterprise architect (Adam) from Cloud Provider Company and communicated the vision and that Innovation was not sure which cloud services to adopt and required consulting expertise to determine the best solutions and approach. Innovation suggested a starting point of Infrastructure-as-a-Service (IaaS) because both storage and disaster recovery services had been discussed, and preliminary executive approvals were obtained. Cloud Provider Company agreed to the terms.

Though there was mild contention in the beginning due to financial issues (Innovation wanted to extend a prior outsourcing contract between Cloud Provider Company to take advantage of the fixed pricing model), Cloud Provider Company convincingly encouraged use of a separate contract specifically for cloud consulting services.

Upon commencement of the engagement, the first thing that Adam required from Cloud Provider Company was the need to firm the scope of the engagement, define a governance framework, and derive an approach for understanding market requirements so that any cloud decisions were beneficial to Innovation's end users. Unfortunately, Adam was unable to converse with the David after the project commenced due to David's unavailability, so Adam searched industry analyst reports and competitor Web sites to understand specific industry demands that might be applicable to Innovation's situation.

A chief technology officer (CTO) from Innovation, unfamiliar to Sandy, sent an e-mail to her requesting a project kickoff as soon as possible. Sandy scheduled meetings to plan the kickoff and the engagement approach, but each time the meeting was rescheduled due to internal issues at Innovation, causing project delays of three weeks. Sandy escalated the issue to the executive steering committee at Cloud Provider Company complaining that she was unable to tell who from Innovation is responsible for what.

After describing the situation to the executive steering committee, both governance and management were identified as top issues on the Innovation account. At that point, the joint teams met and agreed to the following immediate steps to guide decision making and to move the team forward. The governance framework is depicted alphabetically commencing with the financial component. As decisions were made and roles and responsibilities were qualified, the governance framework became more complete and was carried forward into an engagement model and formal project plan:

- Financials:
    - Appoint financial steward.
    - Assess financial impacts.
    - Appoint business case lead.
    - Determine cloud procurement team.
    - Develop funding model.

- Metrics and Tools:
    - Appoint metrics lead.
    - Establish key business value measurements and metrics.
    - Determine dashboard, reporting, and enterprise infrastructure and management requirements, including tools.
    - Determine QA strategy.
- Organization:
    - Appoint executive committee lead.
    - Appoint program management office (PMO) lead and form PMO.
    - Appoint cloud business requirements lead and formalize requirements processes.
    - Establish and appoint team members and key contacts from Innovation and Cloud Provider Company to participate in reviews with Innovation business stakeholders and product development teams to understand cloud opportunities and business impacts.
    - Establish and appoint Innovation's architect to partner with Cloud Provider Company's enterprise architect.
    - Establish and appoint strategic roadmap development leader.
    - Establish joint executive sponsorship and review cadence.
- Principles, Policies:
    - Appoint policy lead.
    - Determine information privacy classifications.
    - Review corporate policies for regulatory, multitenancy, and business development requirements.
    - Establish cloud adoption principles and policies.
- Processes:
    - Appoint process lead.
    - Develop a cloud portfolio management process and strategy.
    - Establish cadence for risk and mitigation reviews.
    - Establish service management strategy.
    - Establish joint executive reviews and cadence with communication plans.
    - Conduct joint agreement of cloud candidates and prioritization to occur between both companies.
    - Conduct joint planning of project kickoff.

- Plan reviews of cloud-specific roles and responsibilities.
- Review business and technical architecture (from existing EA), including security to assess cloud opportunities and enablement requirements.

Over a short period of time, each of the items in this framework was addressed, and the team was able to develop a formal engagement plan. The impact of governance was not the development of the plan; the impact was that business decisions were made, accountabilities were established, and management processes were put in place to ensure that the decision framework evolved and was executed. The team was able to later launch a project kickoff and move forward with refinements and execution of the plan. In this example, Cloud Provider Company provides an example of effective governance where issues were escalated to decision-making authorities and appropriate actions taken; while Innovation provides an example of poor governance.

Summary

This chapter described practical considerations for enabling governance in an enterprise where cloud is a part of the organizational landscape. We addressed new and expanded responsibilities introduced as a result of cloud and some guiding principles that should be considered for integrating cloud into your enterprise. Understanding the significance of governance and your executive stakeholders' ability to describe the value of governing your enterprise cloud adoption strategy will add to its longevity and reuse across business units. Senior stakeholders should regularly ask how proposed cloud decisions and associated projects would leverage and impact your EA, and along with senior cloud architects they should engage enterprise architects in evaluations, brainstorming, and cloud decision making. While the roles of the user experience and test architects are not new, responsibilities are expanded to support cloud adoption, and the importance of addressing security considerations during cloud exploration sessions and decision making discussions are stressed.

This chapter is a reminder that it is important to govern your business contracts and finances by appointing financial stewards. This appointment helps ensure that funding and appropriation of funds are in order and governed by qualified individuals. Governance of financials also involves traceability of cloud investments to the rightful business and IT owners.

Because cloud solutions often involve outsourcing, provided is guidance for governing in the presence of outsourcing where the need for setting clear direction and SLAs for externally provided services are emphasized. As with outsourcing and as was discussed in Chapter 4, "Identifying Cloud Candidates," cloud adoption out of frustration with IT suggests that course corrections are in order to prevent any underlying issues from adversely influencing your strategy and cloud adoption decision making. An example might be establishing an integrated business and IT governance framework that integrates with your enterprise architecture as was depicted in Figure 5.1 or if you recall from Chapter 4, the course corrections were alignment of business and IT budgets and empowerment of technology and infrastructure teams to converse with end users.

You might choose to leverage the services of Cloud Service Brokers (CSBs), and should that be the case, vendor management, communications, and relationship accountability are all instrumental to your success. Example decision categories were described for your CSB evaluation and selection processes:

1. Decide the business purpose for engaging CSBs.
2. Determine how you want to leverage CSBs and what specific services they will provide.
3. Determine what decision rights and levels of authority you want to place in your CSB's hands considering that their primary responsibility is to act as a proxy on your behalf for a scope of work and for a predetermined period of time.
4. Establish viable pricing strategies for CSB services and specify that the pricing model will depend on the role and responsibilities determined for your CSB.

When it comes to governing innovation, enterprises are faced with establishing budgets and a capacity for research, development, commercialization, learning from failures, and rewarding innovations. Example cloud innovations were provided with a focused discussion on the objectives of governance, which is to propel (and not stifle) ideation from all enterprise stakeholders while a board of governors is appropriate to evaluate ideas and determine the level of innovation and the submitters' eligibility for rewards. Some evaluation criteria for rewarding innovators was shared along with the importance of validating the usefulness of ideas to consumers when assessing the business impacts, which is a key criterion for promoting an idea to a business innovation.

NOTE

If there is no marketability, then an idea may be a good one, but it is not a business innovation.

A business scenario—Innovation and Cloud Provider Company—described the impacts of poor governance and the excess churn and unnecessary costs to the Innovation Company due to indecisiveness and a duplication of roles, responsibilities, and effort. Good governance was demonstrated by Cloud Provider Company, which led to effective decision making and enabled business operations to move forward.

When it comes to governing your enterprise cloud adoption strategy, what matters most is enabling the right people, processes, information, and technologies to obtain the appropriate levels of accountability and oversight so that effective decisions are made at the right time by the right parties. Effective governance and management ensures that the execution of your strategy is successful and enduring. Recall that management is the action or execution of decisions that are made and might very well change as your enterprise cloud adoption strategy changes. Some key management processes were outlined and elaborated throughout the chapter. Governance, on the other hand, is your decision framework, which will change less often than management. It is about who makes decisions and their decision rights. Both governance and management are most effective when applied together.

The next chapter covers techniques for mitigating risks associated with cloud adoption.

Endnotes

1.　Ross et al. 2006. Enterprise Architecture as Strategy. Harvard Business School Press, Boston Massachusetts.

2.　The Washington Post reported the incident. "Outsourced $2 Billion Computer Upgrade Disrupts Va. Services." See http://www.washingtonpost.com/wp-dyn/content/article/2009/10/13/AR2009101303044.html.

3. "Google's '20 Percent Time' in Action." May 18, 2006. See http://googleblog.blogspot.com/2006/05/googles-20-percent-time-in-action.html.

4. "Google '20 Percent Time' Going to Help Japan." March 17, 2011. See http://www.physorg.com/news/2011-03-google-percent-japan.html.

5. "CityOne Game for Business Process Simulations." See http://www-01.ibm.com/software/solutions/soa/innov8/cityone/index.html.

6

Mitigating Risk

If you invest in a volatile business, then you are cast as being "risky." If you apply for a mortgage after a recent bankruptcy, you are considered "high risk." If you are a "low risk" investor, then you probably prefer bonds over stocks. Most people would agree that risk is "The impact of an event factored with its probability of occurrence" where the impact is either favorable or unfavorable. This chapter focuses on mitigating the occurrence and the business impacts of unfavorable cloud adoption experiences in your company.

Cloud Risk Management and Response Strategies

A small Internet-based retailer named Retail Stores, Inc., is going through a particularly eventful time of year and decides to leverage an Infrastructure-as-a-Service (IaaS) provider to supplement its in-house Web hosting capability during peak times. The sourcing decision and use of a public cloud service provider falls under the accountability of the IT department. Although the provider is responsible for delivering IaaS services, the situation is risky for Retail Stores as it is investing and reliant on external resources for a key business capability. Additional risks are present since Retail Stores is accountable for delivering a quality performing Web site with positive user experiences irrespective of the sourcing strategy. Retail Stores, Inc., has at least five risks to manage. First, the system quality of service attributes may not meet the needs of its users; this might be in terms of response time, availability, or elasticity to meet the needs of peak demands. A second risk is whether the system meets the needs for recovery in case of a disaster. Security is the third risk and not because cloud computing is insecure, but Retail Stores, Inc., must ensure its end-to-end security model and/or policies are still in force when moving to the cloud model. Determining whether the return on investment will be achieved is the fourth risk that must be assessed. Finally, the fifth risk, insignificant business impacts, involves assessing the suitability of the cloud model in the context of the Retail Stores, Inc., organization, and of course the use of pilots, and a focus on IT transformation, helps reduce this risk.

Risks are present in any solution where another organization provides service delivery for a consumer or subscriber. In the case of cloud computing, this is a unique risk as cloud is inherently transactional. For example, a cloud provider might refund the fees paid for a service in the event of an outage, but perhaps not proportional to the business impact; a refund of IaaS fees might add up to $1,000 for a service whose outage resulted in $40,000 dollars in lost sales. If you compare this transactional-based business model with most traditional outsourcing situations you will find that traditional outsourcers are not transactional based and would have service level agreement (SLA) penalties that are more directly related to the business impact of the outage. Retail Stores needs to weigh the balance between possible negative outcomes with the benefit of taking the risk of subscribing to this service.

Risk response planning is an aspect of managing risk. Responses are derived based on anticipated adverse effects of risk or opportunities presented as a result of an occurrence. The following are some example risk response strategies and example cloud applications.

Risk mitigation involves taking some kind of compensating control when a particular risk is probable or after an occurrence to reduce the business impact. Mitigation is typically applied to eliminate or reduce the chances of the occurrence. Here are some examples:

- You may choose to work with a cloud provider that you have worked with in the past to mitigate the risk of cost overruns due to a longer project startup cycle and provider uncertainties.

- If you are leveraging an IaaS provider (as in the Retail Stores example) and your IT organization discovers that your provider does not encrypt its backups, you might encrypt information before sending it to the cloud for storage. This would allow you to take advantage of your provider's cloud services while mitigating the risk of vulnerabilities associated with having sensitive information in clear text on their system, assuming you keep the encryption keys local.

- Conducting a readiness assessment of moving applications to cloud prior to deciding which applications to cloud-source from external providers is an example of risk mitigation response that is commonly applied by companies in the early stages of cloud adoption strategy development as was discussed in Chapter 3, "The Life Cycle of Your Enterprise Cloud Adoption Strategy." The idea is to identify what applications are suitable for cloud internally and determine the projected payback and total cost of ownership of cloud enablement. Perhaps, for instance, it is more feasible to cloud enable some customized legacy systems because the capability is critical to your global business operations. Without which, the capability is limited to local consumption. In this example, the assessment outcomes influence your cloud adoption roadmap and transition plans. Keep in mind that the readiness assessment identified is only as effective as its criteria, and your success is dependent on how well you address the outcomes of the assessment including identified issues, risks, and recommendations.

Another risk response strategy is to transfer the risk by contractually stipulating that another organization is responsible for the risk. This might be accomplished by purchasing insurance or by establishing a governance structure where a systems integrator becomes responsible for managing your cloud service provider. Some companies view the adoption of on-premise "private" clouds as a way to transfer risks. Although the "transfer" approach does not make another party solely accountable for the risk, it provides a method of compensation and a point of contact so that you can more effectively govern and manage business outcomes.

Organizations can respond with risk avoidance or risk aversion. In the Retail Stores scenario, the organization might consider the impact of the risk too great to undertake any action. If that is the case, Retail Stores might limit the window of opportunity for using IaaS to peak seasons or avoid participation in any IaaS adoption activities. The practice of risk aversion stems from a dislike of taking risks. In such instances, Retail

Stores might proceed with the least risky option such as limiting the type of IaaS services to those that might appear as safer choices, having the least amount of direct impact to end users, such as backup or disaster recovery services.

You might simply accept the risk. Companies often consider this approach in lieu of mitigation when the cost of mitigation is higher than the cost of the risk. Perhaps the cost to Retail Stores for a service is greater than the cost of the negative impact if the risk comes to fruition. In the Retail Stores scenario, the IT organization chose to accept the risk and take advantage of IaaS services that were made available by a notable public cloud provider for peak-time workload processing because the probability of an unrecoverable failure on the provider's behalf was unlikely and the business impacts were insignificant relative to the expected performance and downtime issues associated with using existing IT infrastructure.

While apprehensions pertaining to the value of cloud adoption are subsiding, expressed concerns persist relative to quality of service (QoS) guarantees, risks associated with consumption and governance of information during and once contracts end, and deficits in cloud portability,[1] which hinder your ability to effectively integrate with other applications and data and force you into a vendor lock-in situation should you decide to buy. You (the consumer) are accountable for mitigating such risks and the impacts on your company.

This chapter presents an approach to minimizing the probability of occurrence and the business impacts of some notable risks associated with the adoption of cloud, followed by explicit actions that you should consider as you develop and refine your enterprise cloud adoption strategy. Throughout this chapter, you find applicability of mitigations to older alternatives to cloud, such as IT outsourcing for extended clarity and as a point of reference. Strategically planning your adoption and incorporating cloud into your EA as discussed in previous chapters, mitigates business risks by influencing positive outcomes of your cloud adoption. You are mitigating the risk of escalating costs by planning the offload of workloads to experts that conduct business for you with greater efficiencies; while at the same time strategically planning return on investment (ROI) optimization by extending cloud investments within your business unit and across your company as much as possible, while taking advantage of the benefits typically associated with economies of scale. As with any investment, there is always the possibility that something could go wrong or not exactly as you expected and therefore risk mitigation is in order.

Focusing on several key areas facilitates successful cloud adoption. The next section reviews these key areas offering risk mitigating elements that can be referenced and utilized to meet specific cloud business requirements. These key areas include

- Enterprise adaptation
- Balancing information transparency and privacy
- Service level management
- Quality of service
- Globalization

Enterprise Adaptation

With the inception of cloud and the abundance of emerging offerings in the marketplace, you might experience anxiety or a sense of being overwhelmed, facing a growing amount of choices. As a part of your decision criteria, you most likely require assurances that your choices of adoption will positively meet the desired business outcomes whether it is profitability, productivity, improved collaboration, penetration of new markets, or improved innovation. Aspects of assurance include creditability of providers and their capacity to integrate cloud offerings within your current business models and systems, acceptance of your cloud decisions by key stakeholders, and of course implementation of key strategies that require cloud adoption.

Challenges to address for enterprise adaptation of cloud computing involve addressing the following questions:

- How do we select cloud providers that are conducive to our business strategy?
- What if we are not equipped to make sound cloud computing choices?
- How do we mitigate the risk of stakeholder rejection (e.g., fear of loss of control, security, or ROI) of cloud adoption strategies as a business imperative?

How Do We Select Cloud Providers That Are Conducive to Our Business Strategy?

When considering cloud providers review the checklist presented in Figure 6.1 and evaluate each area to mitigate the risk of investment losses that stem from inadequate selection. The following list examines each of these checklist items in more detail.

✓ Compliance

✓ Credibility

✓ Customer-Centricity

✓ Expertise

✓ Financial Health

✓ Total Cost (Products, Services, Price)

✓ Resiliency

✓ Transparency

Figure 6.1   Checklist for selecting cloud providers

- **Compliance:** You must adhere to government or industry regulations and corporate policy mandates. When it comes to compliance, you must ensure that your providers conform to your regulations and corporate policies. Take, for example, the Payment Card Industry Data Security Standard (PCI DSS) regulation, which is designed to reduce credit card fraud by taking measures such as requiring encryption of credit card transmissions across public networks. Now suppose you are audited and it is determined that your transmissions are sometimes encrypted but not in a consistent manner. It will be inexcusable to respond with something along the lines of, "It is not my fault, the provider did it," or "Unfortunately, I did not have the bandwidth to complete any compliance verifications during the provider selection process."

NOTE

A comprehensive listing of some common industry and government regulations is included in the Epilogue, "Thinking Beyond the Race."

As with traditional outsourcing, your organization is ultimately accountable for your sourcing decisions, and therefore as you go about establishing and executing your provider selection criteria, make sure your
candidates are aware and adhere to corporate mandates that might require
obtaining security clearances before any business activities can commence, or training may be mandated as a precursor to on-premise cloud
deployments; expect embedded compliance in product offerings and services such as controls for those with powerful user and system rights; and
plan continuous monitoring of provider environments so that you know
what is going on and how they are performing—remaining mindful that
your provider's environment is a representation of your business.

- **Credibility:** Obtained through your ability to trust your provider. It is
based on capabilities that matter most to you as a consumer. For example,
your candidate providers' ability and willingness to partner with you to
produce new cloud product offerings. If this capability matters to you,
then it adds to provider credibility.

  Credibility is validated by your candidate providers' reputation and experiences. If, for instance, your candidate has implemented cloud solutions
internally or they maintain proof-points of uptime and availability of
cloud provided services, then this establishes confidence and builds trust
in the investment.

- **Customer-centricity:** Representational of customer loyalty, customer
satisfaction ratings, and responsiveness to customer requests. Providers
that are customer-centric are able to communicate in business terms the
value and essentials of cloud adoption as it relates to your business needs.
They are more likely to understand you as a consumer and concentrate on
helping you reach and maintain your market presence and competitive
advantage. And they will likely be more flexible during contract negotiations. This is a trait you should look for in provider candidates through
direct interchange, customer references, and even social media such as
blogs.

NOTE

Defensive behaviors or evasiveness when asked about clients might be indicators of your candidate provider's upcoming service performance. Aside from moving on to other candidates, you might mitigate the risk of unmet service expectations by taking the opportunity to bring the behavior to their attention and clearly establish service delivery criteria and expectations. Discussions on help desk services is an example talking point, considering that some clients prefer Web-centric, self-service features while others prefer traditional "phone call" interactions or a combination thereof. Choose providers that can and will support your business model and those that are sensitive to end user experiences.

- **Expertise:** It is obvious that you should choose providers with expertise in consuming and delivering cloud solutions. Industry specialization and expertise are also important. Expertise is deep skills in certain areas and includes certifications. For example, Provider A's expertise is SaaS with specialization in customer relationship management (CRM) for telecommunications clients, and interestingly enough they have storage efficiency depth, which is needed. Always look for expertise that will influence and sustain your business strategy. Industry awards and global recognition are viable means of validating your candidate provider's cloud expertise.

- **Financial health:** The financial health of your provider has direct correlation to your business operations and is therefore a critical aspect of risk mitigation. You should review their financial status periodically and on demand, and you should include your explicit requirements during SLA negotiations and upon creation. Here are some key elements that you should examine:
  - How the company has performed financially over the past few years and how this compares to competitors
  - Net worth
  - Operating cash flow
  - Balance sheet
  - Income statement
  - Dividend payments, if publicly traded
  - Earnings per share

- Percentage of company profits that stem from global markets now and percentage that is forecasted
- Whether the company pays its taxes
- What employees are saying, tweeting, and blogging about the state of financial health, retirement services, and suppliers
- Whether the company is able to pay for employee and supplier services

---

NOTE

The amount of time a provider has been in business and the amount of client implementations or "sales" might provide comparative insights as to how well your candidate is currently performing and offer clues as to future performance. For example, consider the provider that has been in business for seven years with two client implementations compared to the provider that has been in business for two years with also two client implementations. Which would you prefer? The size of the company, complexity of the implementations, client satisfaction, and business outcomes of the implementations become key evaluating factors.

- **Total offering and service costs:** Collectively examine the total offering and service costs compared to other vendors and more importantly within the context of your enterprise cloud adoption strategy. While you might narrow your scope of selection to storage clouds, for example, the selected provider should offer a holistic set of services including project management (which for some reason is easily overlooked when it comes to the subject of cloud), strategy, planning, and governance at fair and quality price points.
- **Resiliency:** A provider able to adapt quickly to technological advancements and changing market pressures is an important attribute. Resiliency also means integrated risk controls throughout all layers of their enterprise architecture, which you will confirm, in an effort to solve expected and unexpected business problems. The net effect of your candidates' involvement in acquisition and mergers, for instance, should be seamless to your business operations.

- **Transparency:** When it comes to transparency, you need to subscribe to cloud services that meet your requirements, preferably from an intuitive catalog of offerings, and you need visibility to all charges as they are incurred as well as the performance of your provider when you want and need it. Your provider must be forthright and willingly provide timely and accurate disclosure of information.

What If We Are Not Equipped to Make Sound Cloud Computing Choices?

Many organizations commence cloud adoption on a small scale, such as for a specific project or for a single department to gain a better understanding of the business opportunities and to experience the value of cloud in the organization. This approach is a good way to "try out" solutions before investing in more strategic, companywide initiatives. A case in point is a mid-sized communications service provider, uncertain of business growth, decided to adopt Software-as-a-Service (SaaS) solutions for a specific business unit's program, working with a known cloud provider.

The goal of the program was to (at an undetermined point in time) extend the SaaS model to other business units, but the risk response strategy took priority because of the uncertainty of the investment, which contributed to commencing adoption with a small business unit. They selected this unit because of confidence that they would receive the best revenue margins by reselling SaaS instead of any other cloud service types.

You might also take advantage of cloud consulting services (ensuring that any organizations that you hire or partner with have both business and technical service integration experiences) so that they guide you to make effective cloud adoption decisions. Here are some considerations:

- Choose subject matter experts and consultants that have experienced strategy and cloud implementations internal to their own companies so that you know they have experienced the impacts of their recommendations.
- Expect them to be able to recommend, operate as, or govern cloud service brokers (CSBs).[2] Recall from Chapter 5, "What About Governance?," that the role and responsibilities of the CSB can vary so be sure to clearly articulate and explicitly document your expectations.

- Partner to develop the right cloud adoption strategy for your business. This involves evaluating the capacity of your own organization as well as determining health assessments for potential cloud providers making use of the financial and delivery criteria described earlier in this chapter. You need to ensure that your targeted cloud services integrate effectively with your existing business and technical strategy, and your consultants should help you identify any organizational change requirements that support adoption decisions.

- Leverage market insights and analysis capabilities of consultants so that you select the best cloud services considering price, quality, market demographics, channels, and uptake potential of cloud solutions and services.

- Rely on your consultants to understand your business so that they can effectively help you choose viable adoption entry and end points.

How Do We Mitigate the Risk of Stakeholder Rejection?

Key to success in this area is to understand and effectively articulate your business pain points and needs. This should be followed with a key set of cloud adoption use cases illustrating how the use of cloud addresses the needs and eliminates pain points. You must be able to communicate your business case to stakeholders in a way that the messaging resonates, which means in addition to knowing your situation, you must know your recipients' roles and responsibilities so that you understand the best approach to deliver and communicate your case. Consider the following examples:

- Emphasize how the use of cloud can mitigate business risks such as lost customers and declining profits due to system performance and quality issues as was illustrated in the Retail Stores scenario. Or how adoption (public or private) might save you from investing in tools where continued use beyond a project is unlikely, which might contribute to wasteful spending. Or show stakeholders where the exacerbation of negative business outcomes due to manual or ineffective business processes, or inadequate disaster recovery procedures is likely to continue without the use of cloud. There are also reports that imply that by outsourcing data and applications to cloud, a company can reduce security exposures by utilizing the expertise of the best in the business to ensure that their data is secure.[3]

Other examples are provided throughout this chapter as well as in Appendix B, "Cloud Case Studies and Common Questions."

- Illustrate how the use of cloud removes barriers to entry for small and large companies around the globe, saving in capital and operational costs now and over extended periods of time. If you can, support this statement with projections to the impacts on your profit margins.

- Illustrate how time and effort spent on manual processes can be automated or augmented with cloud-sourcing, making mergers, acquisitions, and channel partnership alliances occur swifter and smoother than past business transactions.

- Compare the use of cloud with time-sharing that allows a large number of users to interact concurrently with a single computer, dramatically lowering the cost of computing capability. Cloud operates in pretty much the same fashion where users are able to interact with a single cloud that contains pools of compute capacity (servers, storage, processes, and others) that are consumed when needed. As with time-sharing, the cloud delivery model contributes to lowered costs for conducting business.

- Server farm facts and analogies might present an effective means of connecting and communicating the value of cloud with stakeholders. A server farm is a collection of computing systems in the form of clusters and maintained by an organization to accomplish business needs that require capacity beyond one machine. Server farms have primary and backup servers with failover and redundancy so that your business continues to operate in the event of server failures, but the costs to maintain can be steep. In the past, you might have invested in in-house server farms and relied on outsourced service providers to run the farms and manage your operations. Today, you can rely on server farms at significantly lowered costs with even greater IT capacity and managed infrastructure in the cloud.

In summary, take the time to get to know your real business needs and opportunities for cloud so that you develop a solid business case. Follow that up with appropriate messaging so that you connect with stakeholders and allow them to understand the value of using cloud to effectively solve business problems and create opportunities for innovation.

Establish shared understanding and responsibility when it comes to managing business risk. Your corporate social responsibility standards, for instance, must be communicated throughout your global channels and you must conduct proactive monitoring to ensure adherence across such channels. Considering the rapid pace of information exchange in our society, can you imagine the potential damages to your reputation if your providers are involved in ethical violations such as unfair labor practices? It just might not matter to an alarmed public that internally you are conforming to all labor laws.

One of the larger problems within enterprises is a stronger need for cross-collaboration and joint decision making between business and IT teams. This omission often hinders business performance as a whole. A way to mitigate this risk is through augmented responsibilities and role reversals so that stakeholders better appreciate each other's responsibilities and think outside their immediate domains when making business decisions.

As an example, evolve your IT leadership responsibilities to incorporate business strategies. The strategy team should fully understand enterprise business objectives so that business needs are addressed appropriately be it through the use of cloud or other delivery models. In other words, infuse business leadership in what some might perceive as traditional IT responsibilities. You might, for example, empower IT leadership to develop marketing strategies and cloud campaigns.

At the same time, evolve your business leadership responsibilities to incorporate IT strategy. This might include business partnering with IT leadership to introduce innovative yet secure strategies—yes the reference to security is intentional here given that security is a joint business and IT responsibility—and engaging IT leadership in what some might perceive as traditional business responsibilities.

NOTE

An interesting and related article was published by *McKinsey Quarterly* titled "Reshaping IT Management for Turbulent Times."[4] The article speaks to "Factory IT," which emphasizes driving efficiency, optimizing delivery, and lowering unit costs, while "Enabling IT" focuses on helping organizations respond more efficiently to business needs through innovation and growth. While I recommend the article and agree with both IT models presented, I also believe that there should be reshaping of business organizations to support the emerging IT organization and to more efficiently manage enterprise risks.

Effective organizational change management reduces the risk of rejection of cloud adoption as a business investment strategy by employees and business partners. Rejection generally stems from some sort of fear, for example, fear of dissolution of work, or hesitancy to step out of one's comfort zone and undertake new ventures due to fear of failure, and so on. Explicit mitigations are to quickly communicate the value to employees first, such as alternate career choices within your company along with the implications on your business as a whole, such as improved transport of citizens in emergency situations like a natural disaster due to cloud-enabled communication channels, and invite employees to partake in adoption efforts including education and training programs in which they will benefit. A conversation (backed with action) with employees on the opportunity to grow and transition from developing systems to developing social skills so that they will excel at leading cloud enterprise integration efforts is an example, another is the opportunity for some employees to exert their energies to research and develop business transformation case studies so that the use of cloud for activities such as idea management, business process optimization, or business intelligence is identified, socialized, and optimized throughout your organization and your partner community.

While this section discussed risk mitigation with emphasis on gaining stakeholder and business partner acceptance, discussions continue as a part of transition planning in Chapter 7, "Planning the Transition."

Information Privacy and Transparency: Striking the Right Balance

Many analyst reports pertaining to barriers to cloud adoption cite information security at the top of the list with an underlying theme of balancing information privacy and transparency. In other words, your provider must safeguard your information as well as your customers' information, yet allow access to authorized users and authorized usage in accordance with service level agreements (SLAs) and regulatory stipulations. Next is a discussion of explicit mitigations for balancing information privacy and transparency, as illustrated in Figure 6.2:

1. Conduct audits.
2. Apply information classification policies.
3. Share appropriate information.

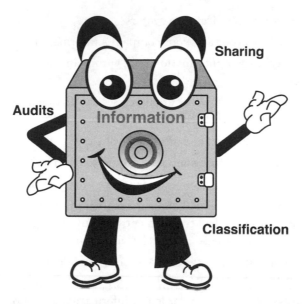

Figure 6.2 Balancing information privacy and transparency

Plan audits of your provider's data centers. Formal audits should be conducted by third parties and through onsite visits, while informal audits can be as convenient as daily reporting on the health of your provider's environment and success rates at blocking threats.

There are risks associated with not sharing information as was mentioned in a Taco Bell lawsuit where faster online defense messages could have helped the company's reputation in response to digital messaging that alleged that Taco Bell's seasoned beef did not meet USDA requirements.[5] There is the Wikileaks[6] situation that soberly reminds us to carefully develop and understand the significance of SLAs. Recall that services were shut down by providers due to alleged security breaches, and more important is the heightened awareness that transpired of the need for shared responsibility to control access and govern the use of information within and external to organizations.

To address risks of this nature, the Cloud Security Alliance (CSA)[7] suggests providers of critical services demonstrate information security management and control by achieving International Organization for Standards (ISO) 27001 certification or at best a subset of business functions certified with ISO 27002.[8] In addition to common sense, here are some key questions that you should ask and expect answered and addressed during audits:

- Who has access to physical data centers?
- Who has access to your and your company's information?
- Is there traceability of information flow within and across clouds? To what extent?
- Are employees audited? What are processes and frequency to block insider threats? What is their background check policy when hiring?
- What are access, storage, and retention policies for audited information?
- Is your provider abiding by and performing to contract?
- Is your provider willing to produce evidence of regulatory compliance?
- Can your provider and global outsourcers (if applicable) show evidence of cooperation with local law enforcement or regulatory agencies that may require access to information and relative assets?
- What types of vulnerability tests does your provider conduct and is this to your level of satisfaction?
- What kinds of security are afforded to information at rest or in flight? (Ex: encryption.)
- What certifications does your provider hold—are they relevant and up to date?
- Does your provider have an acceptable risk management strategy? For example, does it encompass risk response plans?
- How are SLAs managed?
- What are disaster recovery procedures?
- What governance, management, and architectural principles does your provider apply and how does this compare to other providers?

In addition to audits, you must understand your enterprise information classification policy. This policy defines several different sensitivity levels of information and their commensurate security controls. When selecting a cloud provider or cloud solutions, the classification of your information should be considered. For instance, if the information you want to process is confidential data based on your enterprise classifications, then consider adoption of private clouds rather than external public cloud offerings. If your information is public, then public cloud adoption might be more appropriate. Of course, a precursor to this process is to understand your workloads and to determine which enterprise information classification category applies to you, as this guides information sourcing as well as sharing decisions.

Organizations sometimes consider a hybrid approach to cloud adoption. By protecting confidential information via encryption or by redacting sensitive information prior to submitting the information to their cloud provider, they are able to protect their most sensitive information assets while still benefiting from the cost benefits of sharing and exchanging information using public cloud computing. The point is to seek mitigating controls, either contractually, through SLAs or guarantees, or internally by protecting sensitive information before it egresses your organization.

Consider the following example where mitigating controls include contractual agreements, SLAs, and protection of information upon entry and exit of the cloud environment: A government agency decided to adopt SaaS solutions that would be hosted in an off-premise commercial cloud. The requirement was that the commercial cloud provider secures all materials including Internet exchanges. Detailed security SLA's address integrity, confidentiality, accessibility, single-tenancy, ports, and protocols such as secure sockets layer (SSL) and transport layer security (TLS) for Web traffic. The commercial cloud provider is also required to ensure compliance with regulations such as Federal Information Security Management Act (FISMA) and Federal Risk and Authorization program (FedRamp). As a cloud exit strategy, the agency required that data be exported to a destination and permanently destroyed from the commercial provider's system. The SLA included validation that controls are in place through government required accreditations along with scheduled and on-demand audits of the commercial cloud provider's data center.

Service Level Management (SLM)

Service level management (SLM) is critical for cloud-sourcing and in many ways to a greater degree than traditional outsourcing because the risks of poor SLM can be costly. SLM is the process of negotiating service level agreements (SLAs) and ensuring that SLAs are delivered when and where they are supposed to be delivered. When they are not, SLM also provides methods for invoking performance improvement plans (PIPs) for remediation of chronic failures in SLA attainment. SLM involves comparing actual performance with predefined expectations and taking the appropriate actions. The following are some explicit mitigation actions, with emphasis on service level negotiations and governance of contracts in conjunction with integrated service management:

1. Establish enterprisewide communication protocols for contracts to ensure that cloud adoption guidelines and policies are rapidly socialized and adhered to by authorized buyers and designees. Buyers, for instance, must know which providers and services are approved as well as those that are not. Procedures for granting exceptions to guidelines and policies should be documented.

2. Contract negotiations should at a minimum involve your administration department, including policy experts, legal, your enterprise architect, security, and other key business and IT leaders to ensure that agreements are viable and so that terms and conditions are fair.

3. Negotiate mutually beneficial contracts, which most likely require revisions to standard contracts. For example, in addition to understanding and merely accepting the details of standard contracts, negotiate trial periods that allow you to explore options and terminate contracts more easily if necessary, and negotiate incentives such as client reference and joint case study participation or online product promotional activities for providers in support of contract flexibility.

4. Include scheduled and on-demand "right to audit" clauses to be conducted by credible third parties with expertise in assessing and validating information systems security. Statement on Standards for Attestation Engagement (SSAE) 16 is quickly becoming the standard in this area, succeeding the previous Statement on Auditing Standards (SAS) 70 report. Experienced cloud assessors are of course beneficial. A couple of red flags to watch out for are 1) your provider is unwilling to allow audits and/or 2) they insist that audits be conducted by insiders or parties with whom you disagree. Such cases are clues to control the scope to noncritical, non-confidential options or move on to other providers.

5. Negotiate termination clauses such as your right to dissolve agreements at any time at little or no additional charges—no charges might be difficult but certainly a point of negotiation; expected return locations of your information and assets; return formats (for example hard copy reports and XML formatted data may be sufficient for public, nonclassified cloud use); and notify providers on what to do with your information once a contract ends keeping in mind that there are regulatory agencies that may require information to be archived but not destroyed for e-discovery and other legalities. In any case, require demonstrable confirmation that exit criteria is applied (for example, disk wiping removes information

completely from hard drives with unrecoverable options, so in addition to insisting on disk wiping, you might consider observing the activity as it transpires).

6. Although standard liability clauses are usually available, work with your legal team and your provider to establish fair liability clauses and adequate recourses in the event of security or other contract breaches. This is particularly needful to prevent undue costs to your organization for provider course correction and actions such as system outages. Remediation should be negotiated during the SLA process, but there is no doubt going to be unexpected occurrences so fair liability clauses should address these circumstances as well.

7. It is common for one cloud provider to use the services of others. Obligate and hold your provider or systems integrator with whom you are directly conducting business accountable for service level agreements and performance, including those of downstream providers.

8. Is it required that providers own your information and, if so why? Essentially, you should own your information, and you should express this during contract refinements along with specifics, such as "intellectual property is not to be shared, sold, or even discussed without expressed and written consent." You must also make provisions in case of provider bankruptcy or acquisitions, without which your assets are likely to become inaccessible. Work with your legal team for appropriate nomenclature for such circumstances.

9. Through partnership with your provider, apply integrated service management (ISM) principles as depicted in Figure 6.3 for business and operational effectiveness and to mitigate any risks associated with cloud adoption. The essence of ISM is enablement of consumer visibility into the performance of services internal and external to cloud, greater control of your environment, automated processes that contribute to reduced errors and cost avoidance, along with increased operational efficiencies.

    For example, given that you are sharing the use of cloud services using either single or multitenant paradigms, if your provider relocates to a new data center, adds or removes suppliers, or perhaps peaks and valleys in consumption become unpredictable, you expect no adverse impacts to your operations. And while you may have already specified this in SLAs, applying ISM principles grants insights into changes before they occur and allows you to validate impacts so that you can better anticipate the appropriate next steps.

NOTE

Suffice it to say do not limit ISM to systemic aspects only; remember that your enterprise performance is comprised of business and technology, so focus on the impacts of enterprise cloud adoption and risk mitigation from business perspectives as well as within cloud-specific environments. For instance, in the area of change management, are employees adequately trained to manage teams in a heterogeneous environment that now encompasses cloud? In the area of work management, have you developed a strategy for balancing and distributing employee workloads to cloud? And one more, from a knowledge management perspective are you able to leverage information provided in the cloud in a timely and effective manner so that you drive business profitability through the use of managed hosted cloud solutions and services? This holistic approach to ISM ensures that you are conducting integrated and end-to-end service management.

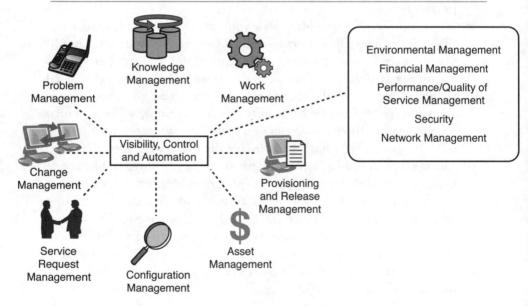

Figure 6.3   Principles of integrated service management

You should insist that all activities listed in Figure 6.3 are conducted and do not just put the responsibility on providers as related efficiencies must occur internally. Remember, although your sourcing providers are responsible for various aspects of your value chain, you hold ultimate accountability for the final product. And should your providers want activities to remain seamless to you, for example incident management, mandate continuous monitoring so that you are always in tune with what is going on with your information and assets. You can use the following as a reference for establishing and managing service levels. While mitigations in each of the areas are fairly intuitive and have been touched on throughout this chapter, Performance and Quality of Service Management warrant further discussion. You can also find descriptions of each of the categories in the Glossary.

Performance and Quality of Service

A first step in mitigating the risk of inadequate performance and QoS issues is to require provider notification of all discrepancies as well as corrective measures taken. You should feel free to challenge corrective actions for the good of your company. Systemic or chronic QoS incidents require deeper problem management and development of a performance improvement program to resolve these recurring issues.

A second step is establishment and continuous review of performance measurements so that impacts of discrepancies are understood, preferably prior to occurrences.

A third step is to establish and apply remediation that encourages your provider to avoid similar mistakes in the future.

Table 6.1 provides some QoS attributes and mitigation considerations as you prepare your cloud adoption strategy. Each should be considered along with the contents provided throughout this chapter.

Table 6.1   Checklist: Performance and Quality of Service Mitigation

QoS Attributes	Description	Example Mitigations to the Impacts of Performance Inadequacies
Availability	Availability is the amount of time your cloud is actually operating in comparison to the total time it should be operating and usually referenced in 9's. For instance, five 9's implies that cloud services are up and available to you for consumption 99.999% of the time during the year or 5.26 minutes per year of downtime, excluding planned outages.	The most appropriate mitigation is to avoid single points of failure (SPOF), which means providers should employ distributed models for information processing, and embrace partnering for effective use of alternate service providers, as well as replicate data centers for rapid recovery and continuity. This is particularly significant in situations where outages are unacceptable or the negative implications are too costly for your business to financially recover. Also, ensure the availability measure you're using is aligned to the business value of the service. For example, if you are engaging a SaaS provider for your corporate e-mail solution, ensure that the SLA measures the availability of the mail service instead of an infrastructure component, such as the network or servers. If your provider does not meet your minimum SLAs, you may mitigate by eliminating your service provider as an SPOF by, for example, having multiple providers working in parallel as an ecosystem that is prepared to partner and backfill for each other as required.
Consumability	Consumability[9] implies that your cloud solution has the right design, installation, configuration, quality, information, integration and maintenance. Consumable cloud solutions enable you to achieve faster time to value, they reduce your total cost of ownership, and they reduce support and maintenance costs.	Some mitigation activities are to conduct viability assessments, with an emphasis on strategic motivators such as data center transformation, user experience, and integration of cloud solutions across people, process, information, and technology early in the cloud adoption life cycle so that issues are surfaced and addressed prior to the need for service consumption.

Table 6.1   Checklist: Performance and Quality of Service Mitigation

QoS Attributes	Description	Example Mitigations to the Impacts of Performance Inadequacies
Portability	Portability allows for an easier transition or move of your assets from one provider to another or between a public and internally hosted environment.	The use of open standards and interfaces helps mitigate the risk of locking consumers to specific providers and induces portability of clouds across platforms. Any services that your provider can offer to ease portability such as export software to close down cloud environments and are welcomed. Portability attributes should influence your decisions relative to provider selection.
Reliability	Reliability is also referenced as dependability. Reliability provides assurance that cloud services are not only available (mentioned above) but perform consistently and according to your security requirements and SLAs when expected. As an example, when you contact your provider for a quote do you get the same results as your co-worker if you both consume services at the same time or within the expected timeframes where rates are consistent?	A good way to mitigate risks associated with unreliable cloud services is to establish scenarios and test for consistency in availability and performance prior to contract finalization. This process also involves evaluation of other consumers and their experiences with providers and service capabilities.

Table 6.1   Checklist: Performance and Quality of Service Mitigation

QoS Attributes	Description	Example Mitigations to the Impacts of Performance Inadequacies
Scalability	When it comes to scalability, your resources shrink or grow based on demand. It is like the "Just-In-Time" model of manufacturing where capacity is there when needed and excess capacity is perceived as waste and therefore avoided. As with the other QoS attributes, scalability encompasses optimization of business capacity (e.g., adequate utilization and staffing of employees when and where needed to support business growth and environmental changes).	Scalability mitigates the risk of services becoming unavailable or performing poorly and in particular at inopportune times. Scalability should be automated as much as possible for faster commissioning and decommissioning of services when and where needed and to minimize variable costs. Resource pooling and cloud bursting are two example scalability techniques that you can expect from providers.
Serviceability	Serviceability involves early diagnosis of faults to prevent system downtimes. Should something go wrong, you need problems fixed and issues resolved quickly and with precision. Serviceability is also referenced as supportability, which implies that proper resources are in place to quickly diagnose and resolve matters.	From a business perspective, you want your providers to establish proper processes to detect and fix defects and inadequacies in real-time and as fast as reasonably possible. This involves more effective use of call center resources along with automatic notification of events and autonomic processes or self-healing. Customer service, including self-service capability, is an important aspect of serviceability.

Globalization

As with offshoring and outsourcing, globalization is significant when it comes to cloud adoption. Benefits such as reduced barriers to entry into new and emerging markets and a global pool of resources (business processes, applications, compute, and humans) are made available and readily accessible to support your business needs. Many small and large businesses, for instance, are taking advantage of disaster recovery capabilities in the cloud as a way to mitigate the risk of natural disasters and other business uncertainties. However, while there are advantages to globalization, there are also risks.

Some countries for instance mandate that applications, data, and intellectual property reside within the country of origin or designated locations, and some require that the same citizens that build the clouds manage and operate the same cloud environments. You must understand such requirements and integrate these considerations into all phases of your enterprise cloud adoption strategy including Requests for Information and Proposals (RFIs/RFPs) from candidate providers.

Concerns about physical security of data centers where consumers have no control are justifiable considering the numerous reports of related incidents; this includes internal and external organizational threats. Therefore, in addition to developing provider selection criteria and audit checklists as described earlier in this chapter, you should expect and probe for proof of physical environment security. At a minimum, check for proper authentication protocols for data center entrance and exits, protected internal event logging and monitoring of facilities with adequate encryption, external sensors that are in operation and adequately secure premises, along with strong intrusion-detection for firewalls, systems, and data from both internal and external sources.

Summary

Recently, a couple appeared on the first episode of *Million Dollar Money Drop*, an American game show, and wagered $800,000 in answer to a question pertaining to Post-it Notes. According to a report published on *ABC News*,[10] the couple felt confident in the wager and provided the correct answer, but game show representatives thought the answer was incorrect and, as a result, the couple lost all $800,000. Later, the game show acknowledged the mistake and offered the couple an opportunity to play again on the show. Who would have thought such a situation would transpire? What could have been done to prevent the error? While subjective, what are some appropriate recourses to provider errors?

In a cloud setting, it can be challenging when it comes to determining the right level of recourse since you have little insights into the operations of your provider. It is therefore more critical than ever to think and plan for the unexpected early in the life cycle of your enterprise cloud adoption strategy through development of explicit service and operational level requirements, establishing reasonable and attainable agreements, and executing established mitigations such as those highlighted in this chapter. Examples include demanding proof of compliance, conducting performance audits, and gaining visibility into your provider's environment and business operations as much as possible.

This chapter opened with a discussion on cloud risk management and risk response planning. Once the context was established, practical examples were applied that described how to mitigate risks associated with cloud adoption, such as information security breaches, cost overruns, and inadequate operational performance by making explicit mitigations—many of which are implicit with older alternatives to cloud such as IT outsourcing, time sharing, and in-house server farms.

Three common organizational challenges were posed as questions, with mitigating responses:

1. Can we do something to prevent selection of cloud providers that are not conducive to our business strategy? You will find included a checklist for choosing cloud providers (refer to Figure 6.1) along with in-depth discussions.
2. What should we do if we are not equipped to adequately evaluate and make sound cloud choices yet we are interested in the business of cloud? Included are practical insights from other companies.
3. How do we mitigate the risk of stakeholder rejection of cloud adoption as a business imperative? This section included a discussion on how the use of cloud can reduce risk for your organization.
   Balancing information privacy and transparency can present challenges as organizations strive to find the right levels of equilibrium, while service level management principles remain consistent but with a focus on integrated consumer and provider management. Service level management can mitigate risks of system outages and performance issues that stem from inadequate contingency planning. Globalization has implications (positive and negative) to your cloud adoption strategy that are similar to traditional outsourcing and offshoring. Each of these topics was addressed in this chapter.

The next chapter considers and continues this discussion as it guides you through some essentials for enterprise cloud transformation and transition planning.

Endnotes

1. An interesting report was published by the Leadership Council for Information Advantage titled "Creating Information Advantage in a Cloudy World: Intelligent Governance Strategies for Cloud Agility." See http://www.councilforinformation advantage.com.

2. Gartner has introduced the notion of cloud brokers. The roles of brokers, system integrators, and service integrators are all applied synonymously in the context of this book.

3. Stevens, Nicole. 2007. "Cloud Tipped to Transform Global Markets." June 7, 2011. http://news.smh.com.au/breaking-news-business/cloud-tipped-to-transform-global-markets-20110607-1fq5q.html.

4. See "Reshaping IT Management for Turbulent Times" by McKinsey Quarterly. December, 2010. https://www.mckinseyquarterly.com/Reshaping_IT_management_ for_turbulent_times_2707. They speak about a new model for managing IT. While I agree, I believe there should be reshaping of both business and IT for sustained survival and to manage enterprise risks.

5. See the published article "Taco Bell Makes Spicy Retort to Suit" http://online.wsj.com/ article/SB10001424052748704832704576114280629161632.html.

6. Vijayan, Jaikumar. 2010. "WikiLeaks Incident Shouldn't Chill Info-Sharing, Ex-CIA Chief Says." Computerworld, August 4, 2010. See http://www.computerworld.com/s/ article/9180130/WikiLeaks_incident_shouldn_t_chill_info_sharing_ex_ CIA_chief_says.

7. The Security Guidance for Critical Areas of Focus in Cloud Computing V2.1 is published by the Cloud Security Alliance. Details can be found at http://www. cloudsecurityalliance.org/csaguide.pdf.

8. ISO/IEC 27001:2005 specifies the requirements for establishing, implementing, operating, monitoring, reviewing, maintaining, and improving a documented Information Security Management System within the context of the organization's overall business risks. See http://www.iso.org/iso/catalogue_detail?csnumber=42103.

9. Consumability is a term that is reportedly coined by IBM. See http://www-01.ibm.com/ software/ucd/consumability/.

10. "$800K Mistake: Game Show Gone Wrong." ABC News. News Videos. December 27, 2010. See http://abcnews.go.com/GMA/video/800k-mistake-game-show-wrong-12483511.

7

Planning the Transition

Hindsight is 20-20 or so the saying goes. The implication is that your vision is clearer when you look back because you can see actual outcomes of actual events. The mere fact that you should learn from yours as well as the experiences of others makes this saying a good idea, but it also begs the question, "In our rapid paced world, new economic environment, and increasingly complex society, how can we effectively glance at the past yet reflect long enough to apply experiences for our future?" This chapter discusses transition planning considerations, including (but not limited to) the business of cloud computing. Intertwined are discussions on change management and the necessity of rapid insights into information and experiences (positive or not) to prepare your company for an effective transition in achieving the benefits and transformation opportunities available with cloud computing.

Relating Transition and Implementation Planning

Your decision to move forward with investing in cloud requires carefully thought out transition planning. This involves analysis of business, technological, and organizational change. Clarity and distinction between transition and implementation planning is first in order.

Transition planning focuses on strategic activities that are necessary to achieve the objectives of the enterprise cloud adoption strategy. Implementation planning is a bit more tactical as it focuses on the multiple threads and projects, that must be completed for the transition to be successful. Both are change agents and are required for an effective enterprise cloud adoption transformation. Transition planning is all about understanding the required activities to prepare your company for your target state; in this case, your target state is enterprise cloud adoption strategy development. Your transition plan ensures your readiness by identifying resources (people, processes, information, technology, and governance) and companywide actions that prepare you for effective execution of your enterprise cloud adoption strategy. Essential elements of transitional planning include the following:

- Review of lessons learned such as previous outsourcing and transformational experiences. What worked, what didn't work and why? What risk mitigation strategies were employed? What did the organizations learn to do differently?
- Recommending organizational changes such as new design authorities, changing roles, revised scope for Enterprise Architecture, training, communication plans, or other governance changes.
- Recommending new or augmented business models for penetrating new markets, geographies, or increasing market share.
- Development of actionable roadmaps.

NOTE

The transition plan forms part of the target state cost/value assessment. It is important to compare not just the current state versus the target state but also take into account the steps and costs associated with getting to the end state. A transition plan is often "executed" by the creation of successive candidate projects to perform the steps of the transition; the planning of the successive candidate projects is categorized as implementation planning.

Your implementation plans are steps that occur to plan for realizing cloud projects. During implementation planning, consumers confirm providers, business solutions, and service level agreements that were strategically formed during transition planning. Some organizations include application development in this phase; however, for the purposes of this discussion, the focus is preparation and planning for the implementation. Figure 7.1 illustrates the relationships between transition and implementation planning. Both are considered when developing your enterprise cloud adoption strategy.

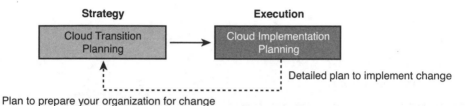

Figure 7.1   Transition and implementation planning relationships

The Business of Cloud

While the service delivery and infrastructure aspects of cloud are obvious, user experiences and the business aspects are often overlooked. Change to your business model, however, is at least as important as the technological change and more impactful to the business. In fact, without proper planning of the transition, your cloud initiatives are likely to generate unresponsiveness causing your strategy to become stale, nonactionable, and susceptible to failure.

Consider some structural pitfalls of a traditional computing model:

- Servers are owned by individual business units, and cost is allocated based on the number of servers.

- Personnel and support costs are not measured so the cost of maintaining an IT organization is allocated as uniform, equally distributed overhead.

- Service level agreements (SLAs) are defined and managed but not in a workload-sensitive fashion.

- Business units wait in queues for IT services delaying time to market.

- Capital is spent to extend IT capabilities in new geographies or business units.

In such an environment, there is no transparency of end user charges for services rendered or the chargeback model is one of equal distribution across the enterprise (regardless of whether you are using services). With the inception of cloud, an important transition consideration and business model change is that now business leaders have direct influence or "say so" when it comes to providers, service levels, and adoption as a whole. Figure 7.2 illustrates a summary of business aspects of cloud and changes that you can expect to your business model, which include the following:

- Self-service
- Speed, rapid development, and service delivery
- Flexible pricing, pay per use
- Café style services
- Leaner

The following sections examine these aspects in greater detail.

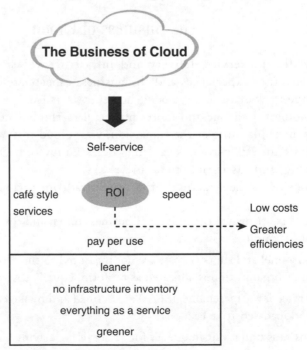

Figure 7.2 The business of cloud

Self-Service

Self-service is an important benefit of your cloud transition as it empowers you to choose the services that want at your own pace. In a self-service environment, the way you buy software and hardware is different from traditional purchasing since you buy from a storefront or service catalogue. The challenge is that you might already have procurement processes in place and with the inclusion of cloud, your procurement processes require adjustments to incorporate self-service along with traditional-style buying patterns.

Along with the empowerment aspects of self-service is recognition of the need for personal contact and help-desk support. For instance, you may have some employees that prefer the chatting mechanisms because they like the quick, crisp responses to inquiries, while others might prefer personal contact such as a telephone call. You know your organization and these are cloud business capabilities that you should consider as cultural readiness, while negotiating what's best for your organization with providers.

A flexible governance model is required that establishes authority for ordering and approving changes in your environment because surely you are not interested in anyone and everyone ordering the standup of new environments because it is now easy and convenient. In a nutshell, the self-service aspects of cloud require planning well in advance of implementation discussions.

Speed, Rapid Development, and Service Delivery

You are required to deliver with speed and agility, which is why you invested in cloud or why you are now giving cloud computing consideration for transformation, flexibility, and realization of new opportunities. As such, you need to ensure your enterprise cloud adoption strategy and product or software development life cycles are complementary. As an example, you can leverage cloud applications (such as SaaS analytics) to swiftly access and analyze consumer behaviors and respond with adequate inventory and product pricing scenarios if you coordinate the timing of SaaS adoption to precede the release of new products. In addition, your transition plans should include enterprise mobilization and allocations for research and development for continued market discovery such that you reap optimal returns on your investments.

NOTE

Some of you may presume that product development and speedy service delivery have nothing to do with you if you are a consumer of cloud services, but that is not the case. Many companies are consuming public cloud services, for instance, to speed up and improve the test and deployment cycle times as well as product development cycles that for instance involves software development. And many are pursuing cloud because of the specialized services and efficiencies, such as global scale and rapid access to critical information. As an example, predictive analytics solutions that are available in the cloud are quite popular for advancing global merchandising and retail sales. These cloud enabled capabilities and skills are compelling for many companies because they simply cannot be matched in-house.

Key questions to address:

- Are leaders in your company aware of your cloud adoption goals and the potential benefits to their organizations?
- Are leaders in your company aware of how cloud computing could deliver on their tactical and strategic goals?
- Are you thinking of all the value propositions of cloud computing rather than IT improvements only?

A benefit of cloud is the rapid provisioning capability that enables your enterprise to deliver goods and services faster with little to no cost of ownership. A related benefit is the elimination of "just in case" over-capacity. What does this mean? Well traditionally fluctuations and spikes in workloads have been catered to with overcapacity principles in anticipation of unexpected demands. This was brought about due to lengthy setup and configuration cycles. Cloud changes this mode of operation for you. With rapid provisioning, there is much less of a need for you to engage in and pay for excess capacity (including both people as well as IT capacity) as was the situation in the past.

Rapid provisioning does introduce a change in traditional risk adversity options as it requires collaborative decision making in an effort to drive effective adoption of cloud such that risks of unfulfilled business events (foreseen and unforeseen) are mitigated. As an example, your transition plan should encompass capacity planning that addresses unpredictable circumstances such as when and if a primary cloud provider cannot deliver on short notice, in which case alternative providers are a viable option. You might not finalize "how to" details during transition planning; however, you can agree to acceptable business policies and standards for your organization, which will carry forward into implementation planning and project execution.

As you plan for implementation, be sure to consider and ask providers about their fast-track, agile approaches to cloud solution delivery including development of documentation. You might also discover that some activities and work artifacts are not required within your own organization. At the same time, there are key elements of development life cycles (for both software and products), such as viability assessments, requirements baselining, testing, and quality assurance that may cause more harm than good if eliminated; however, you might be able to speed up delivery cycles. While you can find more elaborations on this subject in Appendix A, "Augmenting Your Delivery Model with Cloud," some common points of implementation planning that you might prepare your teams to discuss with selected providers follow:

1. Share your vision, your target state, and your budget. In other words, communicate your enterprise cloud adoption strategy with your delivery teams and providers.
2. Discuss predefined use cases of the cloud service offering so that the focus on contract development and signature is validation and refinements for any customization. Validate with your go-to-market strategy.
3. Develop a use case model and request product demonstrations to validate fulfillment of your strategic business opportunities as well as your service requirements.
4. Discuss predefined test cases of the cloud service offering.
5. Conduct at least one workshop with providers to collectively define and gain consensus of the offering and capabilities as well as to ensure that they understand your vision. Since cloud solutions can be sourced from numerous angles such as outsourced providers, service brokers, in-house, and others, a key service description attribute to record and consider when scoping the effort is the source.

6. Complementary to steps 2 and 3, commence project implementation with refinements to requirements and design components applying an agile approach. This differs from traditional methods where project start includes requirements gathering and more of a waterfall approach to solution delivery.

NOTE

In previous chapters, you learned of the significance of business agility and that this is one of the principle benefits of integrating cloud into your enterprise architecture. Complementary, you need to practice agile solution delivery considering that traditional methodologies are too cumbersome and quite frankly, too slow. Without the practice of agile solution delivery where iterative parallel delivery cycles (design, development and test) or "sprints" transpire, you could very well defeat the purpose of your enterprise cloud adoption strategy.

Flexible Pricing, Pay Per Use

Proper metering and billing are both easy and complex with cloud—easier due to the pay per use aspect yet complex because your organization now needs to precisely understand which department owns what and who should pay for what services. You might be one of those enterprises that have some understanding of which systems or business transactions belong to what business units, but not at workload-specific levels. Shared services in particular can be difficult to track without proper instrumentation. Similar challenges exist in the business process arena, for instance, who should pay for the credit score process—a sub process of an overarching account opening business process? The message here is as follows:

- Workload instrumentation such as dashboard upgrades for more visibility and transparency might require enhancements.
- Internal invoicing processes might require adjustments.

- Due to pay per use, it is possible that some business units may end up paying more or less than what they did before as a result of chargeback precision.

One of your transition planning responsibilities is to determine what communications strategy and mechanisms are most effective for notifying stakeholders of the business impacts and benefits of cloud computing.

The other aspect of this topic is establishing the proper pricing strategy that is conducive to your budget and planning processes. Pay per use is good, but some consumers need to plan on a monthly, quarterly, and yearly basis. Providers must accommodate such needs when building service offerings, invoicing, and establishing service levels. Flexible pricing and the tools required to get you where you need to be in your journey to cloud adoption are critical success factors for your transformation.

Café-Style Services

Many organizations, even those that apply EA, continue to have different business models per business unit, either for historical reasons or because the funding model allows for unique or proprietary requirements. You must agree to standardized services (for example, bundles) and service levels (for example, gold, bronze, and silver, no warranty). At the same time, as a consumer, you do not want to feel as though your choices are limited or that you are paying for what you do not use, right? Take, for example, cable television channels where you think about how many channels you watch compared to what you pay. Are you paying for the services you receive or are you locked into paying for more than what you need? How does your provider support change to standardized services to support specialized customer requirements? Regardless of the type of cloud that you are consuming (public, private, or hybrid), discussions with business leaders that express the value of café-style offerings that balance standardization and consumer-flexibility must be a part of your transition planning activities.

Leaner

You most likely have adopted lean principles, hence the title of this section. You can now launch new services and offerings with fewer staff and without the traditional delays and costs of procuring and storing infrastructure. This means you are operating leaner, giving you strategic and competitive advantages over many as you leverage your new and improved cloud enabled business model. In fact, you can start operating along the lines that large data centers and excess resources are really not necessary for you any more as a consumer of cloud services. This "infrastructureless" model allows you to try out innovations in new and emerging markets faster, and it adds to your green objectives such as reduced power, overhead, and waste.

Digitization, which is at the core of cloud computing, continues to have a profound impact in our world. Check writing was replaced with online services and mobile services. Use of cash and a physical wallet are both fading with the widespread adoption of mobile technology. Some aspects are already happening today considering that you can check in at airports using your mobile device, and soon you will be able to shop at your favorite stores with the same experience, no credit cards and no wallets.[1] According to CNNMoney.com companies including Citi, Google, MasterCard, and U. S. Bank are example service providers. In essence, digitization of business processes using enablers such as cloud allows you to conduct business with less on-hand inventory, attributing to your lean business objectives.

It is possible that you will consume cloud services from multiple providers, meaning the concept of federated[2] clouds is in order. While the implementation details relative to federation are seamless to you at this stage, it is important for providers and systems integrators to share their approach with your teams so that they are aware and can make informed decisions relative to contract development and negotiations.

Typically in a distributed computing environment, a large proportion of infrastructure capacity sits idle. The use of cloud allows for much greater utilization of the infrastructure and thus reduces costs. During peaks such as holidays, seasonal ads, or voter registration periods, where more capacity is required, larger virtual instances can be provisioned and then de-commissioned after elections. You will see in the case studies in the appendix that at times up to 300% return on investments were achievable with reductions in labor costs and capital expenditures.

The transitional topics discussed in this section should be considered as you develop your enterprise cloud adoption strategy as guiding principles, and lean, agile concepts as described in the "Speed, Rapid Development, and Service Delivery" section should be incorporated. Following are lessons learned from project experiences that should be considered as you plan your transition to cloud.

Practical Experiences and Lessons Learned

This section describes specific enterprise transition planning activities and considerations that should be reflected in your enterprise cloud adoption strategy. The experiences are shared to emphasize the value of implementation planning such as:

- Establishing proof of concepts and pilot programs
- Organizational change including addressing legacy environments and applications
- The importance of matching business workloads to appropriate cloud delivery models
- Outsourcing considerations
- Buyer/seller experiences
- Test strategy considerations

Proof of Concepts and Pilot Programs

Proof of concepts and pilot projects help you determine the suitability of your organization for cloud. For instance, after conducting a successful pilot rollout of remote desktops, a client concluded that the organization was ready for strategic launch of desktop cloud solutions with multiple teams leading the charge because of their knowledge and gained experiences. What a great opportunity to demonstrate thought leadership and drive the corporate remote strategy. This example is not intended to imply, however, that all pilot initiatives run smoothly as in this same example there were endorsement issues at executive levels that directly contributed to rollouts spanning longer than the teams had hoped. Nevertheless, positive outcomes included incremental transformations and productivity improvements. The point being that you should identify pilot opportunities as a part of your transition planning while at the same time leveraging your experiences from piloted or proof of concept efforts to influence your transition.

Organizational Change

The following principles should be incorporated in your enterprise cloud adoption strategy to guide transition planning:

1. Establish mutually beneficial contracts.
2. Establish integrated supplier (provider) management.
3. Establish integrated change management.

The need to establish contracts between consumers and providers is obvious, so why call out specifically that your contracts should be mutually beneficial; isn't the objective simply to have cloud services provided as cheaply as possible? The point is that, unless there is mutual incentive to continuously optimize workloads running in the cloud, your providers have no reason to offer assistance or advice for more efficiencies or optimization. The question becomes, "Are you treating your provider as a commodity or a business partner?" Now for standardized workloads that really have been commoditized, there might not be the need for shared incentives; however, for mission critical components, care should be taken to set up contracts appropriately or quality and cost efficiency will deteriorate over time. Mutually beneficial contracts can mitigate a wealth of problems that could occur and hinder your cloud adoption, and as such explicit contract suggestions are provided in Chapter 6, "Mitigating Risk."

As a consumer, you might be of the opinion that by using cloud, the need to focus on the operational aspect of your business will go away. Clearly the labor required to run specific workloads that are now cloud-sourced is eliminated; however, there is a need for establishing and maintaining integrated supplier (or provider) management[3] to at a minimum monitor and continuously evolve business relationships. It is important for you to understand that the scope of integrated supplier management in the context of this book involves building stronger connections with providers and augmenting traditional IT operational skill-sets with leadership and management considering that as you divest yourself of resources due to cloud-sourcing, you might need to train your existing resources for new skill-sets or hire subsequent resources that can manage your providers.

Change management is the continuous process of aligning an organization's people and culture with business change, as illustrated in Figure 7.3. As mentioned in Chapter 6, effective change management is a form of risk mitigation that addresses minimizing negative cloud adoption experiences.

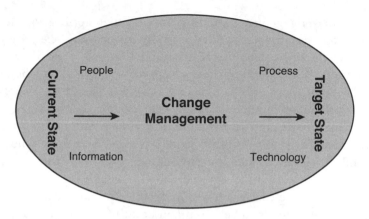

Figure 7.3   Effective change management mitigates risk.

Changes should be planned and integrated across cloud consumer and provider domains to maintain business continuity and to prevent service quality issues. This is important in cases where a service is completely or partially developed within the organization of the cloud consumer. Integrated change management is also necessary whenever there is opportunity for a change in your provider's environment that adversely impacts services that may be critical to your business operations and productivity.

Addressing legacy processes, applications and environments should always be considered when developing your transition plans. For example, a recent experience with a large enterprise required coordination of corporate release schedules with the deployment of a provider's cloud-based data center that commenced with virtual test environments. We ran into a few challenges due to aging applications that could not be deployed to the virtualized environments and some applications were ineligible for retirement due to complex processing (specifically dated application libraries) that had been running for years, and the thought of change generated a fear of unrecoverable business disruption. The good news is that we were able to identify such issues early on due to preliminary legacy analysis and build in contingencies. While there were some exceptions, release coordination and adequate contingency planning enabled enterprise consumers to optimize use of the new cloud test environments and drive quality throughout the organization with fewer resource requirements.

On another engagement, attempts to virtualize application development and test environments were initially unsuccessful because of the omission of the operations teams (individuals who run the data centers and maintain the software) in the decision making processes when developing the cloud adoption strategy. One issue was that current tools were dated and therefore unable to track what is in a cloud image, which would make configuration management nearly impossible (software upgrades, patches, etc.). Another issue was that the people who manually build development and test environments through the use of shell scripts and so on were in no way compelled to change their processes. In this example, course correction was inevitable. When it comes to legacy applications, SaaS tends to be a common point of consideration, but it is the underlying application architecture that enables SaaS capability. This in itself is why each domain of your enterprise architecture must be considered when it comes to cloud adoption.

Here are relative highlights of the revised, three-year enterprise cloud adoption strategy that encompasses implementation planning for an internal "private" cloud:

- Derived considering the expertise and inputs of the business, IT, and operations teams
- Incorporates current corporate release schedules for systems and infrastructure changes
- Includes a "target state" roadmap with prioritization, where the first two months entail resource upgrades (people, process, information, and technology) to get to end of job
- Contains a deployment strategy for moving environments to an upgraded, cloud data center
- Considers components of legacy applications that can be cloud enabled such as the data tier rather than excluding an application in its entirety
- Incorporates incentive plans for leveraging cloud resources first as opposed to building solutions in-house
- Contains an iterative release or "rollout" schedule for the organization that includes training and guidelines for using the environment, while concerted efforts are taken to minimize the business impacts and end user experiences

When it comes to cloud considerations, your speed and throughput to the cloud should be considered, which involves evaluating your own equipment and devices as they could contribute to delays in processing and service interruptions. Consider the following:

Jan uses high speed Internet services from a cable provider in her home office. Lately she has observed noticeable delays when transmitting data using Internet services in addition to unplanned service outages. At one point she thought delays were due to her "in home" wireless router considering that it was quite dated, and while a contributing element, she soon discovered that the real issue was her communication service provider's (CSPs) continuous maintenance at inopportune times. Unfortunately, this impacted her ability to work productively at home so while she upgraded her wireless router, she also switched carriers.

In this example, had Jan decided to consume cloud services prior to switching carriers, she would have experienced the same frustrations with Internet performance issues and service interruptions because they stemmed from her (or her CSP) and not the cloud provider.

As a consumer, you might be wondering, "Why should I care about the network, as I am just consuming services from someone else's cloud environment?" In general, the performance of your network, adequate bandwidth, and so on, is taken for granted, but that should not be the case. Someone else's cloud environment might not be on premise anymore but it is also your environment. You should be careful to evaluate your infrastructure to ensure that it will support increased capacity and the anticipated business outcomes during transition planning. Here are some example network-specific consumer-based transition planning activities and considerations that were derived from project experiences:

- Wireless network coverage and expansions that extend coverage across campuses with guest network and appropriate security
- Remote access services to provide a highway for bringing your own technology and remote worker campaigns
- Data center optimization with new network core and planned server farm migrations for added security and control
- Preparation of use cases for network upgrades to support Internet capacity and growth due to cloud business consumption

Workload Considerations

Proper matching of workloads with possible cloud delivery models must be initiated before implementation planning commences to avoid inappropriate downstream decisions and before any unrealistic delivery expectations become prematurely locked into the mindsets of key stakeholders. This is particularly true for providers and systems integrators if you are working with tactical organizations that have no time for anything but the job at hand.

NOTE

Providers, if you agree solely to offering infrastructure services to consumers, then that is exactly what they will expect. Be careful in your communications, without which, you will have a harder time getting consumers to look "up the cloud stack" even though you might realize that other cloud service types and additions such as governance, business process automation, and so on are needful to fulfill service commitments.

This notion of matching workloads with cloud delivery models is just as important for consumers. As you plan your transition, you should work with enterprise stakeholders as early as possible and jointly with providers to discuss workloads that can be cloud-sourced. Chapter 4, "Identifying Cloud Candidates," describes approaches for identifying cloud opportunities that are driven from a business perspective to guide companywide or at best comprehensive decision making.

As depicted in Figure 7.4, the more mission critical a service, the higher the quality of service (QoS) requirements, which generally leads to private cloud consumption. Security concerns are often nonnegotiable and can be legally mandated. This is certainly an area of cloud transitioning that you do not want to overlook or ignore. Although mentioned in this chapter, Chapter 6 provides more detailed discussions on mitigating risk, including practices to mitigate security breaches.

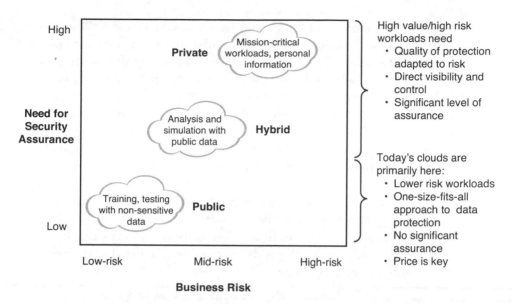

Figure 7.4 Associating business workloads with cloud delivery models

Outsourcing Considerations

Relying on external cloud providers is in many ways similar to outsourcing IT operations. Historically, many outsourcing deals have gone awry because the organization receiving outsourced services did not implement the necessary organizational changes to ensure QoS for entire contract durations. Recall that outsourcing deals are generally much longer in duration, and the perception is that you are locked into agreements that can cause outsourcing providers to become complacent in delivery, especially once the excitement has worn off (this is certainly not always the case, but it does happen). However, cloud's rent-style, shorter term contracts enable you to start and stop services quickly; it is your choice and is a motivator for providers to meet and exceed QoS commitments.

You might be wondering, "What is the difference between planning your transition to cloud as opposed to planning your transition to a traditional outsourced provider?" If you think about it, in an outsourced situation you transfer services and assets to a service provider. In a cloud setting, you rent services and assets from a service provider. So from a transition planning perspective, you still need to prepare contracts, establish service level agreements, and be prepared to conduct business on your own or with the help of other providers once your contract ends. In an outsourced situation, you have an option to transfer permanent ownership of your assets and services to your provider; by contrast, while in a cloud setting you never owned the assets or services, so instead your task is to figure out what to do with rented or leased assets. Do you renew contracts? Should you invest in in-house purchases? Furthermore, you need to determine the right time for making and communicating such decisions. In an outsourcing situation, you might want to communicate such decisions early on with your providers to at a minimum maintain effective business relationships; by contrast with cloud, such communications are not required because arrangements are contract centric with fewer opportunities for human interactions. On the other hand, your transition considerations should always be discussed and firmed with your implementation teams.

Buyer and Seller Considerations

An area of opportunity in transition planning is the inclusion of buyer and seller perspectives. This, of course, has a direct correlation to your end user experiences because buyers need to know what to look for and how to pursue cloud investments, and sellers need to be able to effectively communicate cloud offerings.

The previous section discussed the essentials of balancing flexibility and standardization in the form of café-style cloud service offerings. To continue the discussion, buyers expect solutions that will meet their business needs. They generally are not interested in the bells and whistles and instead appear focused on solving business problems. Therefore, sellers need to know and be able to effectively communicate the personalization aspects of cloud adoption relative to business needs, while both buyers and sellers should be involved in cloud deployment initiatives so that you produce the right mix of standardized, yet personalized offerings.

Buyers want to know that providers understand their market and the potential of cloud undertakings on the organization. As with any investment, they care that cost takeouts will continue and that business will evolve or expand as a result of the investment, and they expect sellers to partake in investments. From an implementation perspective, buyers appear most interested in the amount of time it will take before they are able to start using the cloud services in addition to rapid return on investments. Suggestions on what to expect of providers when it comes to faster time to market were discussed earlier in the "Speed, Rapid Development, and Service Delivery" section.

If you are a cloud service provider and you receive a request for work that encompasses cloud-specific requests, you need to ask the question "who is the buyer?" and, if possible, connect with them. In this example, the buyer refers to the person(s) who will ultimately pay and be responsible for cloud service adoption. Why does this matter? Buyers (not the process or the procurement specialists) are most likely experiencing an element of pain that is driving pursuits that are greater than what is expressed in Request for Information and Proposals (RFI/RFPs).

Knowing who will ultimately pay for and is responsible for cloud services is significant as it helps you build a valuable and winning response. In this example, you might be tempted to focus on your solution offerings (which other vendors probably have as well); however, if your buyer is pursuing cloud explicitly for a purpose (for example, test cycles are complicated and require inordinate amounts of time to execute, or data centers are nearing capacity), then you need to specifically address those needs in your response. Yes, by all means include your offerings, but focus on the value that you bring to address the problem first, such as faster delivery of quality products and services at reduced costs than traditional means with reduced capacity.

The point is that buyers might not know exactly what they need, but they do know what they are experiencing and how much they are willing to pay for cloud services. Your challenge is to generate a winning response that emphasizes capability first as it relates to the consumer and then price.

Be careful to assure that buyers and sellers understand how to communicate the value of cloud adoption. Too often, sellers have expressed that the benefits of cloud adoption are difficult to communicate without getting into technical details. This usually occurs because they are engaged too late in the product development and communications processes to understand the business rationale and drivers behind the cloud offering. Buyers need to understand what to look for in cloud providers as well as their solution offerings and therefore should engage early in the cloud adoption life cycle.

Test Strategy Considerations

Key to implementation planning is determining your test strategy as you will need to validate that cloud services selected will perform according to your expectations (your business units and IT) and will not disrupt your current business operations. The degree of testing will vary depending on the scope and magnitude of your project. The following are some strategic considerations that you can reference as a checklist for developing your master test strategy:

- Determine test and quality assurance stakeholder roles and responsibilities
- Determine test management and automation tools requirements and develop an acquisition strategy
- Define and secure test environments at the appropriate locations (on or off premise depending on your cloud adoption strategy)
- Expect that cloud solutions are thoroughly tested prior to your use. This includes interfaces to other cloud services or commercial off the shelf (COTS solutions)
- Focus on capability and integration testing while conducting security validations of cloud solutions (security considerations were addressed in Chapter 6)
- Plan for data migration testing to the cloud as applicable
- Ensure that test cases are traceable to in-scope cloud workloads, use cases, and business requirements
- Establish entry and exit cloud test cases

Enterprise Cloud Transition Plans and Roadmap Examples

The following illustrations depict three practical examples of transition planning activities. Figure 7.5 contains excerpts from an enterprise cloud adoption roadmap that extended 2.5 years for a financial services client whose cloud position was to operate as a consumer and provider of internal cloud services with the possibility of adopting public cloud services in the future.

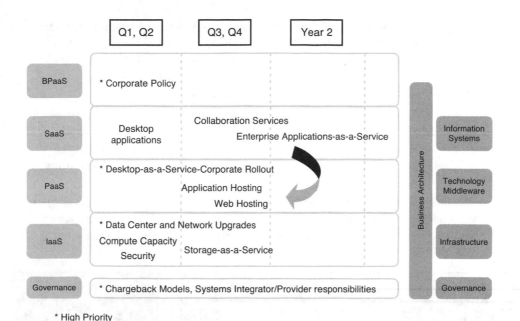

* High Priority

Figure 7.5   Example cloud adoption roadmap

The very nature of cloud adoption required review and possible refinements to corporate policies and was taken into consideration. In this particular case, the enterprise cloud adoption strategy is horizontal (cross business unit impacts) with initial emphasis on Desktop-as-a-Service, chargeback models, and a data center strategy. SaaS applications are expected to run on private PaaS environments, and enterprise applications are planned for internal and external public cloud adoption. Corporate policies were reviewed for determining partner roles and in-house security when joint cloud initiatives were underway, as well as to derive internal billing and invoicing strategies.

To the far left is a depiction of the cloud ontology or "stack," and to the far right is a mapping of EA high level domains that were reviewed to influence cloud adoption decisions as well as to determine impacts of the adoption on the enterprise. As discussed throughout this book, a best practice is to update the EA so that cloud adoption guidelines and practices are standardized in your company. EA updates were a critical success factor for this client as a driver of integrated organizational and technology changes.

What is notable about this client's view on EA is the vertical representation of the business architecture (BA). The perspective is that BA influences all domains of EA and should therefore be considered when making decisions in each of the areas. The same is applicable to cloud. Your BA (which represents your business processes and BPaaS) will have influence on SaaS, PaaS, IaaS, and governance so be sure to consider these points as you think through your strategy.

Figure 7.6 shares portions of the financial services transition plan to a green data center. The plan was an outcome of the enterprise cloud adoption strategy work depicted in Figure 7.5. In this example, the adoption of cloud is expected to reduce energy consumption and carbon emissions, promoting the company's green data center agenda which is depicted in the IaaS layer of the roadmap. The detailed implementation plan is project specific and includes roles, responsibilities, timelines, and approved tasks where the transition plan outlines high level activities that should carry forward into the project plan.

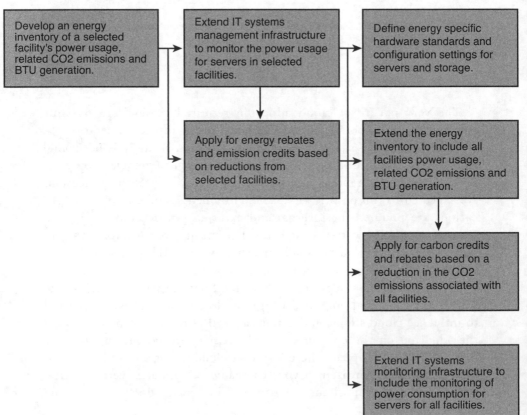

Figure 7.6 Example transition plan for a green data center

Figure 7.7 is a roadmap of emerging trends in IT infrastructure technologies. This comprehensive roadmap includes cloud computing with a
duration that ranges from 2010 through 2013.

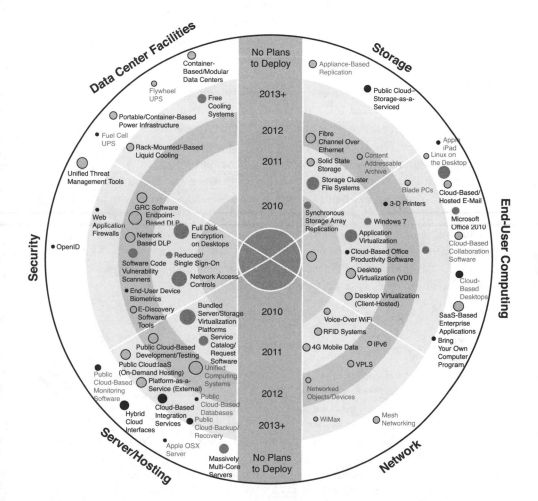

Figure 7.7   Example roadmap, emerging IT infrastructure trends[4]

Summary

This chapter provided transition planning considerations and example
roadmaps to support development of your enterprise cloud adoption
strategy. The motivation was to share practical experiences because the

transformative nature of cloud and services adoption varies depending on your business requirements.

The "business of cloud" was discussed along with analogies to traditional computing and outsourcing as well as the implications for enterprise operations. You also learned about strategically managing and integrating change as well as the necessity of insights into information and the experiences of others to prepare you for a successful and rapid transition to cloud.

It is important for buyers to effectively communicate their business requirements and financial commitments up front and match that to provider offerings. Providers on the other hand are accountable to meet buyers' expectations. Correspondingly, some strategies were incorporated to facilitate positive buyer and seller experiences.

Lessons learned and practical experiences were an intentional focus in this chapter because when it comes to transition planning the process is not scientific and often the learnings of others can be the secret sauce for your success. As such, example transition plans, roadmaps, and implementation considerations were provided for your reference. The next chapter emphasizes the financial considerations and enables you to prepare business cases specific to your environment.

Endnotes

1. You can find the article on mobile wallets here http://money.cnn.com/2011/01/24/pf/end_of_credit_cards/index.htm.

2. See an example federated cloud pattern—derived from a real case study—in Chapter 2, "Business Value of Incorporating Cloud into Your EA."

3. Additional details on integrated supplier management processes can be found in the CMMI standard.

4. Infrastructure Executive Board, "Emerging Trends in IT Infrastructure Technologies." December 2010 Update. Arlington, VA: The Corporate Executive Board, 2011, p. vii, 1, 13.

8

Financial Considerations

Dan is a chief technology officer (CTO) for a business division in Brand, Inc., a midsized global company. He has been invited to present his ideas for moving Brand forward with cloud adoption to the chief financial officer (CFO) and the chief operating officer (COO). Considering the audience, Dan realizes the focus should be on the financial implications of cloud and that conversations should include but go beyond current in-house conversations that emphasize the pay-per-use benefits. Dan also realizes that the CFO and COO take direction from the CEO and want to make the CEO's strategic imperatives realized as quickly as possible. Dan knows that some business units have adopted cloud to address minor business needs, and he plans to leverage such insights along with economic indicators to support his business case. Dan organized topics for presenting his business case, which this chapter amplifies, as follows:

1. Discuss the financial implications of having and not having an enterprise cloud adoption strategy.
2. Dan realizes that it is appropriate to share his strategy to drive more efficiency in managing costs and his vision to reduce both capital expenditures (CAPEX) such as asset purchases and operational

expenditures (OPEX) or day-to-day expenses such as production support and maintenance of acquired assets. Although financial analysis is not Dan's profession, he will discuss correlations to the income statement and balance sheet where appropriate.

3. Describe techniques that were and can be applied to measure the impacts of cloud adoption with an emphasis on financial risk mitigation, time to market improvements, profitability, and cost benefit analysis.

Communicating the Financial Benefits and Implications

The adoption of cloud is reported as a facilitator of global job growth over the next five years[1] in places such as the European Union. Although this is good news and considering that the economic outlook is growing more favorable each day, it should not be surprising to find your company operating more cautiously when it comes to undertaking new business endeavors. C-suite stakeholders are consistently enforcing required justifications for investments in business technologies. Even though cloud adoption is on the rise, you must be prepared to communicate the financial implications of cloud adoption as well as your success strategies.

Your ability to capture and relay the financial implications of conducting business with and without a strategy is prudent and will strengthen your business case for moving forward with execution of your enterprise cloud adoption strategy. This chapter explores key financial considerations that should be communicated as well as incorporated into your EA for current and downstream project effectiveness. The opening scenario with the CTO from Brand, Inc., will be elaborated to help quantify topics covered in this chapter.

Some notable benefits realized from the adoption of cloud are a reduction in capital expenditures and lowered unit costs. Figure 8.1 (lower bar) acknowledges that there are financial benefits with no EA strategy in place, but the results are unpredictable and might not be the optimal solution for addressing your business needs. However, if you strategically plan your adoption with an intent of reaching corporate business objectives, reduce (not just shift) both capital and operational expenditures, and optimize cloud investments across your company, the benefits are more profound and predictable (upper bar).

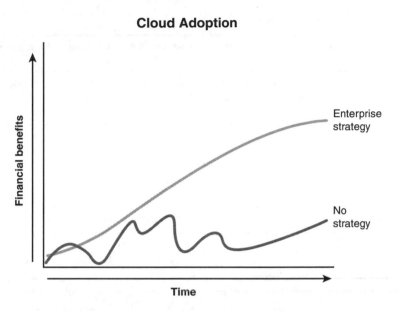

Figure 8.1 Financial benefits of your enterprise cloud adoption strategy

---

NOTE

It is important to capture both tangible and intangible benefits when it comes to communicating the value of your enterprise cloud adoption strategy. A tangible cloud benefit can be measured easily in dollars and with certainty while an intangible benefit cannot be measured easily in dollars or with certainty. Table 8.1 is an example benefits worksheet for Brand. This worksheet will be used as inputs for the financial business case summarized in Table 8.3 at the end of this chapter. You can find more elaborations of benefits in relation to specific case studies in Appendix B, "Cloud Case Studies and Common Questions."

Table 8.1 Cloud Adoption Benefits Worksheet for Brand, Inc.

Tangible (Easier to Measure in $$ with Certainty)	Intangible (More Difficult to Measure in $$ with Certainty)
Reduced IT expenditures (hardware, software, and overhead) due to cloud-sourcing the right business processes and solutions when needed; no unnecessary capital outlays.	The right ideas will surface through the use of a hybrid cloud idea management solution, which will add to Brand's business competitiveness and differentiation.

Table 8.1 Cloud Adoption Benefits Worksheet for Brand, Inc.

Tangible (Easier to Measure in $$ with Certainty)	Intangible (More Difficult to Measure in $$ with Certainty)
Increased sales due to "multitenant" collaboration with the right stakeholders for collective intelligence, enabled with cloud.	Easy to connect and integrate resources across, within, and between clouds and enterprises.
Faster business growth and expansion due to reduced barriers to entry (costs and duration) required to expand business operations.	Improved employee morale and willingness to experiment and "step out of the box" of traditionalism due to employee education, training, and human resource commitments to support the transition to cloud.
Improved business agility and continuous process improvements will result in fewer merchandise returns and discounts due to strategic replacement of manual, error prone, and redundant business processes with proven, reusable cloud business solutions and enablers.	Timely, strategic information expedites future cloud adoption business decisions so that the value of the cloud service portfolio continues to grow in a strategic versus haphazard manner.
Improved time to value of solution delivery (e.g., requirements determination, development, and testing) due to adoption of ready made cloud solutions that augment or replace existing business and IT processes and capabilities.	Green efficiencies (power, waste, carbon emissions) due to cloud adoption.

The following are some key financial considerations that will help you prepare and communicate your business case followed with in-depth elaborations in the following areas:

- Managing your money
- Communicating opportunity costs
- Associating cloud workloads and business profitability
- Deriving return on investment (ROI) metrics
- Determining metrics and agility indicators
- Understanding time value of money (TVM) and net present value (NPV)

Managing Your Money

As suggested by the corporate executive board in its review of the future of corporate IT, you can expect that increases in the percentage of company spend to vendors will continue as cloud applications and infrastructure adoption persists.[2] This business trend is evident today as companies move from adopting cloud at the edge of the enterprise (to address business requirements that are not critical) to using cloud for mainstream business processes, enterprise applications, infrastructure, application development, and innovation.

While consumers are finding the use of cloud important for solving both business critical and noncritical requirements, this background is a reminder that just as it is important to manage consumer/provider relationships, as was emphasized in prior chapters, it is imperative that consumer executives and other business stakeholders control and manage their money wisely such that every dollar spent is spent for the right reasons and in the right direction (as depicted in Figure 8.2). In fact, this was an executive's primary objective for developing the enterprise cloud adoption strategy on a client engagement where we examined the EA to determine the highly prioritized strategic initiatives and positioned the adoption of cloud accordingly. Your enterprise cloud adoption strategy, derived from EA, generates cloud roadmaps and downstream projects granting you better insights, management, and control of where and how your money is spent.

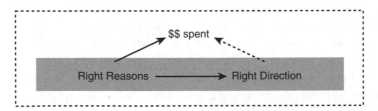

Figure 8.2   At the top of every executive's agenda should be ensuring that every dollar spent is spent for the right reasons and in the right direction.

Cloud computing affords the opportunity to reallocate funds for innovative, competitive advantage (investments and activities) instead of spending money on costly collateral or for capital equipment that could easily end up underutilized. Does it make sense to insist on a private cloud, which involves investment costs to build and configure your cloud environment, when the applications and data (for example collaboration and funds allocation systems) are classified as public and there are relative services ready for you to consume?

You must also take into consideration the level of effort required to develop and execute your enterprise cloud adoption strategy that can range from 6 to 10 weeks. The amount of resources depends on the complexity and scope of the initiative. For instance, if you are focusing solely on infrastructure transformation then the number of resources are less than if you are considering both data and infrastructure cloud-sourcing.

If strategically planned, you have the opportunity to manage opportunity costs (discussed in the upcoming section, "Do Opportunity Costs Matter?") and contribute positively to your overall profit margins (the ratio of net income to net sales, which is generally expressed as a percentage) by steering spending toward cloud assets that add value to your organization for the short and long term. Capital preservation is also likely with cloud adoption.

There are costs that you should discuss with stakeholders and incorporate into your strategy as guiding principles for cloud adoption. You should, for example, explicitly specify viable pricing options that are acceptable for your company as well as those that are off limits. Example pricing options[3] are as follows:

- **Pay per use:** Rates scale up and down depending on cloud usage. Two common aspects of this model are typical for consumers: 1) You subscribe to the cloud services that you need and pay at a designated point in time (e.g., monthly); or 2) charges are metered to precisely match usage down to the millisecond, and you are charged accordingly. Referencing the opening business scenario, Dan is leaning toward the subscription based service model as a recommendation for Brand, Inc., as this model better aligns with the company's budgeting and forecasting processes and he likes that Brand would not be locked into a long-term contract or encouraged to buy more capacity than is required for discounted rates.

- **Pay per number of concurrent online users:** This model is most suitable for global businesses with multiple groups of employees who work at different times in different locations.

- **Pay for unlimited clients:** You do not need to know how many licenses you will need because the licenses are unlimited.

- **Pay per seat:** This is the traditional pricing mechanism where consumers pay a rate per license, and vendors offer deals for volume purchases but might also include penalties for reducing the number of seats before contract renewal.

Types of Costs to Consider
Some cost types that should be considered when evaluating total costs of cloud adoption, each of which should be analyzed prior to and during contract negotiations, include the following:

- Fixed
- Variable
- Direct
- Indirect
- Hidden
- Tangible
- Intangible
- Recurring
- One-time

The cost of doing business is your fixed costs. These are costs that you can expect to pay for the very existence of your business, they remain fairly constant, they are time related (for example weekly, monthly), and they remain in effect until a management decision is made to change. Some example fixed costs are capital expenditures such as data center rent or loan payments; or the purchase of required equipment to run your business such as hardware and software. Another example of a fixed cost is up-front payment to providers for services to be rendered. These up-front costs are more prevalent in traditional outsourcing environments or for investing in and setting up on-premise cloud environments.

Variable costs are optional and can change depending on sales (pay for what and when you actually consume services) and volumes (where, for example, discounts are offered to cloud consumers for repeat business or large quantity purchases). Unlike traditional outsourcing, where up-front costs to providers are expected, in a cloud-sourcing situation you can specify fixed options, which might work better with your budgeting processes or you can select variable options and pay for services when and based on what is actually consumed.

Dan discovered that 15 percent of IT-specific spending is associated with maintaining complex applications and infrastructure due to system redundancies and no business information model or master data management (MDM) strategy. He concluded that the variable costs associated with these issues are hindering Brand's capability or willingness to expand business operations because the implications of mergers and acquisitions are difficult to assess and systems integration processes are elongated due to poor quality of data and inconsistent usage of data and systems across geographies.

Direct costs are usually variable in nature and can be specifically associated with cloud adoption. Example direct costs are the labor costs incurred to develop and execute your enterprise cloud adoption strategy. Costs directly tied to producing or consuming cloud services such as educating employees to select cloud providers or setting up performance dashboards to monitor the impacts of cloud on your organization are examples of direct costs.

Indirect costs may be either fixed or variable. These costs are generally referenced as overhead and can be difficult to tie directly to cloud adoption. Example indirect costs are salaries for administrative staff, charges for Internet services, and property taxes.

You should incorporate guidelines that help stakeholders avoid hidden costs as they can and will eat away at your profits. Hidden costs are expenses that are not included in the purchase price of cloud offerings. Some examples are unexpected provider price escalations, or the financial impacts of risk occurrences such as system downtimes, which can include lost sales and employee overtime compensation.

As a part of his homework in ensuring that cloud adoption will add value to Brand, Dan discovered what he terms "profit leakages," which are activities that siphon away the company's profits. One area where leakages are prominent is in the retail division where excessive discounts and merchandise returns are the norm when it comes to managing customer issues. These issues primarily stem from manual and/or inefficient business processes that contribute to incorrect orders getting shipped to customers. Dan understands that the use of a cloud-based point of sale (POS) system with integrated order management (OM) and loss prevention (LP) that(OM) and loss prevention is reusable across the retail division could eliminate some significant hidden costs, including those associated with merchandise that never gets returned.

Tangible costs are those that you can easily measure in terms of dollars and with certainty. A cloud usage fee is an example tangible cost, and likewise is the level of effort required to develop your strategy. If, for instance, you decide to include storage as a service as a part of your cloud adoption strategy, there are tangible costs associated with the decision that can be measured.

Intangible costs are not easily measured in terms of dollars. An example intangible cost is loss in employee morale due to concerns that the use of cloud will eliminate his or her job, or in Dan's case, the impacts of one customer communicating to another her experiences when receiving orders from Brand, Inc.

Recurring costs are those associated with the ongoing use and evolution of your enterprise cloud adoption strategy. Example recurring costs are renewal of cloud service contracts and costs associated with iterative deployment of applications to cloud per your roadmap, which might include application development or security services to ready applications for cloud. Referencing the opening scenario, Dan identified ad-hoc projects as a benefit of developing an enterprise cloud adoption strategy. This would streamline both recurring and one-time expenditures, which are discussed next.

One-time costs are those associated with project startup and initiation of your enterprise cloud adoption strategy. These costs typically include activities such as network upgrades, team orientation, effort expended to conduct executive interviews, and market research to determine the business value of incorporating cloud as a business technology.

NOTE

Unlike with SOA[4] the one-time or startup costs for consuming public clouds are reduced. This is primarily due to a shift from fixed to variable cost models as described earlier. If your organization is currently operating in a service-oriented capacity, there is increased probability that the amount of time required to on-board stakeholders to a cloud-sourcing model will be streamlined.

Understandably, the amount of one-time costs and savings for private cloud consumption is dependent on your internal capacity and pricing strategies, but you can expect faster ROI and cost savings due to more reliable charges for services rendered, more accurate chargeback models that will (or should) emerge as enterprise best practices, and the underlying benefits of private cloud consumption that include price optimization due to economies of scale.

Figure 8.3 illustrates projected benefits of private cloud consumption for development and test activities—if strategically planned and executed. To the left, IT spending is consistently on the incline while the right side of the chart shows that with cloud adoption, there is a potential for reduction in annual (recurring) operating expenses by 43 percent. The diagram also depicts the possibility of one-time cloud deployment expenditures as discussed previously, although the amount is not quantified. This business case was successfully presented to a South African company. The case study is detailed in Appendix B.

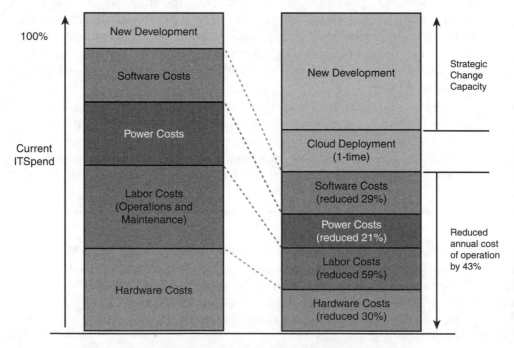

Figure 8.3   Example business case, private cloud test, and development projections

Do Opportunity Costs Matter?

Yes. It is important to consider and communicate the opportunity costs associated with enterprise cloud adoption as this emphasizes the value and will influence prolonged usage of your strategy. Opportunity cost is the cost related to the next-best foregone choice available among choices. For instance, a person who decides to quit his job and go back to school to increase his earnings potential has an opportunity cost equal to his lost wages for the period of time he is in school. In Figure 8.3, the opportunity cost of continuing business as usual is reduced annual costs of IT operations by 43 percent—in other words, this is what was forgone by not implementing a private cloud. Here are example opportunity costs of your enterprise cloud adoption strategy:

- Lost revenues due to inability to anticipate and respond to market demands
- Increased vendor costs due to isolated business procurements (multiple vendors paid for similar services and an inability to take advantage of volume discounts)
- Reduced profit margins due to hidden and unplanned support costs of complex business infrastructure (people, process, information, technology)
- Lost customer revenues due to cloud-sourcing with no tangible or intangible business benefits
- Financial penalties due to cloud information security breaches

Dan found that the value of lost opportunities due to development and execution of his proposed enterprise cloud adoption strategy are substantial, equating to a 4.44 million increase in income for Division A, which is a 30 percent increase in forecasted revenues and a 20 percent increase from the previous year's actual performance. You can find elaborations of this analysis in Table 8.2.

Cloud Workloads and Business Profitability

As mentioned in the previous chapter, in traditional data centers and server farms it is normal to expect low utilization to capacity ratios of IT assets. From a financial perspective, this contributes to return on investments that are not good, your debt to equity ratios are probably higher than you would like, and your financial risk (the perceived uncertainty of your ability to pay for financial obligations) is increased while your risk tolerance levels are lowered. On the other hand, your enterprise strategy provides you with intelligence so that you invest in cloud when and where you need it, contributing to optimal capacity and utilization. This, of course, mitigates your financial risk, increases your company's risk tolerance levels, and has the potential of strengthening both your income statement and balance sheet.

Efficiencies associated with strategically planning and executing the offload of business workloads to cloud is an example of taking steps to positively impact your profitability. Profitability in this context means contributing to positive net income (total revenues – total operating expenses). By examining your entire business infrastructure through the lens of EA (as depicted in Figure 8.4), you holistically determine cloud business opportunities and you are more effectively able to simulate business impacts on your organization.

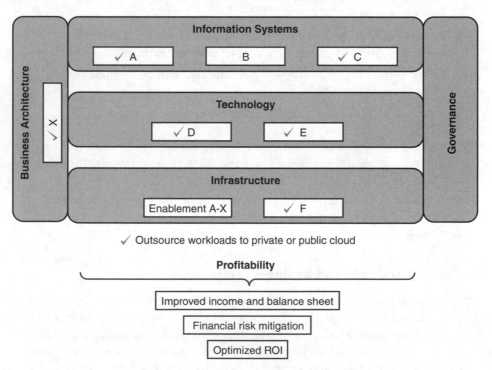

Figure 8.4 Associating cloud workloads and business profitability

For instance, if a workload is not deemed suitable for cloud, then your strategy presents alternatives such as traditional outsourcing, asset retirement, or you might suggest leaving well enough alone and moving forward with business as usual. If a workload is suitable for cloud, you are able to examine your enterprise landscape and determine whether any upgrades are required to support your decision or whether you can use existing assets. The sooner you make such decisions the easier the integration, which will save on rework and associated labor expenses now and in the future.

Your EA also contains industry and regulatory requirements that you can quickly reference to guide strategic cloud adoption decisions. For instance, regulations such as Gramm-Leach Bliley (GLBA), Sarbanes-Oxley (SOX), the Financial Industry Regulatory Authority (FINRA)—the largest nongovernmental regulator for all securities firms conducting business in the United States—require protection of customer data and reporting of security breaches. You can reference such guidelines to determine appropriate sourcing options (public, private, hybrid, community, traditional outsourcing, or in-house sourcing) for a designated workload.

Dan specifically sought out unit and item pricing stipulations along with payment processing and privacy regulations for global operations. He plans to validate compliance with cloud service providers upon acceptance of his proposal.

In essence, strategizing the right workloads to outsource to cloud has the potential to impact your profitability in three ways:

■ **It improves your income statement and balance sheet:** In Figure 8.4 workloads A, C, D, F, and X were identified as cloud candidates (some private and some public). Through review of the business architecture (BA) it is determined that some workloads are disqualified from being outsourced to cloud because processes are nearing retirement, while others are critical to the business and require evaluation. This approach prevents executives from spending time on initiatives that are of low priority, which adds to wasted spend, while ensuring that downstream projects add value to the business. Recall that your business strategy is typically depicted as a part of your BA, and both should be leveraged to understand your business processes and the strategic direction of your company.

Your strategy stimulates reduction in capital and operational expenditures due to purchase of cloud assets as you need them along with payments for cloud services as they occur. Positive cash flows, less debt, and avoidance of standing depreciation costs for what used to be carried as on-hand capital equipment are some of the financial benefits. In essence, the cost of doing business in the cloud has positive influence on both your balance sheet (your net worth) and your income statement (your net income).

■ **It mitigates financial risks:** Examining your enterprise portfolio in the manner depicted in Figure 8.4 allows you to better understand your business and IT assets and integration points for cloud while governing your portfolio enables you to better leverage your assets so that you effectively use cloud now and in the future. Holistic analysis of your portfolio of assets also contributes to faster and more effective business decisions relative to cloud adoption.

Dan researched and will recommend use of a hybrid idea management system to stimulate ideas for improving business operations from internal and external stakeholders. His suggestion is to commence with a public cloud to gain insights into the public's opinion on a retail-related subject or idea (e.g., fashion merchandising), while managing differentiating ideas that surface internally to mitigate the financial risks (e.g., legal fees) associated with exposing confidential, intellectual property.

The adoption of cloud not only adds to your business elasticity by equipping you to strategically plan growth and shrinkages but also reduces your financial risk due to sustainable earnings and rapid business growth. Your retained earnings for instance are positively impacted in that labor and time savings can be monetized and used immediately or retained for investments in future advancement of your business.

■ **It optimizes your ROI:** Return on investment is the money that you earn as a percentage of the total value of invested assets. ROI is calculated by dividing your return on an investment by the cost of the investment. There is ROI advantage in both private and public cloud adoption where payback for investments is faster and costs are more precise than traditional sourcing.

Key ROI Metrics and Business Agility Indicators

ROI metrics are applied to measure the effectiveness of your enterprise cloud adoption strategy on your business performance while business agility indicators[5] measure your potential for success currently and in the future. The following are some key ROI metrics, each of which has influence on your financial performance and takes into account cloud adoption with and without your strategy:

- Percentage of profit margins that stem from cloud adoption
- Percentage of savings in capital and operational expenditures
- Percentage of savings due to green efficiencies (for example, power consumption, water usage, carbon emissions)
- Percentage of reduced cycle costs from ideation to implementation
- Percentage of reduced costs due to business process outsourcing to cloud
- Percentage of costs eliminated due to cloud adoption
- Rate of cloud adoption
- Annual spend (categories and amount) before and after execution of your enterprise cloud adoption strategy

As mentioned in Chapter 2, "Business Value of Incorporating Cloud into Your EA," your business agility has a positive influence on your business performance. This includes your financial performance because the more agile your company, the greater your ability to anticipate market demands. Here are some key agility indicators that are applicable to your enterprise cloud adoption strategy and, of course, you would tailor for your specific business scenario:

- Time to identify differentiating market opportunities
- Time to make cloud decisions
- Time to integrate cloud into your business strategy
- Ability to predict growth in target markets with certainty
- Time from strategy to execution
- Time to collaborate across supply channels
- Time to respond to business events and change

Time Value of Money (TVM) and Net Present Value (NPV)

With the adoption of cloud, you can expect your benefits to accrue in the near term as well as in the future, and therefore it is significant to understand both TVM, which is the process of comparing present cash outlays (your goal is to minimize this amount) to future returns, and NPV, which is the discounted value, as of a specified date, of future cash inflows less all cash outflows. In essence, you want to understand the present value (today's dollar value) of your expected, future cash inflows that result from your investment in cloud, keeping in mind that if the NPV of your potential cloud undertaking is positive, it is a good indicator of positive cash flows, and if the NPV is negative, you should think carefully about this undertaking since the cash flows generated from your cloud investments are most likely negative. The formula for finding the present value of X dollars received in "t" years from now when "r" is the discount rate is depicted in Figure 8.5.

$$\text{present value} = \frac{\$X}{(1 + r)^t}$$

Figure 8.5   Formula for computing present value

You derive the overall NPV by summing the PV amounts for each year. If, for instance, you choose to purchase cloud backup/retrieval and disaster recovery services to prevent system outages and to avoid the costs associated with extra disk storage and data center expansions that are required to support your business's growth, the overall NPV of your cloud undertaking is positive and reflected in Table 8.2 as $6,355.4 presuming the following:

- In Year 0, you will invest $1,000 in employee education and training on how to use the cloud services.
- In Year 1, you will receive $4,000 total revenues.
- In Year 2, you will receive $4,500 total revenues.
- A discount rate of 10 percent is applied due to inflation.

Table 8.2 Deriving Net Present Value, an Example

Data Description	Value	Present Value Computations
1. Annual Discount Rate	10 %	
2. Investments for employee education, Year 0 (cash outflows)	$ -1,000	($1,000)
3. Projected Returns, Year 1 (cash inflows – outflows)	$ 4,000	$4,000 * 1/(1 + .10) 1 = $4,000 * .9091 = **$3,636.4**
4. Projected Returns, Year 2 (cash inflows – outflows)	$ 4,500	$4,500 * 1/(1 + .10) 2 = $4,500 * .8264 = **$3,719**
5. Total Net Present Value	$6,355.4	($1,000) + $3,636.4 + $3,719 = **$6,355.4**

1 PV = $4,000 * 1/(1 + .10)1 = $4,000 * .9091 = $3,636.4

2 PV = $4,500 * 1/(1 + .10)2 = $4,500 * .8264 = $3,719

Business Scenario: Brand, Inc.

Table 8.3 outlines elements of the business case Dan prepared for the CFO and COO at Brand. Financial implications are specific to Division A, the Retail Services division, with company-wide projections. Dan's approach is to discuss the financial implications of having and not having an enterprise cloud adoption strategy; discuss correlations to the income statement and balance sheet where appropriate; and describe techniques to measure the impacts with an emphasis on risk mitigation and profitability.

Dan shared the business potential of a 40 percent reduction in business and IT combined capital and operational expenses and a $4.44 million increase in net income and revenues over a 1.5 year timeframe. He expects ROI to continue for several years while a majority will be realized in the first year, and one of his key takeaways is the enterprise cloud adoption strategy will focus on reducing financial risks through steady, increased business cash flows and reduced debt by driving both up-front and capital costs down while ensuring positive net working capital and operational efficiencies. NPV is to be determined but presumed favorable.

Table 8.3 Dan's Business Case

Category	Analysis
Costs (Current or projected costs without enterprise cloud adoption strategy)	Approximately 40% of enterprise spending can be eliminated or marginalized. Distribution is as follows: 15% of divisional spending is due to silo efforts and includes redundant business processes, one-off application and infrastructure purchases, and manual processes that require staff augmentation for quality control. An example manual process is the generation and physical mailing of paper-based invoices. While these are direct costs for Division A business operations, the costs are preventable. 15% of IT specific spending is associated with maintaining complex applications and infrastructure; these variable costs are primarily due to little or no standardization. For instance, there is no business information model or master data management (MDM). This hinders business expansion because the implications of mergers and acquisitions are difficult to assess and systems integration processes are elongated due to geographical inconsistencies and complexities. 10% of costs are hidden and stem from system downtimes and customer related issues including excessive discounts and frequent merchandise returns. The remaining 60% of enterprise spending does not require change at this time.
Financial benefits (Projected savings with enterprise cloud adoption strategy)	$4.44 million increase in income projected for Division A. 30% increase in forecasted revenues. 20% increase from prior year actual performance in Division A. Revenue projections consider market expansion, reduction in capital spending, reduction in operational spending, and the ability to take advantage of asset reuse and enterprise discounts with cloud providers. $468,000 total annual savings due to elimination of workarounds: (9 FTEs, $25.00 per hour * 52 weeks). $1,500,000 total savings to retire 13 redundant systems in 1.5 years: (includes licenses, labor, and maintenance costs). $1,475,000 total savings from business process outsourcing (BPO) to cloud and Division A reuse of cloud services as a starting point. $1,000,000 deliberate focus on service delivery excellence, end user experiences, and hidden cost prevention.

Table 8.3 Dan's Business Case

Category	Analysis
Balance sheet and income statement (Balance sheet and income statement associations)	Balance sheet does not carry cloud solutions as capital since cost is incurred when services are rendered. Large capital investments and liabilities are reduced with the adoption of off-premise clouds and efficient adoption and use of private clouds.
	Increased cash flows anticipated from strategic cloud adoption adds to income statement and retained earnings.
	Income statement excludes depreciating capital expenses since none are added with the adoption of off-premise clouds.
	Operational savings generated now and over time from strategic cloud investments are reflected as reduced expenses and positive net income.
Financial risks (Risks and planned mitigations)	Paying only for what is used can mitigate the financial risk of uncertainty as to whether Brand will receive a return on any individual cloud investment, but it is the development and execution of an enterprise cloud adoption strategy that further mitigates financial risk by positioning Division A and other divisions to maximize payoff in the short and long run through up-front, holistic cloud decision making that aligns with business strategy; and through effective governance of the adoption (including standardization) to ensure downstream project efficiencies continue to reduce costs while sustaining profits.
	Mitigate financial risks through steady, increased business cash flows and reduced debt by driving both up-front and capital costs down while ensuring positive net working capital and operational efficiencies.
Metrics (Applied metrics to measure cloud adoption success with and without strategy)	Ability to predict growth in target retail market with certainty.
	Time to identify differentiating market opportunities.
	Time to make cloud adoption decisions.
	Time to integrate cloud into the enterprise strategy.
	Time from strategy to execution.
	Percentage of reduction in capital and operational expenditures.
	Percentage of reduced costs due to business process outsourcing to cloud.

Table 8.3 Dan's Business Case

Category	Analysis
NPV	To be determined (TBD).
	Presumed favorable considering the following:
	Use of a private cloud exists in the organization today and there are opportunities to reuse the same infrastructure.
	Public clouds are recommended that will contribute to reduced capital outlays and expenditures.
	Projected returns of 4.44 million are currently for Division A (Retail Services); revenues will grow as strategic cloud initiatives commence across the enterprise with planned operational effectiveness and cost takeouts.

Summary

Be prepared to communicate your strategy and the financial implications to a range of stakeholders including your chief financial officer (CFO). Three major lessons emerged from this chapter: First, key financial considerations that are required to build and maintain sponsorship of your business case for cloud adoption should be articulated. Second, ensure that financial considerations are supported by your EA so that enterprise capability gaps are identified and prioritized, and budgets are allocated and governed, respectively. Third, EA adoption of cloud enables your transition and implementation planning to be successfully realized while financial considerations are integrated into your EA so that downstream cloud and related projects leverage the knowledge and guidelines presented and your EA remains current.

Teams need to be mindful of reducing both capital and operational expenditures and conducting cost benefit or economic feasibility analysis. Key areas discussed in this chapter include strategies and techniques for managing your company's capital, the significance of opportunity costs, cloud workloads and profitability analysis, ROI metrics, business agility indicators, and understanding the time value of money (TVM) and net present value (NPV) of your potential cloud investments. The Brand business case shared how some of the key concepts in this chapter can be applied to develop your business case for development and execution of your enterprise cloud adoption strategy.

Endnotes

1. See the article "Europe to Reap Cloud Computing Dividend-Study" at http://uk.reuters.com/article/2010/12/07/cloud-computing-idUKLDE6B61KA20101207.

2. The Corporate Executive Board Company reported that spending is moving outside the company and to vendors as cloud services expends deeper into applications and infrastructure and internal resources become brokers not providers. You can find several articles on the subject on its Web site. In particular, see "The Future of Corporate IT: Externalized Service Delivery" at https://cio.executiveboard.com/Members/Popup/Download.aspx?cid=100175960.

3. Computerworld, December 2010, provided a useful list of generic pricing options. Of course, this list will vary and depends on your company and your product offerings.

4. You can find more on this subject in the book *SOA: 100 Questions Asked and Answered*, Kerrie Holley and Ali Arsanjani, 2010.

5. Carter, Sandy. 2009. *The New Language of Marketing 2.0: How to Use ANGELS to Energize Your Market*. IBM Press. Upper Saddle River, New Jersey. http://www.ibmpressbooks.com/promotions/promotion.asp?promo=136781.

Epilogue

Thinking Beyond
the Race

The race is about to begin. The runners are excited and at their marks waiting for that infamous sound.

"On your mark. Get set, Go!" yells the announcer and everyone takes off.

The runners are caught up in the moment and the crowd yells in excitement as first, second, and third place winners are announced.

Now What?

To fulfill its potential as the next evolution of enterprise IT, cloud computing must become more than an enabler of IT efficiencies. It must become a driver of business transformation. For some it will be about re-engineering business processes like a retailer that needed a better way to manage its global supply chain, one involving hundreds of partners, thousands of locations, and a plethora of silo systems. A global cloud-based supply chain standardizes and integrates disparate and largely manual processes for tendering, contracting, and managing global transportation services. Benefits include increased collaboration and efficiency, greater contract compliance, improved decision-making, and enhanced visibility, which contributes to significant cost savings and higher revenue. A telecommunications carrier needed innovation to differentiate and capture a greater market share. Specifically, a cloud-enabled collaboration platform created an innovation hub where company employees and partners could engage during the development process of new products and features increased the likelihood of market success. Finally, some companies seek to build a whole new business model like a financial services company that used the cloud to launch, preserving capital while creating an entirely new business model in mobile payments.

Your executive stakeholders, chief information officer (CIOs), chief executive officer (CEO), and other C-suite executives, require teams that can collaborate effectively such that strategic imperatives are chosen, decisions are optimized, and pursuits for business solutions that create outcomes that make a difference occur in your company. Every CIO still has to deliver excellence in fundamentals such as usability, reliability, and security. Figure E.1 illustrates visionary plans of CIOs to increase competitiveness. The data is derived from a global CIO study conducted by IBM where face-to-face conversations occurred with more than 3,000 CIOs worldwide, the first of a kind study with CIOs.[1]

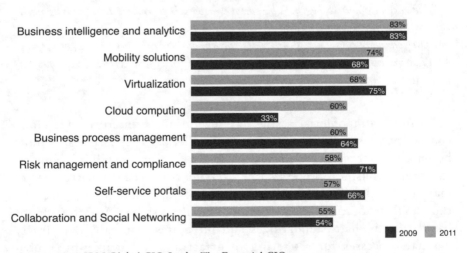

Source: 2011 IBM Global CIO Study: The Essential CIO

Figure E.1   CIO responses: visionary plans to increase competitiveness over the next three to five years

As depicted, cloud adoption made the biggest leap forward, a clear indicator of the business value and strategic recognition; also notice the other strategic assets considered for competitive advantage, many of which will run more efficiently on a cloud platform. Business intelligence and analytics remained at the top of the list while mobility and virtualization followed. The use of virtualization was greater in 2009 in comparison with 2011; business process management (BPM) remained fairly steady, while interestingly risk management and compliance declined in 2011. Self-service portals had a small decline while in investment interests, while collaboration and social networking tools remained fairly steady between the years 2009 and 2011. Each of the capabilities presented will support your cloud investments and should be considered as you develop your cloud adoption strategy.

As you reflect on previous chapters and review the case study presented in this epilogue, you know that new market segments and business opportunities due to technological advances are there for the taking and that you are or soon will be faced with competitive innovations that will challenge your current state. You can expect to experience numerous cloud offerings, and you will have to decide what is right and what is not appropriate for your company. Some thoughts:

- Think about how you can leverage cloud to drive not only cost reductions but how to leverage such capability to deliver high value services and for some to differentiate yourself in the marketplace.

- Study your buying patterns and consider altering to accommodate changing business models albeit through the use of cloud or other delivery models.

- Consider your business processes and contingencies in case cloud solutions become unavailable, meaning contingencies beyond service level agreements and service level objectives (SLAs and SLOs) that generally take affect after the fact. For instance, what steps can you take to quality assure cloud solutions before integrating into your business processes? Are you positioned to discover potential issues before they become problems such as through the use of executive dashboards?

- Study your organization. How well do you collaborate, team, and co-create, and what must you do to ensure that your cloud adoption decisions return sustainable results? For instance, are you applying the same solution approaches and principles today that you did yesterday? If so, what are the current and projected implications to your business performance? Is it time for change?

This epilogue highlights the application of some key principles discussed in this book through the upcoming Project Gold case study—a
small- to medium-sized business (SMB) with approximately 250
employees and is derived from real experiences. To remain competitive
the "Sta-up" company researches the value of cloud and the implications
of adoption. A key business outcome is development of a strategic plan
and roadmap for moving forward. The rationale behind decisions is elaborated throughout for your edification and to stir creativity when it
comes to choosing your cloud adoption strategy.

Project Gold, an SMB Case Study

Stewart is vice president of product development and marketing at
Sta-up International, a global communications service provider (CSP)
company whose corporate headquarters is in North America. Stewart is
excited about the possibilities of using cloud as a vehicle to accelerate
introduction of new products and expand Sta-up's market penetration in
South America. In a team meeting with other senior executives, Stewart
received executive endorsement to introduce public cloud services as a
part of the overarching CSP strategy as a differentiating business capability and service offering.

In his business case, Stewart cited some cloud adoption trends and the
white space that he observed, one of which is a need for cloud offerings for
SMBs in local, global, and emerging economies. In a follow-on session with
the team that he selected, Stewart provided directives and transformational
guidelines as follows:

- **Strategic vision:** Propel Sta-up to become the leading CSP public cloud
  services provider in South America.

- **Strategic Objectives:**
    - Build a partnership business model with cloud service providers
      that enables Sta-up to acquire, re-brand and offer cloud solutions
      to existing and new international customers at attractive rates.
      Include training of sales and marketing teams to effectively pro-
      mote and maintain offerings.
    - Create an attractive, value-add set of offerings for both horizontal
      and vertical markets.
    - Deliver a Sta-up branded cloud AppStore and a performing solu-
      tion within six months that can be shared with end customers.
      This cloud solution must integrate with existing enterprise

systems and support Sta-up's brand of being #1 in the region when it comes to customer service.

Project Gold Strategy Team Organization

Figure E.2 illustrates the Project Gold team membership and organization. A summary of the roles and responsibilities follows. The team is comprised of members from several business units within Sta-up International and is led by Stewart.

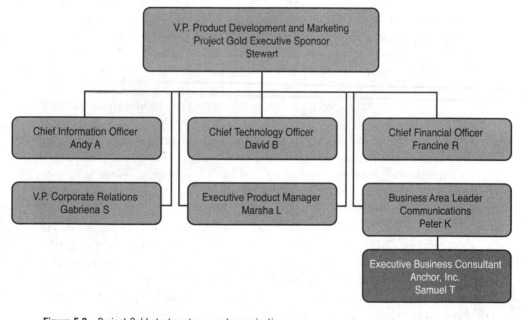

Figure E.2   Project Gold strategy team and organization

As mentioned, Stewart is vice president of product development and marketing. He is the executive sponsor and visionary leader of Project Gold.

Andy, chief information officer (CIO) teamed with Marsha (executive product manager) and Peter (communications business area leader) to understand cloud opportunities and the feasibility of consumption within a Sta-up enterprise. Andy quickly decided that a workshop was essential to pull the teams together for more collective intelligence. He arranged an offsite meeting with stakeholders after two weeks of research to analyze findings and discuss recommendations with Stewart.

David, chief technology officer (CTO) of cloud solutions and chief enterprise architect, provided an enterprise view of the business and technology landscape. David teamed with and provided insights to stakeholders about existing and future enterprise requirements; he worked closely with Andy and took the action to identify and develop an integration strategy along with establishing an enterprise governance framework. David is the primary liaison with cloud service providers.

Francine, chief financial officer (CFO), researched revenue sharing and pricing options from both consumer and provider perspectives. She is focusing on what the right model should be and how to integrate with existing Sta-up business models so that the company benefits from any cloud undertakings.

Gabriena, vice president of corporate relations, legal and regulatory compliance, provides advice and council on international business including taxation, business continuity, and regulatory stipulations. Gabriena is anxious to attend the workshop and has prepared current regulatory requirements that are in effect today at Sta-up.

Marsha, executive product manager, took the action to determine what services made the most sense to consume from the cloud. She began by conducting market analysis for SMBs and internally she studied her organizational capabilities including key business processes that might be suitable for cloud augmentation and her IT service delivery processes and current performance. She will use this data to influence selection of one or more cloud solutions and service providers.

Peter, communications business area leader, researched cloud providers that excel in CSP solution delivery in an effort to jump-start the selection process should the decision be taken to move forward. Peter was concerned about organizational impacts and changes required to become both a consumer and provider. His focus was gaining the organization's buy-in, and along with Francine he focused on funding models and how to measure and charge back service consumption to end users, a core benefit of cloud. Peter recommended that a third party independent business consultant join the team and soon hired Samuel to assist with strategic planning.

Samuel, third-party executive business consultant for Anchor, Inc., specializes in cloud service portfolio development for CSPs and international market analysis. Samuel was selected by Peter. He will attend the workshop as an independent cloud business strategist and subject matter expert. Samuel will help the team determine what to look for in providers, but he will not partake in cloud provider selection.

Figure E.3 is a questionnaire prepared by Andy and David and distributed to the team; the data will be used to facilitate workshop discussions. Recall in Chapter 3, "The Life Cycle of Your Enterprise Cloud Adoption Strategy," that you need to know your own organization so that you can effectively use cloud services. To do this you need to determine areas to assess. In Chapter 3, Figure 3.3 suggested assessment areas as checkpoints for ensuring that there is a common understanding of your organization's experiences and business capabilities so that you make informed and situational business decisions.

Business Innovation:

What products and services do we currently offer?

How can we augment our current services for strategic advantage?

Can we create a shared risk/reward business model with business partners?

Customer / Market Insights:

What role can and will we play in cloud?

What services can we offer to our customers?

How will this new undertaking impact our brand?

Organization and Culture:

Do we have the right organizational structure?

How will internal organizations react to this change?

What cultural changes, if any, must we embrace?

How do we train our teams and who are recipients?

Metrics:

What are measurable KAIs and KPIs?

Are we experienced at measuring our agility?

Enterprise Architecture (Integrated Business and IT Strategy)

Sourcing:

Do we conduct cloud-sourcing today?

How can we leverage existing outsourcing providers to our advantage?

What processes are suitable for offloading to cloud?

What business processes will change?

Will traditional IT delivery processes work?

What service orientation and management processes exist?

Are regulatory solutions in place today?

Are we using the right technologies?

Is cloud the right fit and if not what are alternate choices?

How will cloud integrate with our enterprise systems and architecture?

What will we do with existing IT assets?

Figure E.3 Enterprise capability questionnaire and workshop discussion guide (prepared and tailored for Sta-up using Figure 3.3 as a baseline)

Cloud Strategy Workshop Discussion Points and Key Business Outcomes

Overall, the team agreed that operating as a value added reseller (VAR) is suitable for Sta-up and would complement the CSP business model and service offerings. Peter communicated that Sta-up already has strong network (wireless, unified communications including voice, video, and broadband) capabilities, a large client base comprised of SMB customers, and the business savvy to provide and support individual or bundled services. The company has shortcomings, however, in the areas of IT delivery in that traditional development cycles are long and costly, making cloud-sourcing a viable alternative for new product innovations and enablement. The goal is to build up in-house capability by assisting in development and testing efforts with selected providers. The team is uncertain in its ability to acquire and re-brand cloud service offerings within a six-month window and therefore developed a proposed two-year timeline.

Service Catalogue a Hybrid of Bundled and Standalone Solutions

Essentially, Sta-up will become a private consumer of cloud services, meaning the cloud environment will be hosted in Sta-up's data center in a single tenant capacity. Sta-up will in turn resell select services as public cloud offerings while taking advantage of the private cloud platform to build internal skills and strengthen existing IT capabilities. This approach requires strong collaborations with existing and new business partners as well as a willingness of cloud service providers to share in the risks and rewards. This model is required to support the new VAR-based cloud delivery, and as the team expressed must transpire with a sense of urgency.

During the session, Marsha led a discussion on market insights. She reviewed the data that she researched relaying that public clouds are popular for smaller businesses and that private cloud adoption emerged in prior years and would continue to grow particularly in cases where privacy and regulatory requirements dictate. She singled out the Microsoft SMB Cloud Adoption Study 2011:

Those SMBs paying for cloud services will be using 3.3 services, up from fewer than two services today; Eighty-two percent of SMBs say buying cloud services from a provider with local presence is critical or important; 56 percent of larger SMBs (with 51–250 employees) will pay for an average of 3.7 serv-ices within three years. By 2014, (within 3 years) 43 percent of workloads will become paid cloud services, but 28 percent will remain on-premises, and 29 percent will be free or bundled with other services.²

Marsha, an advocate of collective intelligence and gamification strate-gies to facilitate learning and decision making, expressed that social net-working, collaboration tools, online learning/training with techniques such as serious gaming,³ customer relationship management (CRM), hosted services, and data backups/disaster recovery are popular public and private cloud workloads. Gamification in this context means the augmentation of game mechanics in the work environment through applications, products, and services to promote social interactions and real-time business situations. She is interested in offering such capabil-ity as SaaS solutions.

NOTE

Appendix B, "Cloud Case Studies and Common Questions," contains a list of case studies, and one in particular furthers the relevancy of serious games and describes how integrating serious games and cloud was effectively applied for a travel and transportation client.

Marsha had particular interests in data backups and disaster recovery for Sta-up because they are important applications, yet are not consid-ered business critical by many of the SMBs in the region. To broaden a Sta-up service portfolio, she suggested that the company consider bun-dled cloud offerings that include backup and recovery services since bundling appears to be a buyers' trend:⁴

For instance, we could offer infrastructure compute services that include SaaS applications such as online financial accounting and tax services along with the option to back up data to unlimited storage that we make available in our cloud. That is a much more attractive suite than just offering infrastruc-ture—and if you add to that the managed operations and hosted capability that I know Francine will discuss, the service offering is that much more inviting.

David is in favor of this hybrid approach. He particularly knows and appreciates the interest of SMBs in hosted services and that the approach is typically taken due to internal shortfalls such as finances, infrastructure, or skills deficits. Sta-up is experienced in providing hosted services internally through virtualization; however, there is a shortage of internal cloud skills. This cloud opportunity will augment existing shortfalls.

Business Model Emphasizes Shared Risks/Rewards

Francine commented on the revenue model and pricing structure. She is certain that a Web-based storefront with a hybrid of individual offerings as well as bundles or packaged offerings combined with consumption based pricing that enables users to pay only for the tools or services they need without having to make any up-front investments is an attractive service offering. While her experiences with traditional IT providers have been once solutions are purchased it is up to the consumer to maintain, she is focused on driving a shared risks and rewards strategy, which she views as the path for Sta-up to reach revenue targets faster and for the provider to gain more client testimonials with respect to cloud solutions.

Francine's biggest concern is cost recovery. Because the team concluded that internally the capability is simply not there and it would take too long to build a cloud environment with existing business and IT resources, Sta-up will be making an investment to adopt a private cloud. Francine wants the return on the cloud investment to be positive within the first year of operations, which means the reliance on in-house sales teams with up and cross selling cloud experiences. She has an idea of a cloud marketing and advertising campaign strategy for selected providers that would drive recognition and continued use of Sta-up's cloud offerings.

To minimize costs, Francine suggested to the team to collaborate with an already onboarded outsourcing provider (MZT Enterprises) that manages Sta-up's data center and IT operations in North America because they also have operations in targeted South America markets. Francine feels that the costs to Sta-up should be lowered because MZT is familiar with the existing environments, international laws, and she is aware that although the delivery team might differ, she has experienced MZT's service excellence, and they are known for proven cloud offerings and experienced delivery.

Another financial area of discussion was revenue sharing. Francine wants Sta-up to receive a markup of 20 percent for all services resold.

She is hoping for a growth in customers by 50 percent due to the SaaS, PaaS, IaaS, and bundled offerings over the next two years. If the cloud portfolio stands, she predicts a customer growth rate of 30 percent for years 1 and 2, and 20 percent in subsequent years.

Andy does not agree that MZT should be the choice cloud provider and suggests that others be considered, stating, "We should consider those providers that offer business intelligence and storage solutions as this would be a welcomed addition to our service catalog."

Cost Take-Out

In addition to revenue generated from new service offerings and business growth, the team recognizes opportunities to eliminate costs associated with order management and the introduction of auto-approvals of designated purchases. Traditionally, this process required written authorizations as a part of the workflow, which introduced errors, unnecessary disputes, and delayed settlements. It is expected that the cycle times for new product introduction will improve due to service automation and the rapid availability of applications and servers required to support product initiatives as needed and on demand. The other area of opportunity is the self-service order fulfillment process that replaces dispatching of field agents before a transaction is completed. Combined with order management improvements cloud adoption is expected to contribute to a 25 percent reduction in business processing and IT associated costs.

Regulations Drive Private Cloud Adoption with Public Service Offerings

Gabriena discussed existing corporate, industry and government issued regulations that must be considered as a part of the cloud strategy as listed in Table E.1. She is in support of a private cloud strategy, which will ensure that Sta-up remains in compliance with local regulatory requirements and since international capability is introduced she knows there are other considerations such as the need to host cloud solutions in regional Sta-up data centers with citizenship from the same countries. Gabriena requires that all the standards listed be revisited and augmented to support the expansion of business in South America in order to move forward with cloud adoption and for finalization of the service offerings. She discussed the importance of these regulations citing FDA policies and informing the team that life sciences workloads running in the cloud must be validated in accordance with Good Practice guidelines as set forth by the Food and Drug Administration (FDA) and the International Conference on Harmonisation of Technical Requirements for Registration of Pharmaceuticals for Human Use (ICH). Gabriena and her chief security architect will oversee the process and validate candidate provider's when it comes to local and international regulatory compliance.

Table E.1 Common Regulatory Standards

Acronym	Standard	Description
BITS AUP	BITS Shared Assessment Program Agreed Upon Procedures	BITS is a division of the Financial Services Roundtable, an industry consortium comprised of the 100 largest financial institutions in the United States. They created the Shared Assessments Program in 1998 to effectively and uniformly audit service providers and outsourcers outside the financial services industry. The Agreed Upon procedures (AUP) is an established means of evaluating vendor controls for security, privacy, and business continuity aimed at reducing redundancies and increasing efficiencies in the vendor control assessment process. http://www.sharedassessments.org/about/
*COBIT	Control Objectives for Information Technology	COBIT is a voluntary IT framework published by the IT Governance Institute (ITGI), a workgroup of the Information Systems Audit and Control Association (ISACA). COBIT facilitates the identification of technical issues and business requirements for a given enterprise and provides control requirements and risk mitigations strategies in the context of a maturity model. Unlike ISO 27001, which is applied to a single target within the organization, COBIT is designed to be applied at the enterprise level. http://www.isaca.org/Knowledge-Center/cobit/Pages/Overview.aspx

Table E.1 Common Regulatory Standards

Acronym	Standard	Description
*FDA	Food and Drug Administration (FDA)	FDA's bilateral and multilateral interactions with Mexico and the countries of Central America, South America, and the Caribbean are to ensure that the entire range of FDA-regulated products developed, tested, manufactured, grown, and/or processed from this region and exported to the U.S. meet FDA requirements. http://www.fda.gov/ http://www.ich.org/
FFIEC IS Handbook	Federal Financial Institutions Examination Council Information Security Examination Handbook	The Council is a formal interagency body empowered to prescribe uniform principles, standards, and report forms for the federal examination of financial institutions by the Board of Governors of the Federal Reserve System (FRB), the Federal Deposit Insurance Corporation (FDIC), the National Credit Union Administration (NCUA), the Office of the Comptroller of the Currency (OCC), and the Office of Thrift Supervision (OTS), and to make recommendations to promote uniformity in the supervision of financial institutions. http://www.ffiec.gov/ffiecinfobase/html_pages/it_01.html#infosec
FISMA	Federal Information Security Management Act	The Federal Information Security Management Act (FISMA) defines a comprehensive framework to protect government information, operations, and assets against prevalent risks and threats. FISMA was signed into law as part of the Electronic Government Act of 2002. http://csrc.nist.gov/groups/SMA/fisma/index.html
GLBA	Gramm Leach Bliley Act, a.k.a. Financial Services Modernization Act of 1999	Gramm-Leach-Bliley (GLBA) is an act that allowed commercial and investment banks to consolidate. It carries a number of data privacy requirements around consumers, clients, and their finances. http://banking.senate.gov/conf/

Table E.1   Common Regulatory Standards

Acronym	Standard	Description
ITA	International Trade Administration	The International Trade Administration (ITA) strengthens the competitiveness of U.S. industry, promotes trade and investment, and ensures fair trade through the rigorous enforcement of our trade laws and agreements. ITA works to improve the global business environment and helps U.S. organizations compete at home and abroad. ITA supports President Obama's recovery agenda and the National Export Initiative to sustain economic growth and support American jobs. http://trade.gov/about.asp
*HITECH and HIPAA	Health Information Technology for Economic and Clinical Health Act (also see Health Insurance Portability & Accountability Act)	Title II of HIPAA, the Administrative Simplification (AS) provisions, requires the establishment of national standards for electronic healthcare transactions and national identifiers for providers, health insurance plans, and employers. The AS provisions also address the security and privacy of health data. The standards are meant to improve the efficiency and effectiveness of the nation's healthcare system by encouraging the widespread use of electronic data interchange in the US healthcare system. http://www.hhs.gov/ocr/privacy/
NERC CIP	North American Electric Reliability Corporation (Critical Infrastructure Protection)	The North American Electric Reliability Corporation (NERC) ensures the reliability of the bulk power system in North America. NERC develops and enforces reliability standards; assesses adequacy annually via a ten-year forecast and winter and summer forecasts; monitors the bulk power system; and educates, trains, and certifies industry personnel. NERC is a self-regulatory organization, subject to oversight by the U.S. Federal Energy Regulatory Commission and governmental authorities in Canada. http://www.nerc.com/page.php?cid=2|>}]http://www.nerc.com/page.php?cid=2|20

Table E.1 Common Regulatory Standards

Acronym	Standard	Description
*Patriot Act	USA Patriot Act	"Uniting and Strengthening America by Providing Appropriate Tools Required to Intercept and Obstruct Terrorism (USA PATRIOT) Act of 2001." http://www.fincen.gov/statutes_regs/patriot/index.html
*PCI DSS	Payment Card Industry, Data Security Standard	The PCI Data Security Standard is a multifaceted security standard that includes requirements for security management, policies, procedures, network architecture, software design, and other critical protective measures for credit card and personal information processing and handling. https://www.pcisecuritystandards.org/
*SOX	Sarbanes Oxley	A United States federal law enacted on July 30, 2002, that sets standards for all U. S. public company boards, management, and public accounting firms. It does not apply to privately held companies. The act contains 11 titles ranging from additional corporate board responsibilities to criminal penalties, and requires the Securities and Exchange Commission (SEC) to implement rulings on requirements to comply with the new law. http://www.sec.gov/spotlight/sarbanes-oxley.htm

*Standards and compliance currently in operation at Sta-up. However, each listed standard must be reevaluated and augmented in support of our cloud strategy and our growth in South America.

Enterprise Integration and AppStore Standards

Gabriena is adamant that payment processing must occur through Sta-up's existing portal infrastructure that was shared by David, due to established security protocols and compliance with enterprise data, application, and infrastructure standards. She and David both insist on using existing billing and credit card gateways on confirmation that Sta-up is up to date with COBIT, HITECH, PCI, and SOX compliance along with current enterprise security standards. David set the standard for providers when it comes to interoperability stating that they must generate open application programming interfaces (APIs) and/or Web service interfaces for all cloud business functionality so that integration with Sta-up's existing systems including the portal is simplified and for a smoother transition during on-boarding into the cloud environment and upon exit.

As mobile devices such as tablets become more popular in the workplace, Sta-up recognizes that employees should be allowed to load or consume applications from their devices but do so in a controlled manner. In David's previous role as the chief enterprise architect, he led development of policies for an in-house enterprise application store (AppStore), which his EA team maintains.

The enterprise AppStore contains company approved and fully vetted applications, many of which are publicly available, that were adopted and recommended for business purposes. As David discussed, the same principles are applicable to cloud adoption where (although in its early stages) he maintains a list of approved cloud solutions and providers. Storage-as-a-Service, for instance, is readily available for consumption by numerous vendors; this solution, however, requires policies and enforcements so that company data does not become exposed to the public or susceptible to vulnerability attacks as a result of the adoption.

The EA team has developed procedures for adding and removing tools from the enterprise's AppStore and welcomes feedback on suggested or available tools. For simplicity, in addition to AppStore standards, David would like to have an integrated enterprise AppStore.

Service Desk Support

Sam reminded the team that while self-service is a benefit of cloud, service desk support is highly recommended to support Sta-up's current track record of service excellence and as a strategy for identifying new service offering opportunities based on customer demand. The ticketing system should be integrated with the Web storefront for simplicity and suggested service desk support as selection criteria when choosing cloud providers. He shared a high level process of a ticketing system and standard performance metrics:

- Receive incoming Web, voice, and e-mail requests for support in three international languages and English.
- Open a ticket.
- Record calls and inquiries.
- Assign level of severity.

- Transfer calls or tickets to the appropriate support group.
- Initiate escalation for critical situations.
- Increase support levels if agents cannot resolve an issue.
- Measure and manage the quality of service with agent quality audits, root cause analysis, and SLA monitoring.

Typical service desk performance measurements are as follows:

- Number of customer service requests received at help desk.
- Number of tickets opened.
- Number of tickets closed.
- The average time to respond to tickets (time between opening and the first contact with the requester).
- The average time spent to resolve tickets.

Sustainability and Rewards

A key discussion point was organizational sustainability. Too often, initiatives such as this take off with strong executive endorsements, but as implementation nears, the endorsements dwindle. The team was concerned that the same would transpire here and that the risks of such occurrence would be harmful. Each of the strategic team members agreed to remain involved throughout implementation as steering committee and hands-on subject matter experts. Outcome-based reward systems were discussed as a motivator to each of the leaders and implementation teams. Examples include bonus alignment to the strategic roadmap and key implementation milestones; Formal communications across the company in recognition of team contributions and first of a kind asset development and delivery; and rewards for innovations in business process improvements and cloud adoption strategies. Stewart took the immediate action to institute this outcome-based reward system with Human Resources.

Outcome-based rewards were also discussed in the context of select providers and as a part of the shared risks/shared rewards strategy. A critical success factor is to determine which measurements or leading indicators are used to ensure that the outcomes are realistic and on track. As mentioned, this approach will be discussed and negotiated with vendors; however, a key indicator will be consumption of the public cloud offering and on-boarding of new customers. The team agreed that measuring the outcomes at the appropriate times will generate the best behaviors. If, for instance, measurements transpire at the end of the contract, then it is too late to make appropriate course corrections, which would somewhat defeat the purpose of an outcome-based reward model. The team (David is the focal point) will work with providers to determine the appropriate processes as well as governance of the processes.

The following steps were outlined to sustain Project Gold, including the outcome-based reward model:

1. Ensure that processes are established and properly followed.
2. Ensure that exceptions and undesirable outcomes are identified and addressed in a timely manner.
3. Establish accountability throughout the entire process from strategy through implementation.
4. Establish reporting and audit trail processes and execute.
5. Ensure transparency throughout the entire process from strategy through implementation through communications and Project Gold status meetings.
6. Conduct ongoing measurements and evaluation of leading indicators.

Project Gold Cloud Requirements Framework and Strategic Roadmap

Table E.2 describes the requirements for cloud services. The integrated requirements and strategic roadmap was collectively developed by the team during the workshop and shared with Stewart. After adding service level targets Stewart approved the roadmap and authorized the team to commence development of a Request for Inquiry and Quote (RFI/RFQ) that will get disseminated to cloud service providers.

The requirements aspect of the framework indicates what services make the most sense for Sta-up considering the strategic vision and business objectives and will influence cloud provider selection. The roadmap considers all information collected during the workshop beginning with the questionnaire responses (refer to Figure E.3), requirements, gaps in capability, and transition planning, such as provider selection and training of internal sales and marketing teams, and applies this data to determine realistic delivery windows. As depicted in Table E.2, projected delivery windows are Phase 1 (1-5 months), Phase 1b (6-12 months), and Phase 2 (1-2 years). This strategic roadmap will evolve and is expected to be updated once provider selection transpires.

Table E.2 Project Gold: Cloud Requirements Framework and Strategic Roadmap (Remember, Sta-up will approach cloud service providers as a consumer with a strategic vision and business requirement to resell services.)

Category	Capability	Target Market	Target Delivery
Enterprise Service Management and Integration		Steady state operations and upgrades	
		Cloud Computing Management Platform (CCMP)	
		Service desk support in three international languages + English	
		Enterprise integration (apps, processes, on-premise data centers)	
Service Levels		Service availability (99.95%); Recovery < 20 minutes per event; RTO ≤ 30 minutes	
Payment Options		Pay as you go (hourly or license based)	
		Bring your own license (BYOL)	
		Volume discounts	
BPaaS	Future offering	Small-to-medium enterprise (SME)	Phase 2 (1-2 years)
SaaS	Bundled apps (horizontal markets) Specialized apps for vertical markets (for example, serious games, e-learning)	Small-to-medium enterprise (SME)	Phase 1 (5 months) Phase 1b (9 months)
PaaS	Developer and test environments Virtual desktops Web hosting Communications-as-a-Service	Small-to-medium enterprise (SME)	Phase 1b (6 months)
IaaS	Compute-as-a-Service	Storage-as-a-Service Security-as-a-Service All enterprises	Phase 1 (3 months)

David assigned ownership to each of the roadmap domains and will validate, update, own, and integrate into the EA as cloud adoption standards. Reading from the bottom of Table E.2 to the top, the strategic requirements are

1. IaaS compute and storage: These solutions are intended for SMB and large enterprises and intended to jump-start revenue returns. It is expected that Compute-as-a-Service (CaaS) can be delivered to customers in three months. Storage offerings include backup, archive, and recovery services that can be consumed on-demand or through automatic provisioning of CaaS. Security services are a part of the standard IaaS offering, and example capabilities are antivirus, threat pattern recognition, and intrusion detection services. The owner of this domain is David.

2. PaaS services include communications offerings such as voice and video along and collaboration services such as unified messaging enhancements, Web hosting, virtual desktops, and developer and test environments: The intended consumers are small- and medium-sized enterprises. The services are a part of Phase 1b to allow base infrastructure cloud service components to be put in place first. PaaS services can also be offered as a part of the service bundling strategy and consumed on-demand or through automatic provisioning. The owner of this domain is Andy.

3. SaaS services are vertical and horizontal applications: Required vertical applications are education, tax and revenues, and human services. Required horizontal applications are finance and accounting, project management, collaboration, CRM, security, business intelligence (BI), and reporting. Serious games is a game changer for Sta-up that will emphasize e-learning and business process simulations. The target market at the onset for serious games is education and transportation services. The emphasis on BI is to augment CRM with information on customers who are ready to talk to sales, and to establish nurture streams for customers in the early buying stages. Intended consumers are small- and medium-sized enterprises.
SaaS services are a part of Phase 1 and 1b, respectively, due to ease of integration considerations and because the team requires time to figure out which applications make the most sense in terms of business complexities and ROI to enable as cloud services. As depicted, SaaS services can be offered as a part of the service bundling strategy or standalone. The owner of this domain is Peter.

4. BPaaS services are vertical business processes: Although currently not in scope, the targeted BPaaS service for Sta-up is employee benefits management—a vertical solution with horizontal (cross industry and organizational) impacts. The intended consumers are initially small- and medium-sized enterprises. The services are a part of Phase 2, which can take up to two years to deliver. BPaaS services are bundled with applications, a platform, and infrastructure, and the current intentions are to make BPaaS services available by third-party providers that are accountable to Sta-up. The owner of this domain is Peter.

Overarching are payment options, service levels, and enterprise service management. These services are applicable to SME and large enterprises. The team suggests several payments options to attract customers; these options are

- **Pay as you go:** Allows users to pay for services used whether they purchased licenses or selected metered usage.
- **Bring your own license (BYOL):** Allows existing licenses to be carried forward onto the cloud platform.
- **Volume Discounts:** Users buy in volumes to receive attractive discounts.

Service availability will be measured as Total Uptime Hours/Total Hours within a month. To meet current service levels, Sta-up requires 99.95% availability. The recovery point objective (RPO) is 20 minutes, meaning when the cloud becomes available, all data must be restored to a point within 20 minutes before the disaster, while the recovery time objective (RTO) is .5 hours, meaning the cloud must be available for service within 30 minutes of the outage's occurrence. The team realizes these service levels are stringent and will negotiate with cloud service providers as long as existing customer service levels are not compromised.

Enterprise service management and integration addresses end-to-end management of the cloud solution internal to the cloud and across the Sta-up enterprise as appropriate. Service consultants provide assistance in the areas of steady state operations including software and hardware upgrades, vendor liaisons and integration with existing business support services such as billing and order management; cloud specific management and performance monitoring, including new features, service portfolio upgrades and user management; and integrated service desk support in three international languages and English to support the South American region. Enterprise integration includes front-end and back-office collaboration and connectivity.

Project Gold is a reminder of some cloud adoption business essentials, such as the need for a clear strategic vision with business objectives; the importance of building relationships and teaming across business lines to derive service portfolio requirements even if you decide to commence implementation with a specific business unit; and implementation activities such as the need for service desk support and cultural considerations. The study illustrates the value of collective thinking to stir creativity and innovation when building out your strategic roadmap so that your enterprise cloud adoption strategy is both effective today and sustainable tomorrow. As you read on, you find elaborations of some cloud business patterns, business adoption trends, and emerging technologies for consideration as you develop and evolve your strategy.

Cloud Business Adoption Patterns and Trends

Chapter 3 provided decision analyses for some cloud business adoption patterns. Each pattern is described next. Keep in mind that more than one pattern can be applied to address business requirements, and many are enabled as traditional and new IT solution providers begin to work together to remain competitive.

Business Adoption Patterns

The business adoption patterns are as follows:

- **Allocation:** This pattern is applied to determine what service types to include in your portfolio. Traditionally, many companies entered the cloud space by adopting IaaS and for horizontal business purposes. The trend is shifting to vertical solutions such as BPaaS to address the needs of vertical markets.
- **Broker:** The broker pattern is the use of an intermediary to advise you or to make cloud adoption decisions on your behalf.
- **Bundling:** The selection of packaged cloud solutions that are bundled by providers or on demand for cloud service consumers.

- **Diversification:** The deliberate selection of a diverse set of cloud service types and deployment options in an effort to optimize enterprise returns. Coexistence of both public clouds and private clouds in an organization is an example of a hybrid cloud and a diversification strategy that I expect to grow by large and small enterprises as was indicated in the Project Gold case study.

- **Federation:** Establishes a trust relationship between cloud providers on- and off-premise so that clouds can automatically access one another to fulfill a business request with single sign-on capability. This pattern allows enterprises to move workloads seamlessly across internal and external clouds.

- **Rebalancing:** Regularly shift adoption patterns to match your changing business model and evolving customer requirements. Revisiting and updating your cloud adoption strategy drives rebalancing.

- **Resell:** This pattern is growing and as of late has become particularly popular with Telco providers. A reseller buys cloud services from providers with the option to add capability or resell those exact same services for profit. Resellers are also referenced as value added resellers (VARs) as discussed earlier in this chapter as a part of the Project Gold case study.

- **Self-service:** This pattern is applied when selection of cloud services occurs by the consumer, at purchase. The objective is to self empower consumers to purchase cloud services at their convenience.

- **Sourcing:** This pattern is applied to source solutions. Some options are cloud-sourcing through known outsourced providers, cloud-sourcing through new service providers, cloud-sourcing in-house, or do not source solutions from cloud but instead use alternate means such as traditional outsourcing.

- **Trade:** This pattern is applied to address unused assets that result from cloud adoption. Some options are to sell assets, repurpose within your organization, or rent out the assets for a fee. Spot trade is an example where the value of the sale of the asset occurs immediately as opposed to future trades where value is realized later.

Financial Patterns

Chapter 8, "Financial Considerations," was a reminder that as companies adapt to the ubiquitous data centers and compute resources that are readily available anywhere, anytime, and from any location, they can expect energy costs, IT expenses and up-front investment costs to shrink. Note, however, that in cases of private cloud adoption, some up-front investments are often required.

The Project Gold case study emphasized the expectations of cloud consumers one of which is that candidate providers should be able and willing to partake in a shared risk and shared reward financial strategy. The challenge becomes how to go about developing the right financial model so that it is a win-win for both companies. When it occurs, such partnerships are drivers of successful cloud implementations because the level of commitment on the part of the provider is just as genuine and dedicated as the consumers' level of commitment and dedication. Some techniques include outcome-based contracts, as discussed in the case study.

An example financial pattern for VARs or private cloud consumers is to pay for up-front investments as they grow so that as they reach target revenue levels consumers pay more on capital expenditure investments until paid in full. Other examples might be for consumers and providers to split investment costs and profits or to practice margin acceleration, meaning the cost per unit of CSP cloud service offerings drops as volumes increase, which increases profit margins and sales incentives. The point is that providers are working with consumers to arrange the best financial options as was the expectation of Project Gold. When it comes to revenue generation, the case study reflected a markup of 20 percent of cloud solutions that are resold and incurrence of direct financial benefits due to working with existing outsourced providers.

Financial patterns will evolve to become even more attractive due to more creative partnership models, more predictable markets, which was a challenge for Project Gold due to market hopefulness yet growth uncertainties, and financial models that are and will continue to emerge. Questionable, however, is the value of multiyear IT implementations as such strategies appear to be dissolving with the emergence of cloud and other rapid delivery models. Traditional outsourcers for instance must recognize the value of cloud-sourcing their operations to reduce the cost and improve the quality of services. Complex issues concerning privacy, local, and international jurisdictions are examples of the kinds of financial patterns that are evolving to support the cloud paradigm.

My expectation is that private and public cloud consumers as well as VARs will reap financial rewards as the cost of doing business in the cloud shrinks with inclining business value, and while I don't think we are there yet, tools will emerge that will allow you to better monitor your spending on cloud so that you can clearly demonstrate how this business technology is truly facilitating productivity and advancement of your business. A performance dashboard is a good example of a tool that exists today, while the opportunity is in the area of business intelligence and metrics. And while shared risk/shared reward models offer strategic advantages for both consumers and providers, two challenging areas of consideration for both parties are managing intellectual property and effectively handling the financials when contracts are dissolved.

Industry Verticals: How Are They Taking Advantage of Cloud?

Industry verticals are taking a closer look at cloud with a focus on leveraging the technology to solve business challenges. While cost is still important, it appears that capabilities such as efficient information processing, real-time business processing, outsourcing (BPO), and automation are taking precedence. Both small and large enterprises appear to have an interest in vertical cloud offerings.

Hospitals, for instance, are taking advantage of private clouds to support electronic health records moving away from paper-based solutions. Applications such as shift management and recruiting tools for healthcare institutions can help reduce labor costs, and the accessibility through cloud-enabled communities allows individuals or companies to take advantage of the capability. This means medical staff, doctors included, can take advantage of mobile devices to facilitate patient care. This also means the skills of your teams (business and IT) must encompass industry vertical knowledge, including privacy, security, and regulatory compliance requirements.

The energy and utilities industry is taking advantage of cloud to address increased energy demands. Executives such as Steve Ballmer of Microsoft recently shared how the use of cloud and other emerging technologies can better manage large influxes of data and speed insight to finding affordable energy solutions. He suggests bringing business partnering and business technology advancements to energy and utilities (E&U) companies to improve real-time communication and collaboration, enable massive data aggregation, provide secure access to information, and empower workers with business intelligence on smart devices.[5]

Telcos are taking a more active role by operating as cloud service providers. The Project Gold case study is based on real-life Telco experiences where companies recognize opportunities to accelerate market penetration through the use of cloud. Many are introducing new products and services that traditionally would not fall within a Telco's core competency. Some examples are SaaS and IaaS, while competencies such as managed hosting fall within traditional business models. Many Telcos are reselling SaaS services to augment infrastructure-focused cloud solutions.

Media and entertainment companies are taking advantage of public cloud storage due to fluctuating business needs and requirements to handle streaming media. As discussed in the case study, the benefits of storage are particularly appealing to SMBs, and organizations must be careful as to what data should be placed in the cloud and maintain a line of sight into how to retrieve data should providers find themselves out of a job.

Automotive industries are taking to cloud for what is called "cloud-sourced navigation."[6] This trend enables navigation systems to rely on information that is stored in the cloud as opposed to embedded data-bases where the devices operate in a standalone capacity. Maps, traffic, and weather conditions are examples of cloud-sourced content that is enabled through consistent "online" connectivity. Other examples of cloud-based navigation services are traffic camera visuals and map updates.

A travel and transportation client in China was experiencing excessive data overload due to the deployment of sensors and meters across the city on cars, buses, mopeds, and some traffic lights. City officials struggled with how to use this data to develop a "smarter city." Officials were overwhelmed as to how to even get started considering the wealth of challenges. Cloud was suggested as the business technology that would enable business process modeling and simulations to guide development of a strategic roadmap and the implications of proposed actions.

Organizations are increasingly choosing cloud service providers to transform key business processes in departments such as marketing, finance, and customer service, and the demand for cloud is on the rise. Several industry-specific solutions are described in the case studies in Appendix B; in particular, universities and schools face increasing cost challenges while, in parallel, they are required to roll out online tools for education and e-learning services. This requires scalable infrastructures, along with virtual labs and remote data center access, data mining is often required, and high performance computing or the use of server-based super computers. Cloud enables students, faculty, and alumni to access academia and process solutions effectively and keeps schools up with the emerging technologies that they are in fact teaching. The situation is elaborated in Appendix B.

Solution Patterns

Your candidate cloud provider should have and be willing to communicate its cloud reference architecture, and you should work with your enterprise architect to ensure that the cloud solution fits and adheres to your enterprise architecture and cloud principles. Figure E.4 provides an example cloud computing reference architecture (CCRA) provided by IBM. The main roles and corresponding architectural elements are defined at the highest level, allowing decomposition or drill-down for each element as needed.

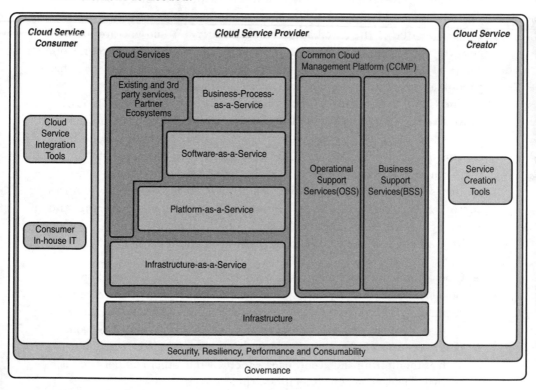

Figure E.4   Solution patterns: an example cloud computing reference architecture[7]

In this example, the CCRA defines three main roles: cloud service consumer, cloud service provider, and cloud service creator. Each role can be fulfilled by a single person or by a group of people or an organization. The roles defined here intend to capture the common set of roles typically encountered in any cloud computing environment. Therefore, it is important to note that depending on a particular cloud computing scenario or specific cloud implementation, project-specific subroles may be defined. Detailed cloud roles and responsibilities are discussed in Appendix A, "Augmenting Your Delivery Model with Cloud."

Evident in the Project Gold case study, it is important to integrate cloud services within your existing enterprise (small and large). You and your provider should discuss integration requirements and the required tools. On a recent engagement, a customer's enterprise billing system used unique, specialized technologies and required sessions between the consumer and provider to develop the appropriate integration strategy. On another engagement, a client wanted to deploy some applications into the cloud to support his private cloud strategy, only that became impossible due to the dated application libraries. When you are looking at enterprise integration there is more to it than application integration. There is data, infrastructure, and business processes. Your provider has to look at integration from all layers of the cloud stack.

The Cloud Computing Management Platform (CCMP) is responsible for delivering instances of cloud services of any category to cloud service consumers. As discussed in earlier chapters, cloud services can be built on top of each other; for example, a software service could consume a platform or infrastructure service, and a platform service could consume an infrastructure service. Bringing any cloud service to market requires corresponding pre-investment, along with respective metering and charging models in support of the corresponding business model.

In this example, the CCMP is split into two main elements:

- **Operational support services (OSSs):** OSSs represent the set of operational and technical services exposed by the CCMP. These services are required by to implement a cloud service. Example OSSs are the service delivery catalog, service automation, and provisioning. Many OSS components can also be encountered in traditionally managed data centers such as monitoring and event management, while other components such as image management are specific to cloud.

- **Business support services (BSSs):** BSSs represent the set of business-related services exposed by the CCMP. These services are consumed and directly impact the user's experience. Example BSSs are the service offering catalog, billing, and pricing.

Security, resiliency, performance, and consumability span the cloud environment. These nonfunctional aspects must be addressed holistically from the view of the consumer through cloud solution delivery. These components address the way your cloud is set up including the hardware infrastructure. Your provider looks at network zoning setup, data center setup, disaster recovery, and a host of other capabilities so that the solution will perform.

Service creation tools are used by the cloud service creator to develop new or modify existing cloud services. Example tools are metering and provisioning.

In Chapter 5, "What About Governance?," you learned about the need and value of governing your enterprise that has integrated cloud as a part of the solution landscape. The chapter emphasized the need for end-to-end business and IT governance. In this example, governance of the development and deployment of cloud solutions is the focus. It is an essential element of the CCRA. You should ask your providers what their cloud governance processes are; for instance, who is accountable for and how will they ensure that single-tenancy environments are built and operating to service commitments? You then want to ensure that their cloud governance adheres to your strategic, enterprise governance model and/or framework.

Emerging Technologies

While business trends and adoption patterns are significant, one area that cannot be ignored is emerging technologies. Take a look two to three years down the road to see what's coming, how you will be able to solve your business challenges, as well as how you will be able to apply your current methods, technologies, and your cloud adoption strategy to incorporate these emerging trends. One of the opening topics in this chapter is a discussion on the CIO's visionary plans where projected use of technologies was elaborated. This section focuses on emerging or upcoming technologies for the year 2012 and beyond. Understanding where technology is headed and how such capabilities can augment your skills and capabilities in support of your cloud adoption strategy can be invaluable. Our planet is becoming smarter and more intelligent. Intelligence is being infused into the way the world literally works—the systems and processes that enable physical goods to be developed, manufactured, bought, and sold; services to be delivered; everything from people and money to oil, water, and electrons to move, and billions of people to work and live. Our intelligent, smarter world evolves by connecting the digital representation (a.k.a models) of three interdependent domains. First, the human world of individuals and communities that includes social networks. Second, our physical reality of geospatial models, physics, sensors, or robotics. Third, the business and IT world of business processes, applications, and data models.

The evolution of the smarter planet will accelerate to capture and model different worlds at different abstractions creating impactful business outcomes for those organizations that leverage and create value from these three merging models of our world. Of course, cloud delivery will be a significant factor in the capability of these models to merge and create value. Cloud computing may become the dominant means for delivery of computing infrastructure and applications on the Internet. As the cloud delivery mechanism takes hold, the control components of software—that is, components that are used to create, configure, and adjust the nature of applications—are going to be moving to the edge of the enterprise but remain outside the cloud. A significant impact of cloud computing is the rapidity and ease of creating new computing functions and services in the network.

Combining existing applications and data with new types of processing functions and technologies derives new value: Big Data, social business, mobile computing, and analytics. This combination process creates a network of applications and data services, jointly referred to as computing services. In this network of computing services, businesses tend to keep those computing services that are critical to their business within their premises and in a manner of speaking, outsource the non-critical computing services to the cloud.

As the industry moves to the new model of outsourcing in the computing services arena, we may see the control components of the computing services networks getting aggregated and moving toward the edge of the enterprise. The control components of the computing services networks are functions used to create, control access, and modify the computing services network. These control components are going to move toward the edge of the enterprise, where they are used to control the interactions between the computing services within the enterprise and within the cloud.

Dynamic and autonomous systems, conversational language solutions, self-optimizing software, and advanced robotics with self-navigating speech capable robots may cause the emergence of new industries as a result of cross-industry systems. As a result a combination of factors, including improved modeling, analytics, rules engines, discovery mechanisms, and monitoring tools, is making it possible to return control of a business's operations to its executives.

It was recently reported that the United States military has a new weapon that could save many American lives. It is the driverless truck or as reported, "drone convoys." This technology (which has some cloud characteristics) moves truck convoys without using drivers. The technology has been in development by Lockheed Martin over the last six years, and according to reports these vehicles become robots that can travel in convoy style with as long as 25 trucks in a row at some 65 miles per hour and remain on course.

"In semi-autonomous mode, if there is a soldier in the vehicle, that soldier can be looking for threats, including IEDs, rather than operating the vehicle," Lockheed Martin program manager Adrian Michalicek said. "And they can avoid obstacles such as a child who might dart into their path."[8] This is an exciting technology that has emerged to keep our soldiers safe. Driverless vehicles are not just offered by the military, however; it was recently reported that Google is experimenting with a self-driving car.[9] The cars are loaded with sensors that feed data to an in-vehicle computer for control and the intentions are to develop safer and more efficient cars.

Imagine your ability (regardless of your physical state of being) to automatically detect and immediately reject your doctor's intention for medical treatment that might be harmful to you. Imagine walking down the street and your mobile device informs and guides you to the appropriate nearby restaurant that serves the proper meals for your immediate situation, because it knows you are a diabetic and your current insulin levels. Imagine an IBM Watson™ capability in an emergency room where all the medical information in the world resides at your finger tips—on a computer system that is accessible by you and your doctors to quickly diagnose your situation enabling medical professionals to keep pace with the constant pace of new drugs and findings when it comes to medical cures and side-effects. Reportedly, IBM is working with medical experts to identify the best ways to incorporate Watson-like technology to the practice of medicine.[10]

The examples in this section offer insights into where we are headed with respect to business technology adoption and adaptation. As was depicted the motivation may not always be for profit as in the case of the "drone convoys and medical necessities" where the emphasis is on saving lives but as evidenced, the impacts are substantial. Can you see how taking advantage of cloud can increase business value and expand the possibilities for your business?

Summary

Business technologies are a part of our daily lives. We are constantly connected, and we do not have to carry around excessive devices any longer to do so. Companies that leverage business technologies such as cloud to more effectively solve problems and those that are willing to step out of their comfort zones and explore new innovations with these technologies are the ones that will remain competitive. I agree with the comments made in the book *World Class IT: Why Businesses Succeed When IT Triumphs*,[11] where the author reminds us that IT is a source of innovation and that CIOs that understand that they are stewards can help spread innovation more broadly.

Today, we're seeing the impact of cloud in companies; some starting in the home and flowing into the business environment through the use of smart and mobile devices.. Focus on an integrated business and IT strategy that will leverage your company's strategic advantage, knowing that business teams are not as successful as they can be without an IT strategy and IT teams are not as successful as they can be without a business strategy. Adding cloud to your integrated strategy makes your adoption that much more valuable, much more effective, and longer lasting. For those that have gotten started with cloud, it is time to start thinking about broadening your horizons so that you strengthen your investments. Maintain your vision yet broaden your scope.

Summarizing this book, the initial chapters described the business value of a cloud adoption strategy and the value of focusing on the enterprise and embracing EA principles to maximize your investment potential and business performance. You then learned techniques to identify cloud candidates in a manner that helps to drive business value. Mitigating the business and technical risks are core techniques toward development of a successful transition plan that must be also governed, financially managed, and secured. Considerations for risk management, governance, security, and financial implications are therefore reflected in many of the chapters.

In this epilogue, it is requested of you to maintain your strategic eye (your vision to develop an effective, enterprise cloud adoption strategy) even when faced with tactical actions and decisions. You are reminded that the days of large companies driving technology are pretty much over and that cloud providers must consider the consumer to be successful in their endeavors. But, how can they if you yourself do not have a strategy? Along the same topic, consider your own organization where consumers buy smart phones, tablets, and other devices and bring them into the workplace. Your business and IT teams should view this as an opportunity to wisely accommodate, which will in turn strengthen your organizational capabilities, prevent unapproved use of tools and additions to your network, mitigate business risks, and add to your team's overall effectiveness. In essence, the question is not about whether adoption will occur but how? It is not a question of whether business value will be achieved but how quickly and how much?

This epilogue concluded with a discussion on some emerging technologies and further the conversation in Appendix C, "More on Cloud Business Trends," as a reminder that such knowledge sharing, awareness, and adaptation is important, just as the other content discussed in this book, toward enabling you to choose the best cloud adoption strategy for your business. The race is approaching. Are you prepared, are you ready for the next one, what is your strategy?

In closing, it is important to build a culture of trust, collaboration, and innovation when it comes to cloud adoption. Such considerations were shared throughout this epilogue along with the need for organizational support and business performance sustainability as summarized in Table E.3.

Table E.3 Sustainability: Business Performance Risks and Mitigation Strategies

Risk	Mitigation Strategy and/or Considerations
Staff is neither using nor selling the new cloud solutions.	Training to be provided to employees, targeted consumers, sales, and marketing teams by providers or designees.
Uncertainty getting started.	Strategy workshop; see Project Gold.
Customers not buying cloud offerings.	Shared risk/shared reward joint coalition between consumers and providers; see Project Gold. Emphasize the business outcomes, which includes increased sales and satisfaction levels due to business and IT transformation.

Table E.3 Sustainability: Business Performance Risks and Mitigation Strategies

Risk	Mitigation Strategy and/or Considerations
Dwindling executive sponsorship.	Strategy team remains on-board as a part of the implementation team. In the Project Gold case study, Stewart would remain the executive sponsor.
Resistance to change.	Outcome-based reward system introduced; see Project Gold.
No new innovations.	Outcome-based reward system introduced; see Project Gold.
No ownership and accountability.	Strategy team becomes overarching executive council (hands on).
Develop Responsibility, Accountability, Consulted, and Informed (RACI) matrix and enforce for all stages of the project.	Establish/enforce project governance and transparency.
Communication strategy that includes providers and business partners.	Establish reporting and audit trail processes and execute.
Processes are not followed or updated.	EA integration and enforcements.
Exceptions and undesirable outcomes identified and addressed.	Cloud Service Portfolio becomes unmanageable.
EA/Cloud leadership and accountability.	Build out cloud center of excellence.
Provider underperformance.	SLAs, SLOs, partnership agreements, shared risk/shared reward joint coalitions.
Stale metrics.	Ongoing review and updates. Includes leading indicators, outcomes, and required actions.
Noncompliance.	Regulatory requirements review and stakeholder accountability; see Project Gold.

Endnotes

1. "2011 IBM Global CIO Study: The Essential CIO." See http://public.dhe.ibm.com/common/ssi/ecm/en/cie03073usen/CIE03073USEN.PDF or IBM Institute for Business Value at iibv@us.ibm.com.

2. "Microsoft Unveils Findings from Its SMB Cloud Adoption Study." EMEA Press Centre. See http://www.microsoft.com/presspass/emea/presscentre/pressreleases/MSSMBCloud Adoption.mspx. And Kass, D. H. "More SMBs Will Pay for Cloud Services in the Next Three Years, Microsoft Study Shows." IT ChannelPlanet. March 29, 2011. See http://www.itchannelplanet.com/smallbusiness_news/article.php/3929361/More-SMBs-Will-Pay-for-Cloud-Services-in-the-Next-Three-Years-Microsoft-Study-Shows.htm.

3. According to ABIresearch, the overall online game market is expected to eclipse $14.5 billion in 2010 and grow to just over $29 billion by 2015. See http://www.abiresearch.com/research/1003591-Gaming+in+the+Cloud.

4. "U. S. SMBs Show Strong Preference for Cloud Bundling." Site News. May 12, 2011. AMI Partners. See http://www.ami-partners.com/index.php?target=news&mode=details&news_id=199.

5. "Steve Ballmer Discusses Cloud Solutions at CERAWeek. TechNet Blogs. March 17, 2011. See http://blogs.technet.com/b/vertical_industries/archive/2011/03/17/steve-ballmer-discusses-cloud-solutions-at-ceraweek.aspx.

6. Magney, Phil. "Automotive Navigation Heads into the Cloud." October 7, 2010. IHS iSuppli press release. See http://www.isuppli.com/automotive-infotainment-and-telematics/news/pages/automotive-navigation-heads-into-the-cloud.aspx.

7. CCRA and CCMP. IBM. See http://www.infoq.com/news/2011/03/IBM-Cloud-Reference-Architecture.

8. "New Lockheed Martin System Turns Truck Convoys into Drones." May 25, 2011. 9News.com. See http://www.9news.com/news/article/200232/188/New-Lockheed-Martin-system-turns-trucks-into-drones.

9. Herrman, John. "Google's Self-Driving Car, In Action." March 4, 2011. SmartPlanet. See http://www.smartplanet.com/blog/thinking-tech/google-8217s-self-driving-car-in-action/6422.

10. Menon, Jay. "IBM's Watson to Bring Rewards Beyond Jeopardy." May 31, 2011. IBM Smarter Computing. See http://www.smartercomputingblog.com/2011/05/31/ibms-watson-to-bring-rewards-beyond-jeopardy/.

11. High, Peter. 2009. *World Class IT: Why Businesses Succeed When IT Triumphs*. San Francisco: John Wiley & Sons.

Augmenting Your Delivery Model with Cloud

The most relevant lesson is the need to continually move to the future. This requires investment... when your model is based on innovation, on continual forward movement... you make these investments.

It also requires risk-taking. Running an innovation model over the long term is not for the faint-hearted. It often compels the enterprise to act when it is not obvious to do so... to place bets that seem risky to those who are focused on short-term gain... and to combat corporate inertia when times are good.

And it means you have to know when to leave behind the sources of your previous success...sustaining an innovation model over the long term—for a decade, much less a century—also means leaving the past... your own past... behind. Companies, as well as nations, need to know when to make this transition.

—Samuel J. Palmisano, chairman, president IBM, excerpts from "The Smarter Future of IT" 2011 CeBIT Published Keynote Speech

While Chapter 2, "Business Value of Incorporating Cloud into Your EA," demonstrated how to incorporate cloud into your EA and Chapter 3, "The Life Cycle of Your Enterprise Cloud Adoption Strategy," emphasized development of your cnterprise cloud adoption strategy, this appendix provides business considerations for augmenting your delivery model, such as the use of data centers and delivery methods with cloud as well as strategies that you should consider to maintain or even improve your brand.

Delivery Models and Cloud Considerations

Your delivery model should have direct correlation with your integrated business and IT strategy and thus your organizational effectiveness. Delivery model (in this context) is the use of people, processes, information, and technology to deliver IT solutions to your customers, employees, partners and suppliers.

The typical IT delivery model keeps most risk residing within the IT organization. The IT organization is responsible for the data center, the hardware in the data center, and the application stack. Financially, the IT costs are fixed, as the data center was on premise, owned, and depreciated over extended periods of time (for example, 20 years) while equipment typically depreciated over five to seven years.

Public cloud computing provides the opposite end of the scale, with the risk of the data center and hardware moved to the cloud service provider, and a variable financial model as cloud services are provided using a subscription or usage-based model.

Consider Figure A.1, which shows a two-dimensional set of options for IT delivery models based on four premise delivery options (on premises, on premises utility, off premises dedicated, and off premises shared), and three financial models (fixed, mixed, and variable).

The adoption and use of cloud enables cloud consumers to augment their delivery model to preserve capital, take advantage of new market opportunities, improve IT effectiveness, or to make IT a center of innovation. For example, some service providers (IBM and others) offer components that allow you to build your own private cloud environment in addition to services that help you create your own public cloud. Both result in an on-premises utility delivery model that you control, an environment that you can grow and expand depending on your business needs. Utility in this context implies the creation of a multipurpose IT infrastructure that provides common functions that can be shared by multiple customers with pay per use options. Utility services include business processes, software, and infrastructure.

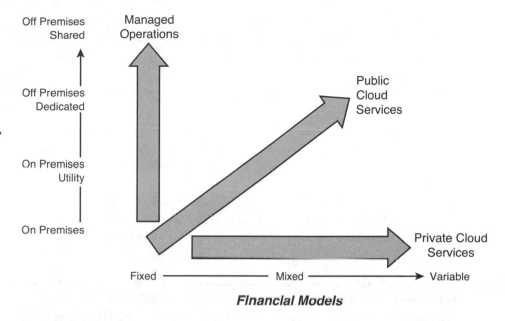

Figure A.1 Delivery models and cloud considerations

A typical fixed (flat rates are charged for service purchases regardless of the amount of consumption) financial model integrating cloud furthers an organization's capability to move to a more consumption based financial model where consumers are accurately charged only for their service usage. In this example, financial modeling occurs on the current and upcoming years. Consider the following real-life business scenarios.

Brand, Incorporated, hires TCP Enterprises (a cloud service provider) to build a private cloud with compute and storage service offerings, where a private cloud indicates that the cloud resides in Brand's data center. In addition, the private cloud would be managed and governed by Brand while operations of the cloud environment, including performance and maintenance, is the responsibility of TCP (refer to managed operations in Figure A.1).

Brand plans to offer cloud services to existing and new customers making it an on-premise utility service available as a public cloud offering. Charges for building the cloud and managing the operations are fixed and extend over a ten-year period, while charges to Brand's end users are consumption based. At the same time, TCP receives a percentage of the profits generated via the purchase of cloud services by Brand's end users making the financial model for Brand mixed, comprised of both fixed (for managed operations) and variable costs (to accommodate both private and public cloud services).

NOTE

This scenario is a growing reality and example of how businesses are partnering to augment their delivery models with cloud. Two strategic relationships surface from this scenario. First, Brand is a consumer of a private cloud offering from TCP where TCP's delivery model is on premises and private cloud delivery. Second, Brand leverages that same private cloud to become a public cloud service provider where Brand's delivery model is on-premises utility and public cloud delivery.

Service providers offer public and private cloud offerings. These are represented in Figure A.1 as off premises dedicated or off premises shared delivery models with a variable as opposed to fixed financial model. In this case, it is a standard practice to charge consumers for actual usage of services. This is usually accomplished with subscription or metered enablement. Consider the following example.

Brand, Incorporated, hired TCP Enterprises to build a cloud that would be hosted from TCP's data center. In this example, TCP is responsible for managing and governing the cloud environment in accordance with Brand's service level requirements. Authorized subscribers to this cloud as specified by Brand are employees and authorized personnel. Brand expressed that the cloud environment must not be shared with other TCP customers. In other words, it is dedicated to Brand. This is an example of an off-premises dedicated delivery model. If and when Brand authorizes TCP to allow TCP customers and other business partners to use the cloud environment, it will become an off-premises environment. Referencing Figure A.1, financial models traditionally were fixed but are moving to variable models to support off-premises delivery models.

The use of cloud within your organization will change over time just as business and IT requirements change and as cloud offerings change. Customers periodically go through periods where their data center and or IT equipment is fully utilized and future growth is constrained or not yet available. Cloud provides a temporary location for IT workloads while additional data center resources become available.

Many of the initial public cloud computing offerings were Infrastructure-as-a-Service (IaaS) offerings, where the service provider owned the data center, IT hardware, and base operating systems. The customer was responsible for installing the rest of the software stack including the application and for operating the cloud workload.

Then Platform-as-a-Service (PaaS) and Software-as-a-Service (SaaS) surfaced. These offerings include more of the software stack, up to and including customer applications and the system management tooling to run IT workloads without involving IT resources. In fact, previous outsourcing and out-tasking workloads have given way to SaaS cloud environments based on a variable financial model.

In a typical data center, some servers might run billing applications, while others run enterprise resource planning (ERP) applications. You might consider adoption of an on-premise private cloud where applications run on whichever servers have free cycles at the time the applications need to run. This separation of applications from the hardware that it runs on is one of several advantages of cloud. Traditional data centers are also larger than what they need to be. Cloud grants you the opportunity to shrink your data center costs and physical capacity and expand in the future as needed supporting more of a Just-In-Time[1] (JIT) strategy.

NOTE

JIT is a business inventory and production strategy that strives to improve a company's return on investment by reducing in-process inventory and any associated overhead. JIT companies focus on increasing efficiency and decreasing waste by receiving goods only as they are needed in the production process, thereby reducing inventory and warehousing costs. Data centers are moving to a JIT model to optimize costs and asset reuse.

Maximizing your investment benefits requires an understanding of how future business and IT requirements are changing. You must understand what cloud options will exist over time, such that you should consider incorporating cloud delivery models into your overarching and integrated business and IT strategy (your EA). While you might not move 100 percent of your workloads to cloud in the immediate future and thus eliminate the need for internal data centers, you now have the capability to streamline data center assets, and you have the opportunity for a certain percentage of risks

associated with current IT delivery processes and requirements to be mitigated by taking advantage of cloud delivery models thus improving service
levels and overarching performance.

Building Efficiencies and Sustainability

Organizations are working to optimize energy and efficiencies in
office buildings, data centers, campuses, and other facilities. Cloud solutions provide analytics, automation, command and control, and asset
management services helping you achieve your desired energy efficiency
objectives by providing information allowing you to optimize building
use and marginalize occupancy costs and space requirements.

In addition, if you purchase cloud services, any required servers and
software assets are not required to reside in your data center, which in
turn improves your capacity for energy efficiency and environmental sustainability. Your ability to use external assets to handle your temporary
requirements such as business peak loads and the fact that you are sharing capacity across larger pools of users certainly adds to your capacity to
optimize utilization of equipment and environmental sustainability.

Your on-premises data centers should be designed to utilize renewable
energy sources, and you should monitor energy efficiencies such as the
power usage effectiveness (PUE) ratio that measures how efficiently
power is actually used by computing equipment (in comparison with
cooling and other overhead) and Data Center Infrastructure Efficiency
(DCiE),[2] which is a more accurate reflection of power usage that takes
into account raised floor power. Provisioning and virtualization management software can reduce server power consumption substantially along
with management functions such as power capping.

You should discuss your efficiency goals and requirements with service providers since your off-premises green objectives should be as
important to you as your on-premises objectives. In fact, providers that
offer eco-friendly cloud solutions could differentiate themselves from
their competition. There might be incentives for cloud providers, particularly if servers are purchased in larger quantities. For instance,
providers may be able to negotiate with vendors to build lower powered
servers, CPUs, and storage, or they may consider customized orders to
include better cooling to prevent excess generation of heat and equipment failures.

A final note on this subject is equipment disposal. Discarded computers don't just take up space in a landfill; they spread toxins into the environment. You need a responsible way to recycle your equipment that is good for business and the environment. You will want to work with companies that recycle end-of-life IT assets, such as servers, hard drives, monitors, and so on, and you will need to choose vendors that will handle your recycling and disposal needs in an environmentally friendly, EPA approved manner, complying with all regulatory requirements and local legalities.

Project and Solution Delivery Model (PSDM)

Organizations (business and IT) need to adapt to the accelerated project and solution delivery life cycle (PSDM) to support the cloud delivery model. Traditionally a project lasts months and requires a large delivery team with various skills to complete the effort. Teams include project managers, data analysts, application developers, testers, subject matter experts, and more. With the adoption of cloud, projects are implemented in shorter timeframes and require fewer resources, increasing end user demands with expectations of faster, improved services at reduced costs.

With this background, and regardless of whether you are a consumer or provider of cloud services, your PSDM needs to support rapid development and embed fast-track, agile approaches to solution delivery as users will likely find traditional phases to be too long and too cumbersome. At the same time, there are key elements of development life cycles (for both software and products), such as viability assessments, requirements baselining, design, testing, performance engineering, and quality assurance efforts, including user acceptance testing, that should not be short circuited. Solution rework, failure to satisfy requirements, and dissatisfied customers are experienced outcomes should this occur.

In the case of outsourcing, it generally takes longer to provision environments as long as traditional development life cycles and approaches are utilized. Understandably, more outsource providers are becoming cloud providers. Use caution when selecting outsourcers and find out what rapid software and product development life cycles are used including automated provisioning of development, test, and acceptance test environments. These precautionary steps prevent you from offloading services to outsourcers to save on costs only to discover that it would have been more beneficial had you offloaded services to cloud.

Business leaders are attracted to self-service capabilities such as building a Web site, dashboard, or application without having to contact the IT department or following stringent protocols. This means that an ability to acquire cloud services to solve business challenges in a self-sufficient capacity is beneficial to organizations. This capability, however, adds a level of complexity to your service management processes as more environments, even if virtual, must be adequately governed, managed, and maintained. A recommended strategy is to require product and IT teams to align with and operate as trusted advisors to business leaders, and establish a governance framework that does not hinder but rather guides cloud adoption and ensures enterprise alignment. Consider the following scenario:

Brand discovered that software licensing and warranties for some legacy applications were no longer renewable since support for the software was nearing end of life by the vendors. The CFO excitedly tells the business that TCP will move forward with cloud solutions to replace the legacy applications. However, the VP of marketing and sales does not agree because one of the legacy applications has been customized to provide key functionality that is required for customer demographical analysis. The dilemma for TCP is to let the legacy system's warranty expire and do nothing considering that performance issues have not been a problem, or replace the legacy system in its entirety because it would be impossible to simply replace only one of the applications.

This is a common dilemma that organizations are experiencing and a prime example and opportunity for the CIO, CTO, and IT delivery teams to collaborate and influence direction relative to cloud adoption. TCP should establish governing policies and procedures so that teams know when to engage the necessary resources, when stakeholder involvement is optional, and when it is required.

NOTE

Although a lower level of analysis is required, and typically by cloud providers, a key consideration is determining which (if any) components of legacy applications can be provided in a cloud environment. This is significant in cases where the application itself may be categorized as unfit for cloud. In such cases, you would explore opportunities to make components of the application available in the cloud such as the user interface or data tier.

Global Delivery Model (GDM)

It is not surprising to find that many offshore vendors are becoming cloud providers to support the low-cost delivery model that cloud brings to bear. Consumers of cloud services are demanding bilingual capabilities (for example, French translations and currency conversions of the service catalog) and a broader reach when it comes to global consumption of cloud services. There is also expressed concern by some consumers on the exposure of data in public clouds, which opens the door to growth in private clouds[3] that sit behind an enterprise's firewall but has global capacity. Considering the proliferation of cloud services that are occurring, globalization could be a differentiator for cloud providers.

You can take advantage of cloud to expand your global delivery model (GDM). A GDM is IT-enabled services that are coordinated and delivered by global project teams. In a GDM, offshore teams execute based on the inputs gathered from the onsite team. A good example of this is systems testing where requirements gathering sessions occur locally and data are disseminated to global teams for quality assurance testing. In such cases, regular reporting and collaborations ensure that at all times offshore actions align with business and local team requirements. Cloud enables you to connect, collaborate, and establish business in international markets faster due to rapid access and provisioning of required services anywhere and at anytime. You might have hired offshore teams to conduct application development or testing, or to conduct activities such as set up and configure infrastructure that is then deployed to your resources as a part of your refresh processes. With cloud, offshore capabilities can be augmented or replaced in their entirety with virtual services. Consider the following scenario:

Your GDM enables you to expand or move to different regions on demand without having to plan and implement lengthy systems updates. Your global data centers could potentially eliminate regulatory issues that surface when transferring data across geographical boundaries with in-policy rapid and automated provisioning services. This is directly dependent on how your cloud solution is configured. For instance, a cloud consumer may not want his/her client data stored in another country due to regulatory requirements. The provider could, in this case, set up a global cloud that is hosted out of the consumer's data center or a dedicated location within the consumer's geographical boundaries.

Cloud and GDM give you the ability to build and run global initiatives faster and more efficiently. An example is leveraging global cloud collaboration tools to build virtual teams and manage communications across projects. GDM also makes it easier for you to transfer work to alternate, safer locations for disaster recovery, failover, and for client risk mitigation, which amounts to faster time to value and business agility, and a common example is the use of cloud to advance supply chain communications so that delivery of goods and services are identified and executed faster, often ahead of the need, and more efficiently. These opportunities present substantial business savings. You and your provider must be careful, however, to comply with international laws including domestic export laws and import laws of destination nations.

Shared Service Delivery Model (SSDM)

Shared service is an example IT delivery model. It is an organization that provides support services that are "shared" across multiple business units. If you are operating as a shared service organization, your IT teams have the capacity to make and stand behind service level commitments, and the capacity to offer and deliver the right services and products at the right time, with high quality. This is because a shared service delivery team is aware of customer needs, they have a focus on driving business value, they know their business performance targets, they know their capacity to deliver, and they know when it makes more sense to pursue alternative delivery mechanisms and sources.

Before adopting cloud, you should know and understand your service capacity, understand your core competencies as discussed throughout this book, and know your market (internal and external) so that you source with cloud and other solutions appropriately.

If you compare SSDM to traditional delivery models, the shared service model is customer focused with an eye not only for today's business requirements but also future demands, while the traditional IT service delivery model operates more like a cost center with a focus on getting things done.[4] The value of traditional practices of buying, configuring, and operating IT assets, followed with retirement has become questionable as to efficiency and effectiveness, and alternative delivery models such as cloud are becoming more popular. SSDM is a shared services approach to supporting users where IT resources are offered as a shared service. Cloud does not change your shared service delivery model, instead it augments capabilities so that you provide greater services and support to your customers. You can think of cloud in itself as a shared service as well as an enabler for shared services such as SaaS.

Business Processes-as-a-Service (BPaaS) is an example cloud delivery model whose economies of scale make it a more attractive approach than traditional delivery models such as business process outsourcing (BPO). This is because BPaaS is a vertical solution that moves the typical cloud conversation from cost reduction to fixing manual or inefficient business processes. In a BPaaS model, business processes are provided externally and customers connect over the Internet to the cloud and consume these services.

It is expected that by 2013, "nontraditional" service providers with specific vertical and business intellectual property will aggressively enter the BPaaS market, partnering and challenging traditional outsourcers, and by 2015, 50 percent of new BPO deals will be delivered as BPaaS.[5] BPaaS may also be referenced as business process utilities (BPUs).

In previous chapters, you learned that it is important to commence at an enterprise level and decompose business requirements into specific components. In Chapter 4, "Identifying Cloud Candidates," you learned how to do this. One example was through the use of your business architecture (BA) so that you ensure that processes, tools, systems, and business demands align. This means that your IT organization knows and understands its service portfolio and operates accordingly. You learned the importance of business value outcomes and the importance of selecting cloud solutions in such as way that value is sustained across organizations. In this model, IT organizations are fused into business units. This value optimizing delivery model might result in the dissolution of traditional IT organizations.[6]

Quite naturally, if you are a practicing shared service organization, then integrating cloud might not present new challenges. This is because you might have already established and applied governance with adequate stewardship for purchasing IT solutions, you should have developed enterprise standards and architecture, assessment criteria of the internal IT organization's service capabilities against external service providers should be available, and funding and chargeback models for IT services should be in effect. A notable benefit is that you might experience a decline in data center capacity requirements and better utilization of your resources, which will lead to cost savings in overhead and power consumption. If you are new to cloud or shared services, you should plan your transition carefully and take the necessary steps to prevent unstructured adoption of cloud solutions.

Information Technology-as-a-Service (ITaaS)

Cloud is popular because of the variable financial model as discussed previously. Up-front costs are marginalized, and there is an ease of doing business in a cloud delivery model where business units can purchase services without traditional IT rigor and approvals. As such, IT organizations should focus more on offering IT-as-a-Service (ITaaS). This means becoming more flexible and adaptable to changing business models and offering insights to solve business problems that might include cloud purchases.

Traditionally, IT organizations were the sole or major source of solutions, but now business units can easily buy solutions elsewhere. Thus the opportunity presents itself for IT teams (whose capabilities may evolve but will not go away) to help business leaders decide whether cloud purchases are the right business decisions. Knowing that in-house delivery will come under further scrutiny, internal capabilities in value add competencies such as service integration, business process design, business performance management, information management, risk management, cloud quality assurance, and test services, and end-to-end solution design and delivery will remain.

IT teams should be careful to maintain an objective eye on what sourcing strategies are most suitable to address business needs for the short and long term, and they must be careful to not project an image that only IT teams can do it right or they will quickly lose the trust of business leaders. Business leaders, on the other hand must maintain an inventory of all IT purchases—expressly those that are not controlled by IT departments—and engage IT leadership and insights when faced with cloud adoption choices to sustain both decisions that are made and positive relationships.

Bring your own (BYO) technology is enabled with cloud and supports the ITaaS vision. With BYO employees are empowered to use their personal equipment such as iPads in the office where the goal is that employees become more efficient, more innovative, and more productive. IT teams should invite BYO as a business enabler in the workplace along with providing management and security controls.

IT organizations need to develop skills, capabilities and governance to better market ITaaS services and ensure adequate awareness and training on how to use such services. Operating as a cloud service provider, IT organizations should manage the lifecycle of ITaaS service offerings which includes pricing and chargeback precision.

An abundance of applications as well as information is readily available in the cloud. This data is typically delivered through SaaS and PaaS. Does this mean that consumers' traditional business, application, or information architecture will go away? Of course not, but this does imply that your teams should look to augment your application landscape with cloud and use that model to guide adoption decisions.

Figure A.2 illustrates an integrated business and application architecture. The diagram is derived from a consumer's enterprise architecture (EA) and for simplicity focuses on enterprise approved business applications and standards. Although not pictured, infrastructure is required for end-to-end solutions and can be offered by SaaS providers. Highlighted in the example are core components that were analyzed to influence cloud adoption decisions and the business fit. Table A.1 offers elaborations, which are derived from actual project experiences.

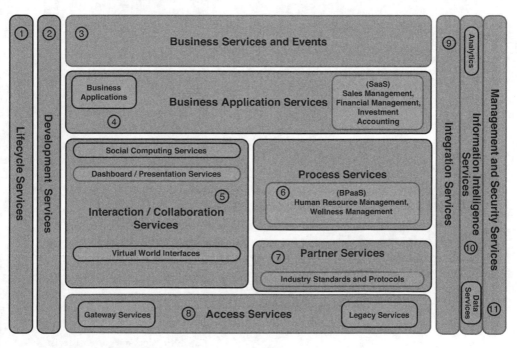

Source: IBM's Intelligent EA, Copyright IBM, 2012.

Figure A.2 Information Technology-as-a-Service is required and enabled by establishing an enterprise, end-to-end solution landscape that encompasses cloud.

Table A.1　Enterprise Application Architecture and Decision Analyses for SaaS Adoption

Component Name	Description	Decision Analyses
1. Life Cycle Services	Life cycle services (e. g., requirements management of services) utilized to standardize deployment of components across the enterprise.	N/A. On-hand life cycle tools are adequate.
2. Development Services	Development services can be utilized to design, build, and test Business & Information Systems components.	N/A.
3. Business Services and Events	Business services and events (e. g., a user enters the room) enable enterprise stakeholders to view, depict, and model digital interactions of people, processes, and activities.	Required. Proposed SaaS capability supports billing and monthly reconciliation processes. Meets corporate standards. Capability does not currently exist.
4. Business Application Services	Business application services such as customer relationship management (CRM), social networking, and SaaS cloud services provide application functionality. Organizations may choose SaaS to optimize software expenses by reusing proven solutions.	Required. Proposed SaaS capability supports billing and monthly reconciliation processes. Meets corporate standards. Capability does not currently exist.
5. Interaction/ Collaboration Services	Interaction services enable communications and can be utilized to create digital communities.	Required. Proposed SaaS capability comes with a dashboard that does not meet company standards.
6. Process Services	Process services are generally used to fulfill a human workflow or automated business process and can include process simulators.	Required. Proposed SaaS capability will augment current order management processes. Capability does not currently exist.

Table A.1 Enterprise Application Architecture and Decision Analyses for SaaS Adoption

Component Name	Description	Decision Analyses?
7. Partner Services	Partner services enable integration of business partners in the overall design. Includes industry standards and protocols including certification.	Required. Proposed SaaS solution and environment must meet ASCA certification.
8. Access Services	Access services enable elevation of legacy application functions (e. g., customer information control system and transactions) into services to fulfill a business process. A gateway server is an example access service that controls and directs entrance into the enterprise and its ecosystem.	Required. Integrates SaaS with portal and back-end systems.
9. Integration Services	Integration services enable mediation, transformation, and direction of information flows throughout the enterprise for access and display on computing interfaces.	Required. Integrates SaaS with portal and back-end systems.
10. Information Intelligence Services	Information intelligence services (IISs) process data provided by applications and can apply analytics and decision support techniques to determine real-time insights and actions.	Required. Need to manage billing, customer, and subscriber current and historical data.
11. Management and Security Services	Management and security services are foundational quality-of-service components required to sustain the environment.	Required. Outstanding is how to ensure integrity of audit logs? How do SaaS providers ensure access to audit logs in a secure manner (and how will this be managed)?

Source: Project experiences and IBM's Intelligent EA cloud-based solutions

Key Cloud Roles and Responsibilities

Figure A.3 offers a list of three key roles and responsibilities that should be considered as a part of your cloud adoption strategy. The roles depicted are service creator, service consumer, and service provider. Each role contains subroles. They are cloud focused and augment traditional service delivery teams and end users. The following relationships are depicted in the diagram:

- A service consumer may act as a service provider. This is common in cases where service consumers buy and resell cloud solutions and services.

- A service provider may act as a service consumer; this is common in cases where service providers use cloud services that are provided by others such as SaaS services to augment an existing service portfolio.

- The relationship where service providers and service consumers can include a service creator to build and/or integrate cloud solutions.

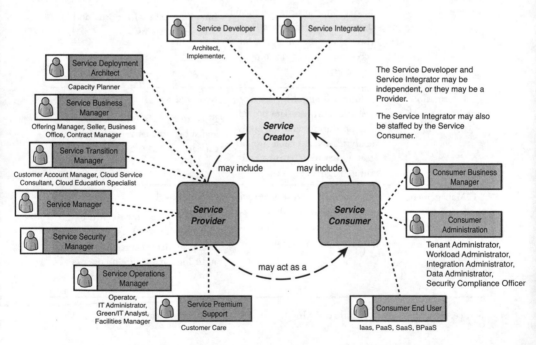

Source: IBM Cloud Computing Reference Architecture, Copyright © IBM 2011.[7]

Figure A.3   Cloud roles and relationships

NOTE

Although the role of the enterprise architect is not illustrated, and as you read in Chapter 2, executives generally view enterprise architects as front-line contacts and a conduit for translating business needs into IT needs. They trust the advice of enterprise architects to guide them with thought leadership on cloud and the application of other business technologies and if resources are ill-equipped or unavailable decision makers might turn to less reliable sources for guidance. Understandably, companies should and are relying on EA resources for cloud purposes.

The following is a list of all the roles depicted in Figure A.3 and descriptions:

- **Service creator:** The service creator develops the cloud services that will be consumed by the end user. The type of service created varies and depends on the service offering itself. Some example creations are virtual images, storage images, and multitenant applications. Here are the sub-roles for service creator:
    - **Service developer:** The service developer designs, implements, and maintains the technical aspects of a service template.
    - **Service integrator (or broker):** The service integrator designs, develops, and implements the interface between the customer's on-premise environment and off-premise cloud entities.
- **Service consumer:** The service consumer uses cloud services. Service consumers can also be buyers of cloud services for an organization. The consumed services vary with the service offering; for example, when it comes to SaaS offerings consumption is of an application while in IaaS or PaaS situations; consumption is of hosted virtual images. A service consumer may or may not be the end user (see consumer end user). Here are the subroles for service consumer:
    - **Consumer business manager:** The consumer business manager holds financial responsibility, accountability, and approval rights for purchasing services.
    - **Consumer administrator:** The consumer administrator over-looks all cloud operational processes and acts as focal point for communications between provider and consumer.
    - **Consumer end user:** The consumer end user requests and uses cloud resources.

- **Service provider:** The service provider hosts cloud services for end users. The type of hosted service depends on the type of offering. Service providers can host services developed by other service developers (in addition to their own services). Here are the subroles for service provider:

  - **Service deployment architect:** The service deployment architect evaluates and configures service settings for successful cloud deployments and ensures that compliance requirements are met.
  - **Service business manager:** The service business manager offers all types of services and manages customer accounts.
  - **Service transition manager:** The service transition manager is responsible for enabling a consumer to use the cloud service; responsibilities include on-boarding, integration, and business process adoption.
  - **Service manager:** The service manager focuses entirely on the service that runs on the infrastructure, ensuring that all IT services and infrastructure meets operational targets and that all configuration items are appropriately recorded.
  - **Service security manager:** The service security manager ensures that service providers appropriately manage all risks associated with development, delivery, integrations, support, and use of the cloud services.
  - **Service operations manager:** The service operations manager manages the infrastructure required for providing cloud services.
  - **Service premium support:** The service premium support provider is responsible for customer support and resolves levels 1, 2, and 3 problems according to service level agreements.

Collaborate, Experiment, and Act!

Along with augmenting your delivery model with cloud comes a change in technique and attitude. For instance, the move toward more effective collaboration to gain and apply the collective intelligence of enterprise stakeholders and business partners; the willingness to experiment and take risks; and your willingness to expediently make decisions and act based on your collaboration and experimentation are three important elements of your cloud adoption strategy and implementation success as illustrated in Figure A.4. Each topic is expounded next.

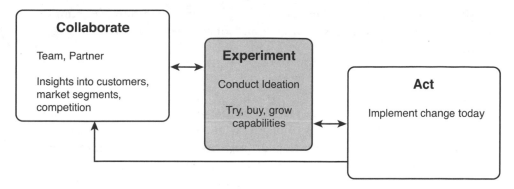

Figure A.4   Collaborate, experiment, and act.

Collaborate

Executive level stakeholders as well as service line leaders and practitioners need to focus on managing essential IT activities so that high value IT services are rendered, and so that information makes it to decision-makers faster and more accurately. This presents opportunities to collaborate more effectively and more importantly compels you to adopt new tools such as cloud that facilitate real-time information exchange and business collaborations. Steps such as establishing company communities and enabling mobile collaborations (discussed in Appendix C, "More On Cloud Business Trends") are excellent ways to strengthen delivery models. Consider the following scenario that demonstrates how cloud was adopted to promote business collaborations for a company.

A company invited employees to participate in an online community jam. The goal was to allow the best ideas to come forward pertaining to new products and services that the company should offer. The format is free-form where themes are posted and jammers respond to a topic or create a new one to support a theme. Jammers were employees from all geographies, all ages, and all ranks. The themes that attracted the most interest were carried forward for vote and on to enterprise projects. This initiative was successful, and as a result a second jam occurred with different themes but related topics, where external customers and business partners were invited as participants. It too was successful, driving change into the organization due to an integrated strategy of ideation and requirements management.

In this example, not only did the collaboration tools promote teamwork and rapid ideation, but an added benefit was the credibility that the company built with both internal and external communities simply by seeking the opinions of others and demonstrating a listening ear backed with action.

Experiment

A traditional source of dissatisfaction between business and IT teams is that the cost of IT services compared to the value of goods and services rendered is unequally proportioned. Business teams have an interest in experimenting with ideas, and as discussed they do not have time for long, drawn out, software implementations, nor do they want to pay excessive costs. There is generally a sense of urgency when it comes to experimentation since the results drive other business decisions. This is why pilot programs, where work is not thrown away but rather provides a foundation for further business solutions, are becoming more profound. Proof of concepts (PoC) is still viable, but work can be thrown away since the PoC is more focused on proving out a technology than solving business problems. Cloud facilitates experimentation with its ability to quickly provision and decommission test environments as needed. Rather than committing to a major investment in software and hardware, the business unit commits and leverages a pilot program subscribing to ready-made service offerings required to validate the business solution.

If, by reading the previous paragraph, there is a conclusion drawn that IT teams are not interested in conducting pilots, well that is not the case. In traditional IT environments, IT teams might have a more difficult time obtaining the funds to conduct pilot work unless funding is provided by business units or work is planned into the budget early enough so that resources get allocated and adequately assigned. This challenge is presented because the assets to be acquired to conduct pilots are just as significant an investment as the assets required for larger projects—meaning software, hardware, and information sources typically have to be purchased or leased and installed. In essence, IT teams are interested in business technologies and driving strategic direction for organizations. What is challenging in traditional environments, which must change with newer delivery models, is the inability to take time away from an already overloaded schedule to experiment or pilot initiatives.

Cloud remedies experimentation related issues as just described in several ways: Pay as you go or subscription style service offerings can be expensed as operational or discretionary spending as opposed to unplanned capital overlays that would be difficult to fund in an out of budget cycle; the cost of cloud solutions is typically less expensive than traditional purchases, which may help your business case; and cloud gives you the opportunity to experiment or "try before you buy" in a controlled environment, affording you the opportunity to test the viability of your ideas before strategic decisions are made that can be more difficult to reverse once the undertaking commences.

Act

You collaborated to gain insights into business, customer, and market opportunities, focusing on improving communication and collaboration throughout your company, and you experimented to understand the viability of alternative delivery models and solutions. The final step, which is probably the most important of all, is to swiftly act! In other words, take what you have learned and quickly put it to work. Each of these steps—whether labeled as such or not—are what you can expect to see demonstrated in your cloud augmented delivery model.

At this point, it is well understood that cloud as well as outsourcing both add to your ability to allocate internal resources from routine activities to more strategic, value-centric assignments. So what are some example value-centric assignments? Strategy and planning of the services catalog that you will consume and possibly resell for profit is an example and important strategic initiative that you would want to ensure that your organization leads. Other examples include conducting market analysis to establish your client base and growth segments, master data management (MDM), business/information intelligence and information dash-boarding—meaning the creation of dashboards that measure key business and IT metrics, such as customer satisfaction levels and time to market.

To support the augmented delivery model, match the IT and business talents of your teams to tasks and consider implementing intern programs to expose IT personnel to the full range of enterprise operations and cloud opportunities. Expect business buyers to show interest in cloud augmented delivery models. Referencing the Brand/TCP business scenario discussed in previous sections, develop strategic and tactical plans to renew legacy systems, hardware, and software. Take advantage of cloud to standardize the IT infrastructure and automated related business processes organizationwide. Take advantage of dashboards that leverage data collected to measure key business and IT metrics, including ROI and revenue, customer satisfaction levels and other information including response time/time to market, system availability/downtimes, and employee satisfaction.

Summary

To keep pace with the accelerated changes brought about by business complexities, emerging economies, and competitive business landscapes, executives and technology leaders are augmenting their traditional delivery models with cloud. This appendix discussed business considerations for such augmentations.

Traditional data center business risks that resided with the IT organization have shifted to an integrated cloud service provider and consumer shared risk model with mixed and variable financial models that help offset data center costs. At the same time, server communications are improving so that data centers can securely connect to other data centers within and external to cloud and effectively share resources. Discussed was the notion of shrinking data centers, the application of Just-In-Time (JIT) business patterns, along with building sustainability and how cloud can contribute to energy and environmental efficiencies.

Other delivery models that might be augmented with cloud deployments including BPaaS, SaaS, IaaS, and PaaS were discussed and are summarized in Table A.2. Example topics include the impacts of cloud on global delivery models and the value-add when businesses adopt an IT-as-a-Service (ITaaS) approach to solution design and delivery where you start with what is in your data center, look at where you want to go, and focus on how to get there. If something is not what or where it should be, for example, Web applications are not performing as expected, you fix the situation hopefully before it catches the attention of your end users. That may mean using cloud or taking other steps.

In an ITaaS model, you treat your business units as customers. Your focus is to keep your customers happy and thus keep business performance high. This does not mean that you overwhelm them with new features that they may or may not use, but it does mean that you consider realizable and meaningful business value and act accordingly. This may mean outsourcing services to cloud, and it may mean keeping the capability in-house.

Table A.2   Augmenting Your Delivery Model with Cloud

Delivery Model	Description	Cloud Augmentation Opportunities
Data centers	Facility used to house computer systems and associated components, such as telecommunications and storage systems.	On premises, on premises utility, off premises dedicated, off premises shared, Just In Time (JIT) business patterns, energy efficiency and sustainability including disposal.
Project and solution delivery model	Integrated project management, application and product development life cycle.	Rapid delivery, agile, self-service, legacy modernization, trusted advisor.
Global delivery model	Companies engaged in project implementations using a team that is distributed globally.	Rapid growth and business expansion, Failover, disaster recovery. Accelerate ramp-up time and minimize capital investments.
Shared service delivery model	Services provided by an organization that are shared across multiple business units or enterprises.	Service level commitments and performance optimization, customer and process-centric as opposed to asset-centric, augmentation precision.
Information Technology-as-a Service	The use of systems to store, retrieve, and send information, with a mindset and capacity to offer end-to-end solutions that involve not only systems but people, processes, information, and technology.	Changing business model flexibility and adaptability, stronger IT organizational effectiveness. IT viewed as a provider of fundamental business technologies and services. Develop skills, capabilities and governance to better market ITaaS services and ensure adequate awareness and training on how to use such services. Supports bring your own (BYO) licenses and technologies.

BYO technology is enabled with cloud and supports the ITaaS delivery model. With BYO employees are empowered to use their personal equipment in the office where the goal is to become more self-sufficient, efficient, and productive. Ubiquitous capability is a benefit of cloud and at the core of BYO. The concept of ubiquity is expounded in Appendix C.

In this appendix, analogies and common dilemmas that organizations are experiencing were shared, particularly when it comes to legacy applications to add clarity as to how and when to engage stakeholders so that cloud decisions are made in a timely manner and with accuracy. Also described were key cloud roles and responsibilities that will likely augment traditional roles and responsibilities. Collaborate, experiment, and act is a common theme and welcomed addition to augmenting traditional delivery methods with cloud.

Endnotes

1. JIT is an example strategic model that data centers are evolving toward. See http://www. investopedia.com/terms/j/jit.asp.

2. Lamb, John. 2009. *The Greening of IT: How Companies Can Make a Difference for the Environment.* Indianapolis: Pearson Education. p. 173.

3. Claybrook, Bill. "Building a Private Cloud: Get Ready for a Bumpy Ride." Computerworld. August 24, 2010. See http://www.computerworld.com/s/article/ 9180941/Building_a_private_cloud_Get_ready_for_a_bumpy_ride. The author indicates that 75 percent of survey respondents said that they would be pursuing a private cloud strategy by 2012, and 75 percent said that they would invest more in private clouds than in public clouds through 2012.

4. Gartner published an excellent write-up titled "Understand Shared-Service Fundamentals and Avoid Perennial Traps." See http://my.gartner.com/portal/ server.pt?open=512&objID=260&mode=2&PageID=3460702&docCode=208647&ref =docDisplay.

5. McNeill, Robert. "The Evolution of Business Process as a Service." October 2010. See http://communities.progress.com/pcom/servlet/JiveServlet/download/106238-2-94461/ 796MKT-BPO%20Evolution-19Oct2010%20PROGRESS%20REPRINT.pdf.

6. "Understand Shared-Service Fundamentals and Avoid Perennial Traps." See http://my. gartner.com/portal/server.pt?open=512&objID=260&mode=2&PageID=3460702&doc Code=208647&ref=docDisplay. Specifically, Gartner speaks about value optimizing and describes this as an IT delivery model stating that in this model, there may not even be a traditional IT organization citing that the CIO may morph into a COO, chief change strategist, or some other role focused on the strategic viability of the enterprise.

7. There is a whitepaper that discusses the CCRA titled "Getting Cloud Computing Right: The Key to Business Success in a Cloud Adoption Is a Robust, Proven Architecture." See http://public.dhe.ibm.com/common/ssi/ecm/en/ciw03078usen/CIW03078USEN.PDF.

B

Cloud Case Studies and Common Questions

The future is ours to win. But to get there, we can't just stand still.
—*President Barack Obama*

This appendix contains additional examples and analysis of cloud adoption deci-sions that were made with and without the use of EA. Incorporated are some common questions relative to cloud adoption that are asked and answered. Commentary throughout this appendix includes lessons learned from project experiences.

Private Cloud Adoption: Two South African Case Studies

These private cloud adoption case studies are based on two IBM cus-tomers in South Africa. The first is a large bank that experienced ineffi-cient application of infrastructure environments and inadequate governance. The second is a large cell phone company that became inun-dated with preproduction virtual and physical environments.

A Large Bank

The benefits to the bank from installation of a private cloud for test and development capacity are indicated in the following list:

- Robust governance and scheduling process for test environments.
- Eliminated test server waste due to lack of governance and management.
- Provided a cloud scheduling process to release servers when testing is completed.
- Provided much faster setup of test systems. The bank reported that test system setup that previously took two weeks now takes two hours.
- Savings to customers due to cutting physical servers in half and optimizing environments to achieve better usage.

The Application Integration and Security team at the bank is responsible for setting up and maintaining the different SOA server environments required to support projects. These environments include development and test, quality assurance, and production as well as disaster recovery environments. Each of these environments may include one or more suites of middleware such as DB2® databases, WebSphere® process server (WPS) clusters, WebSphere application server (WAS) clusters and WebSphere message broker clusters among others.

Building and maintaining these environments involve a multitude of tasks that required coordination and performance by various teams. The main teams involved were as follows:

- Infrastructure team manages the server hardware setup, logical partitioning, and network setup.
- AIX® support team manages AIX installations, patches, configuration, and settings.
- Open systems storage team is responsible for allocating storage resources.
- DB2 support team manages database creation and administration.
- Data security team is responsible for security aspects such as creating authorized users on systems.
- Application integration and security team requests the computing resources from the teams mentioned above to perform their own software installation.

Each of these teams performed a variety of other duties as part of their job, which resulted in working durations for any given deployment being significantly longer than the estimated duration for completing assignments. While each team involved may perform their tasks efficiently, the nature of the manual processes along with the hand-offs between teams inevitably added costs and delays to projects resulting in an additional two weeks for a system to be set up correctly in a single environment.

EA governance and a cloud computing platform was collectively applied to resolve the issues above including enterprise integration of cloud solutions and more effective coordination of team communications. Establishment of decision rights among team members, standards pertaining to provisioning and decommissioning environments, and image management became enterprise standards.

The cloud platform now dynamically provisions, configures, reconfigures, and decommissions test and development servers as needed and provides the following capabilities:

- Provide self-service interface that can be provided to anyone in the organization, alleviating the need for complex engagements with the IT department every time a new environment is required.

- Orchestrate and track the provisioning and decommissioning of related resources such as networking, storage, and computing resources as a single project. Project deployment and cleanup are performed as specified by a calendar.

- Manage the automated installation and configuration of complex software topologies and applications. This also provides visibility into the method and steps used to create any given environment configuration. Administrator sign-off is required before deployment can begin, which provides controlled usage of the cloud.

- Reduce the risk of deployment errors with fast and automatic deployment of environments, since all complex configurations are performed up front and not at deployment time.

- Provide dependency validation for software installations. For example, given a particular platform and OS, what is the software that can be installed?

- Monitor server utilization in real time to provide an accurate view of project resource usage.

- Help system administrators estimate capacity demand early, which allows the business to proactively assign more computing resources to the cloud.
- Host a variety of different workloads, including batch-style back-end jobs and interactive, user-facing applications.

The booking, scheduling, and management of machines is now done through a Web-based interface. The Web interface gives an overview of the entire cloud infrastructure, including which projects are currently defined and how many resources each project uses or will use in the case of future projects. A consolidated view of available and utilized resources in the cloud is also shown through the use of real-time monitoring.

A Cell Phone Company

The cell phone company was experiencing typical concerns for large companies with their test environments. The concerns include

- Test environment resource availability. This was for both hardware and people resource, especially for end-to-end testing.
- There was no good scheduling process for shared resources.
- There was a significant amount of test server waste due to lack of governance and management. For example, every project received servers (virtual and sometimes physical environments) for testing; however, the servers were often not released once testing initiatives completed.

A private cloud was proposed and accepted that would manage the company's virtualized test environments. The private cloud would be used to provide tight governance around automated provisioning and decommissioning of environments allocated to projects. Based on their analysis, the cloud proposal team believed a private cloud for test and development environments would offer the company benefits in the form of:

- Greatly reduced time to procure test servers/systems
- Allow tight scheduling and governance of test systems
- Significantly reduced number of servers used for test
- Significantly reduced number of people resources for test

- Reduced test server waste that is due to poor governance and management
- Elimination of cloud security concerns since the private cloud is installed at the customer's data center

During 2010, the cell phone company's South Africa IT landscape continued to increase in size and complexity, with analysis as follows:

- 1100+ Server Instances—The number of instances has grown exponentially over the past five years.
- 40 percent to 60 percent incline in estimated spend on maintaining current IT infrastructures versus adding new capabilities.
- 87.03 percent average server idle times. The company has an average of 12.97 percent CPU usage across platforms while test CPU is even lower.

The following is the preproduction analysis and technical refresh considerations prior to cloud adoption:

- An estimated 42 percent of servers are used in preproduction roles.
- Preproduction servers consume up to 40 percent of power and cooling (339,509 Watts out of 855,025 total consumption for all environments).
- There are 231 servers expected to reach end of life capacity and performance within the next six months distributed as follows:
    - 149 Windows® servers. Approximately 80 will be in preproduction/staging.
    - 44 AIX servers. Approximately 25 will be in preproduction/staging.
    - 38 Linux® servers. Approximately 20 will be in preproduction/staging.

Here are the actual usage figures for March 2010, as illustrated in Figure B.1:

- UNIX® (24 AIX) Avg. 25.46% Max Avg. 60.21%
- Linux (101 Linux) Avg. 5.07% Max Avg. 27.34%
- Windows (317 Win) Avg. 8.39% Max Avg. 45.86%

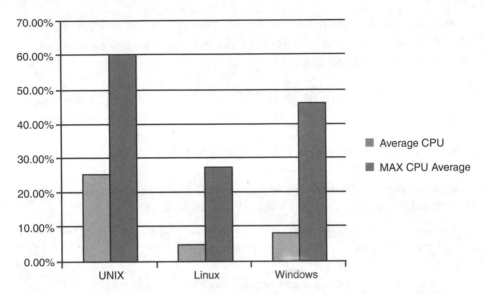

Figure B.1   Cell phone company's server CPU utilization

IBM proposed a private cloud solution to address the company needs that was approved and currently being implemented; here is a summary:

- Private cloud will manage the company's virtualized preproduction environments.
- Integrate into the company's cloud and overarching IT governance processes.
- The approach is to commence with an entry-level system that provides an entire framework and three working HS22 blades to host around 3 ∞ 8 = 24 concurrent virtual machines (assuming one core per VM) and five terabytes of storage. One Blade will be used for CloudBurst®.[1]

NOTE

A technique based on private cloud workloads, cloud bursting, leverages hosted or public cloud resources in support of private cloud workload demands. If the private cloud has the capacity, any hosted or public cloud capacity is not used. In this scenario, IBM offered CloudBurst as a part of the total private cloud solution.

- Scale by buying more HS22 blades, up to 14 in the BladeCenter®. This gives $13 \times 8 = 104$ concurrent VMs (assuming one core per VM, and one blade for management). An additional BladeCenter can be added.
- CloudBurst has the capability to manage external hardware as part of the cloud. This capability could be leveraged as an option to expand capacity.
- Enhance service management capabilities to bring awareness to environments that are not in use and reallocate.

Figure B.2 illustrates typical company benefits resulting from cloud adoption.

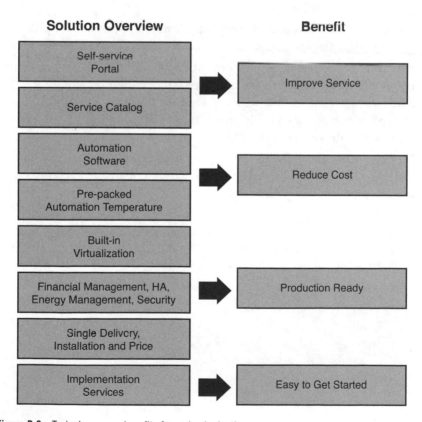

Figure B.2 Typical company benefits from cloud adoption

CloudBurst-specific benefits with illustrations in Figure B.3 are as follows:

- **Self-contained on-premise cloud:** Prepackaged hardware, software, and services based on System x® BladeCenter platform and Tivoli® Service Management products
- **Web 2.0 self-service portal:** Automated request and decommissioning production or development/test workloads utilizing virtualization technologies across server, network, and storage including reservation of compute and storage resources
- **Prepackaged automation templates and workflows:** For most common resource types, such as VMWare and KVM virtual machines (provisioned-to capabilities)

  Service Catalogue across all required application components for provisioning and decommissioning
- **Integrated core service management capabilities:** Real-time monitoring of virtualized resources, energy management, (de-) provisioning, patch management and remediation, security, usage and accounting, reusable library for rapid deployment, prebuilt reports using Business Intelligence Reporting Tools (BIRT)
- **Modular/plug and play:** Incrementally, automatically expandable and scalable; extensibility across data center with integrated cloud service monitoring and management

Capability	From	To
Server/Storage Utilization	10–20%	70–90%
Self-service	None	Unlimited
Test Provisioning	Weeks	Minutes
Change Management	Months	Days/Hours
Release Management	Weeks	Minutes
Pay as you go	Fixed cost model	Granular
Payback period for new services	Years	Months

Traditional data centers ➡ Cloud-like data center management

Figure B.3 Project benefits—based on client testimonials

The private cloud benefits are enabled by virtualization, optimization, rapid provisioning, and decommissioning of virtual environments as illustrated in Figure B.4. The benefits include reduced capital expenditures and reduced operating expenditures. Additional benefits include reduced risk, less idle time, more efficient use of energy, acceleration of innovative projects, and enhanced customer service.

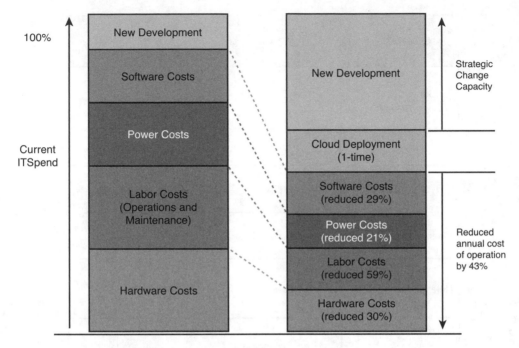

Figure B.4   Sample business case projected benefits

Sample business case results from other customers indicate the ROI:

- **Total 5yr Savings:** $1.9M (43%)
- **Breakeven:** 8 months
- **Net Present Value (NPV):** $1.9M
- **Return on Investment (ROI):** 316%

Projected server and labor resource savings due to use of a private cloud for test and development servers indicate that when 280 application development and test environments were moved to a private cloud, the number of physical servers could be reduced by 62 percent. The time (days) to provision the test environments could be reduced from 33 days to 5.4 days, and the number of test team members needed to provision the environments would go from 16 to 2. Much of the projected savings is due to reduced labor required for test, development, and operational expenses typically incurred during setup, configuration, and maintenance of environments. Savings are also associated with a reduction in the required software licenses.

Overall, in these two case studies, private cloud adoption with applied governance (an EA principle) provided a way to greatly improve test and development environments for speed in setup and configuration, generating savings in hardware, software, and labor expenditures. The EA teams that included senior level stakeholders developed, standardized, and enforced cloud adoption and usage guidelines throughout the company.

Enterprise Reference Architecture and Private Cloud Adoption: Case Study

This example demonstrates the value of developing an enterprise reference architecture that incorporates cloud.

An international financial services company is building foundational enterprise reference architectures to control how IT teams build, deploy, run, and manage IT environments along with the products and services deployed in the environments. This financial services company provides solutions to customers that encompass fraud protection, check guarantee and verification services, and Internet commerce. One particular service offering is situational based card services where customer credit lines are automatically increased or deactivated based on buyer behaviors.

The company initially worked with a provider to develop a private cloud solution; however, there were significant amounts of performance related issues along with an inability to customize solutions to meet business demands without excessive costs. The CTO expressed that similar experiences "could not be repeated" and turned to a different cloud provider for new services. Regrouping its service delivery approach, the company placed emphasis on definition of an enterprise reference architecture (derived from EA) that includes standards, business and IT governance, process management, formalized development and test environments, documentation rigor, and artifacts related to product development, operations, and control. The anticipated private cloud workloads are compute or Infrastructure-as-a-Service (IaaS) and utility services such as Storage-as-a-Service, automated backups, and archival services.

The company believes that the enterprise reference architecture is critical in providing the following:

- Alignment of business and architecture objectives and solution delivery
- Support of situational-aware analytical solutions and services
- Capacity to perform during workload variability
- Development of architectural principles and standards for security, data access, integration, and other application development domains for hybrid cloud and traditional environments
- Design, development, and performance best practices for integrating cloud into the enterprise
- Development of cloud specific infrastructure designs that must be incorporated into network, security, server, storage, virtualization, and managing infrastructure that now encompasses cloud
- Enterprise service-oriented solutions
- Framework in which all support and development activities center
- Governance framework that manages cloud and the integration of legacy systems
- Integrated security framework that guides Payment Card Industry Data Security Standard (PCI DSS) and other regulatory compliance
- Framework that becomes self-documenting to speed on-ramp of new development resources, as well as enhance the experiences of existing development resources

Published Criteria for Provider Selection

The following are published criteria used by the consumer to select cloud provider(s):

- Proven ability to integrate front-end and back-end solutions, including cloud.
- Experience defining and implementing enterprise architecture (EA), applying a structured method to identify business technologies, and developing enterprise cloud roadmaps for private consumption.

- Promote quality and service assurance in the areas of performance, scalability, elasticity, information integrity, security and maintainability of new and legacy solutions.
- Drive standards and governance usage to manage and maintain the reference architecture.
- Demonstrable core capabilities in the following areas:
  - Architecture leadership
  - Complex systems integration
  - Operational support
  - PCI DSS knowledge and compliance
  - Strategic partnership and mentoring
  - Solution design, development, and delivery

Smarter Education: Cloud Case Study

This example demonstrates the value of cloud as an enabler of virtual data centers.

A large U.S.-based university was experiencing significant growth and increased demands on academic computing resources. The need for increased compute capacity to support a continually growing user base, tailored course curriculum, and application requirements, as well as the need to provide service levels that meet customer requirements was exposed as a business risk.

Challenges surfaced when working with IT teams to prepare course images, install in the labs, and ensure that all applications integrated smoothly. And because it took so long to perform the necessary integrations, IT teams imposed deadlines on instructors that were due months before course terms were to commence. As a result, instructors had to wait as long as a year to get the latest applications in the hands of students.

The university introduced a provisioning framework that enabled self-service provisioning of a managed yet virtual computing lab.[2] Users are now able to access environments from anywhere, which allows them to conduct work from dorm rooms or at home, as opposed to having to go to the university lab to complete assignments. Users can select an application image (consisting of the operating system and a suite of applications) either for current use or future use, at a set time and for a set duration. Instructors can create block reservations for an entire class, reserve clusters of servers, and even add new applications without the assistance of IT staff. Once a scheduled session is over, service automation causes a user's virtual environment to be wiped clean, enabling unused blades to be put back in the resource pool for further consumption.

Projected Business Benefits

The projected business benefits as listed are substantial. It is important to note the alignment and traceability of the core business problem to the solution so that value is realized across the enterprise, or in this case, across university campuses.

- Savings in software licensing costs of up to 75 percent
- 150 percent increase in students served per application license
- Higher student satisfaction through more convenient access
- Improved access to the most recent software releases for instructors
- Increased flexibility to shift computing capacity between instructional, research, and administrative needs
- The ability to meet significant growth in enrollment without building additional computer labs

Serious Games: Cloud Case Study (Hybrid: Public and Private Model)

This example demonstrates the value of cloud as an enterprise enabler of serious games.

Large Transportation Business (LTB) is experiencing significant business challenges. In particular, the CEO has expressed that real-world issues such as traffic congestion during natural disasters must be handled better and more efficiently. In the current environment, for instance, should a crisis such as a city blackout occur, LTB is known to lose communications with all vehicles along with the whereabouts of employees and passengers. To meet LTB's long-term goals, a serious gaming solution was designed with a cloud platform. A phased implementation approach would grow use of the game and mature the organization relative to using gaming technologies to solve complex business problems, and proprietary aspects of the game engine is planned. Figure B.5 illustrates the solution.

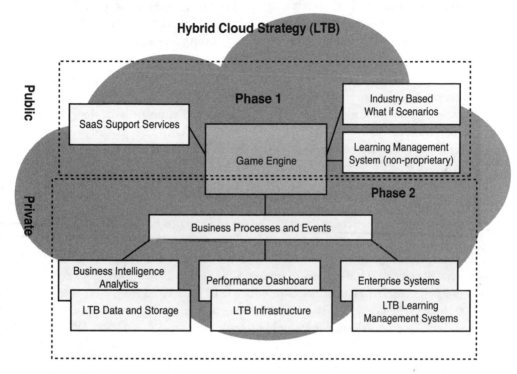

Figure B.5   Serious games hybrid cloud case study

In Phase 1, LTB established a cloud platform for engaging single and multi players. LTB chose an initial public cloud model to take advantage of existing SaaS services that would support the gaming initiative. Public cloud consumption is allowed in subsequent phases for nonproprietary game use.

In Phase 2, a supply chain management game that mimics actual business processes is enabled to support operational decision making. This solution is comprised of enterprise systems integration powered by SOA that runs on a private cloud platform since data at this stage is classified as confidential to the company. The following is the high level implementation strategy:

- **LTB scenario-based skills development:** Create a single and multi-player game that offers preset supply chain scenarios that the player must complete. These scenarios start easy and become progressively more difficult depending on the player's performance. Accounts are created for the players to keep track of their progress via learning management solutions.

- **LTB serious games platform for operational use:** A proprietary gaming platform can be used for broad enterprise operational use. Enabled by streaming live data feeds from different data sources, this platform helps users attain a number of objectives, including real-time visualization, optimized modeling, the collaboration around a complex logistics problem, and event driven scenarios that are invoked by different suppliers to improve situational awareness and readiness for planned and unexpected incidents.

- **Example game rules:** Players access a public cloud platform initially followed with a more secure model as business scenarios become more significant and proprietary to the organization. A Game Master (GM) instantiates a geographic instance of a game and selects a region. The GM then decides which suppliers to invite. Suppliers must work together to meet the requirements of the GM, which will be derived from a business scenario. The GM can then create an event that will affect the supply chain (e. g., a hurricane) or a city blackout.

A summary of the business benefits for LTB are as follows:

- Playful yet serious transportation scenarios and preparation to handle unexpected events.

- Enterprise business process optimization through review and application of LTB's EA with a concerted effort on the business architecture domain as it contains process and event models.

- More efficient handling and simplified access to large data sets due to the cloud platform.

- Analytics measurements that consider human as well as the technological elements, such as metrics tracking of how well personnel are learning and applying knowledge gained to real-life experiences and business problems.

- Greater performance monitoring of players and their capabilities prior to and after playing the game. Performance dashboards are tailored for all ranks within the organization from senior executives to practitioners.

Business Influencers and Drivers of Cloud Adoption

With the rapid emergence of new technologies such as cloud, it is important for business executives and stakeholders to focus on the real business challenges and the needs of the enterprise. By examining some of the key business problems that are prompting companies to use cloud, it is possible to build a stronger business case for adoption.

We have explored many different use cases for cloud from several industries and found common drivers throughout. The use cases demonstrate business value through optimizing resources, lowering costs, and providing solutions on-demand when and where customers, partners, and employees need it. The following are eight key business reasons that businesses are adopting cloud followed with two business use cases. You can find more details on Pam Isom's blog[3] and in the whitepaper, "Strengthening Your Business Case for Using Cloud."[4] This paper was published by The Open Group and ongoing revisions are planned.

- Ability to consolidate information across disparate systems with complete transparency to the user
- Ability to modernize business systems at a low cost and fast speed of deployment
- Ability to move to a remote desktop services model using the cloud
- Need to support high storage capacity requirements
- Rapid deployment emerges as a consistent business value theme
- Ability to provide IT using self-service capabilities
- Need to support mobile services
- Need to support internal and external collaboration for employees and partners

Table B.1 and Table B.2 present two scenarios from the collection of use cases. The examples indicate the primary purpose of cloud adoption and the business requirements that influenced cloud adoption decisions. Both scenarios reside within the category of business assurance.

Table B.1   Scenario 1: Business Transaction Assurance and Continuity

Category	Description
Company background	This financial services company is seeking rapid continuity services that assure business operations and associated transactions, particularly during mergers and acquisitions.
Business problem/description	This company lacks the necessary in-house skills and resources to support the high degree of sensitive assets and data required to support its key business processes.
	Business transaction assurance, disaster recovery planning, and testing of vital business processes for the same are required to comply with enterprise and regulatory guidelines.
Actors	Business operations controller.
	Business procurement management.
	IT operations management.
Business requirements	Provide necessary disaster and recovery backup processes.
	Ensure that business activities can be carried out during times of additional complexity, such as mergers and acquisitions.
	Access to rapid deployment of compatible and simple end user services through browser or end user devices.
Business risks	Current business operation is exposed to disaster and recovery backup processes either being insufficient or not in place.
	Lost information contributing to poor business decisions.
	Loss of business continuity across processes and new ventures.
	Significant loss of assets or revenue flow.

Source: "Strengthening Your Business Case for Using Cloud" as published by The Open Group.

Table B.2   Scenario 2: Secure Business Assurance Services

Category	Description
Company background	This financial services company is seeking transaction verification and hosting security assurance services.
Business problem/description	Security assurance is paramount to business operations, yet there is increased concern over the external service provider's services.
	This business lacks internal skills and resources to develop security services.
	This business seeks to gain cloud computing elasticity benefits, but they are unable to support public service access due to security restrictions.
	Business legislation requires the company to use its own private secure services to control access to secure business services.
Actors	Business operations controller.
	Business procurement management.
	Security and compliance.
	Data center management.
	IT operations management.
Business requirements	Private cloud capability.
	Access, authentication, repudiation.
	Audit and e-discovery compliance.
	Securely partitioned and isolated.
	Disaster recovery.
	Web security authentication.
	Business continuity.
Business risks	Security and compliance breach.
	Lost business continuity.
	Sovereignty compromise.

Source: "Strengthening Your Business Case for Using Cloud" as published by The Open Group.

21 Common Cloud Questions and Responses

As cloud emerges as a subject of great interest, many questions accompany it. This section offers questions you might ask and answers that will anchor successful cloud experiences for you:

1. *Is the development of an enterprise cloud adoption strategy augmenting EA applicable to the small business as well?*
    Yes. The context of enterprise applied in this book has nothing to do with the size of your company. It has to do with your holistic view of developing a strategy that allows you to anticipate, prepare, and solve business problems in a way that your company reaps immediate and long-term benefits. When vetting providers, you should ask about their EA strategy and how they intend to help you integrate cloud with your existing systems. A cloud provider with an integrated EA is more likely to have the proper foundation and controls in place to grow with your business as well as adequate governance to support your dynamic business requirements. Likewise, you should validate and reference your own EA capabilities including governance, security, integration, and performance for cloud service and enablement decisions. Without which, issues with sustaining your cloud adoption and maximizing its value may surface.

2. *Is there a particular business area that our company must pay close attention to when it comes to consuming cloud services?*
    Billing and customer relationship management are common processes for cloud adoption. You need to understand who and how you will be billed for services that you consume, you must understand whether there is a standardized payment gateway or whether you will rely on your provider's payment gateway, and your provider should have certified billing and security measures that guarantee against fraudulent activities. The impact of your provider's capability is closely linked to customer relationship management and service excellence. It is better to address these considerations early on, during the strategy phase.

3. *What are some lessons learned from cloud projects?*
    While the IT capabilities of cloud are significant, organizations can achieve higher returns if they focus on the business value of cloud

adoption with an emphasis on applying the capability for business efficiency, expediency, and agility. This has been challenging for organizations that perceive cloud as purely an IT play because the business units struggle with recognizing the impacts to their organizations.

Traditional solution methodologies can be too time consuming and require excessive paperwork, but at the same time you cannot ignore requirements gathering, testing, and formal documentation. When the right balance goes unmet it generates issues for all parties involved including delayed implementations.

Executive sponsorship and leadership is essential for not only driving cloud adoption but driving the right business model with cloud providers so that investment risks and rewards are fair and adequate. Proof of concepts and demonstrations are not production-ready deliverables; you and your providers need to call a spade a spade so that realistic project expectations are established and managed appropriately.

Buyers and sellers need to communicate expectations and the value of cloud in business speak. There remains a growth opportunity in this arena—this book provides guidance on the subject.

When you are accustomed to operating in a traditional hosted manner, it can be difficult to change. One way to guide adaptation is to maintain your traditional environment as a contingency until cloud environments are proven; and by all means, do not overlook the value and necessity of quality assuring the interoperability cloud solutions in your environment.

Finally, some organizations don't shoot high enough in terms of what's possible to do for business value in adopting cloud computing.

4. *What are industry verticals and what is the market potential for cloud?*
   A vertical cloud aims at addressing the needs of a given business within a vertical market. Some example vertical clouds are those developed to support healthcare services. Other examples are automotive, manufacturing, and banking specific cloud solutions. Vertical markets are an excellent opportunity for cloud consumers because of the specialized, expert capability that is available to you. Such markets are also, at this time, an excellent opportunity for providers, since the cloud market currently is not overly saturated with such capabilities.

A horizontal market is a market that meets the needs of a variety of industries, rather than a specific industry. Storage and compute as a service are example horizontal cloud solutions. Horizontal markets are the norm and present excellent business opportunities for cloud consumers and providers. Your challenge will be choosing from among the various cloud offerings, which means you need to ensure that select services align to your business strategy, goals, and objectives.

5. *What is the role of communications service providers (CSPs) and cloud?*
CSPs are well-positioned to capitalize on this new market opportunity using the assets they already have in place such as networks, customer connections, brand strength, strong service levels, and management of small and large customer base. CSPs are good candidates for cloud consumption as well as becoming a provider because of their foundation. Some key capabilities required for CSPs to remain successful in the cloud market are

- Extensive product development and marketing experience with numerous sales channels to leverage and promote your cloud offerings. You can consider offering fewer products with more features or you might consider offering more products with fewer features. You also need to consider pricing strategies that work for you. For instance we know that with cloud a benefit is consumption based pricing, but exactly how should that work for you and your organization. Does it make sense to offer subscription style services, or is it more efficient to charge per use down to the minute? You have to consider the cost to enable this capability, your target market, as well as the payback.

- Customer data handling including demographics, billing, and credit information for postpaid accounts, service subscription information, usage data, and personalization are some examples.

- A strong brand where you are known for financial stability, local community presence, secure maintenance of customer data, and respect for privacy.

- Highly scalable/high volume networks and systems to guarantee highly automated service fulfillment and customer care.

- Strong regional market position and perception as a trusted service provider.

- Establish partnerships with competitors as well as friends, and develop an ability to integrate third-party applications and services into your service portfolio.

6. *What are your experiences with SMBs and cloud adoption?*

   Our experiences are pretty consistent with published industry reports in that small and medium sized businesses (SMBs) are rapid adopters of cloud computing, particularly in the Business Process-as-a-Service (BPaaS), Software-as-a-Service (SaaS), and Infrastructure-as-a-Service (IaaS) areas for compute and storage services. Virtual desktops, at least with my clients, are starting to gain momentum.

   SMBs typically look for lightweight, mobile solutions to control costs and maintain client responsiveness. If you recall the situation of the small business owner named "Jack" in Chapter 1, "Business Value of a Cloud Adoption Strategy," then you can relate to the fact that SMBs are not particularly interested in all of the bells and whistles because they generally have a smaller budget. They are instead focused on affordable services that they need to drive value and client impacts. If SMBs can consume services at a fraction of the cost that it would take to build a data center or create applications they will and are doing so. You can find more on this subject in the epilogue.

7. *What can my company do to prepare for cloud even though adoption is not an immediate goal?*

   It is a good idea to ready your organization for cloud before you attempt to implement. You can take actions such as research strategic advantages that your adoption will bring and ensure that you have adequate network capability. You should educate your teams on cloud, review lessons learned from other companies, and start to review your EA domains including business, applications, information systems, and technology/infrastructure architectural building blocks (ABBs) to see where cloud adoption makes sense and to determine the foundational components to put in place. Reading about case studies and engaging with your peers is another great pursuit for readiness. Materials throughout this book will help you ready your organization whether your decision is to move forward with cloud adoption today or tomorrow.

8. *What are some financial advantages to consider?*

   For the CFO, the challenge is to think of new ways to utilize technology in the business that helps deliver the strategic objective of
   the company but at an acceptable cost. Removing the burden of routine maintenance and management and accessing business applications via cloud offers enterprise stakeholders a prime opportunity to
   refocus energy on more strategic aspects of business and IT operations, freeing up time and resources, which can be used on growing
   the business.[5]

   Essentially, cloud shifts the business model for the customer from
   the high capital expenses of a physical data center and hardware,
   which are now the investment of the cloud provider, to operational
   expenses via a subscription or usage based business model. For users,
   cloud arrangements can bring about cost reductions and data center
   efficiencies.

   If a user needs temporary additional space, they can simply tell the
   cloud service provider to up his quota for the time being, rather
   than purchase additional physical capacity, which would only be
   needed for a short period and then left idle.[6] This also means that
   computer resources as a whole are generally used more efficiently,
   contributing to greener, leaner, and more optimized data centers.
   This topic is expounded in Chapter 8, "Financial Considerations,"
   where the impact of an enterprise cloud adoption strategy furthers
   financial benefits and mitigates financial risk.

9. *There is a fear factor around security in public cloud implementations.*
   What are some of the concerns, and how are cloud service providers securing
   their public clouds?

   One source of comfort is to recognize the subject matter expertise
   that is required of cloud service providers. Many specialize in security and ensuring reliable cloud solutions as this is the core of their
   business model. On the other hand, cloud adoption does not eliminate the need for security. Cloud providers should proactively offer
   cloud security strategy and road map solutions to help guide clients
   through the security and privacy concerns of their cloud initiatives.
   When users place data and applications on centralized servers, they
   lose the ability to maintain complete control of that information.
   With the rise in the adoption of cloud, critical and sometimes sensitive information that was once safely stored on personal computers
   now resides on the servers of online companies. Examples of such

information include users' e-mail accounts, banking information, and full backups of individuals' hard drives. One of the biggest risks of storing data in the cloud is the possibility that data will be accessed by unwanted parties. While some cloud services encrypt user data when it is stored, you have to ensure that the right levels of encryption are applied. Some providers store data in clear text, leaving data especially vulnerable to security breaches.

Data stored in the cloud might also be provided to marketers. According to a report by the Pew Internet and American Life Project, 90 percent of cloud application users say they would be very concerned if the company storing their data sold it to a third party, 80 percent of users say they would be very concerned if companies used their photos or other data in marketing campaigns, and 68 percent say they would be very concerned if companies that provided these services analyzed their information and then displayed ads to them based on their actions. You can find more on this subject in Chapter 6, "Mitigating Risk."

10. *What types of workloads are being deployed on public and private clouds?*
Typical entry points for public cloud workloads include those for collaboration such as instant messaging, Web conferencing, e-mail, idea management, and file sharing or those that are self-contained. Typical entry points for private cloud workloads include those that have a significant amount of interaction between various components that can't be moved immediately to a public cloud, and those workloads with regulatory compliance and/or proprietary information requirements. Along with determining public and private workloads, here are some common application considerations for consumers when it comes to determining cloud candidates (these application-specific considerations augment the content that was discussed in Chapter 4, "Identifying Cloud Candidates."

- There are multiple users (preferably across business units) for the service.

- Services are loosely coupled which makes them more interoperable and vendor and device agnostic.

- There is a geographical reach if required (e.g., language support and capacity for consumption).

- Services comply with corporate information security and regulatory requirements.

- The lifetime of existing, replacement services is nearing retirement and/or service warranties are expiring.
- There is a favorable cost and user experience.
- There is help desk support according to your specifications.

11. *Are there common workloads that are fit for cloud?*
    Yes. Some common workloads are
    - Application development and test
    - Business intelligence and decision support services
    - Business applications
    - Collaborative services
    - Archival, storage, and information retrieval services
    - Disaster recovery services
    - High performance computing
    - IT infrastructure/hosting
    - Web infrastructure/hosting

12. *Should companies do away with their data centers and move everything to cloud?*
    Some companies are looking to minimize their IT investments, and moving workloads to the cloud is a viable option, especially with startup companies with minimal IT requirements that want to leverage the scalability. Established IT organizations will look to leverage cloud for some but not all content, and as discussed there is a move toward enterprise applications into cloud. Cloud offerings are maturing, and you should keep in mind that not all workloads—for example, some legacy applications—are suited for cloud. You should also be mindful that while you can minimize hardware purchases by using a pay per use model, not all of your hardware needs can be addressed via cloud.

13. *How much should I expect to save from moving to cloud?*
    The amount of savings depends on how constrained you are with your data center and legacy resources. Those that do not require a large data center investment will find cloud savings to be significant up front and downstream, such as cost avoidance from having to build new data centers or expand existing servers and infrastructure. The case studies in this appendix offer specific examples of experienced benefits and projections including a total ROI of 300

percent or greater. You can find more financial discussions associated with planning your cloud adoption in Chapter 8.

14. *How do I compensate for network connectivity, availability, and response as*
    I move workloads out to the public cloud, which has to interact with our
    distributed workforce and retained IT workloads?

    The same network techniques that an IT organization has been
    using for data center consolidation can be applied to public cloud.
    At a high level, you need to make sure that there is sufficient net-
    work bandwidth between the public cloud location and your
    customers interacting with the cloud. Network measurements
    for response time and latency should be taken as part of providing a
    quality service. Workloads with noninteractive traffic are better
    suited for centralization. Network techniques such as WAN acceler-
    ation and content caching can be used to complement application
    changes to leverage centralized IT workloads. Chapter 7, "Planning
    the Transition," describes some lessons learned from a project and
    some key network considerations.

15. *What are some key integration considerations when it comes to adopting*
    cloud?

    You have to consider the integration of cloud with your existing
    business processes, applications, data, and security. For example,
    your enterprise application portfolio, upon SaaS adoption, is
    extended, and your portfolio must be governed accordingly. In turn
    you might assign a CTO that is dedicated to managing external
    cloud providers; there is an element of organizational knowledge
    transfer and training associated with cloud that you will need to
    address; and most cloud solutions come with a front-end user inter-
    face or dashboard. You will want to establish a plan for integrating
    that interface with your existing dashboards. Many companies, for
    instance, require that their current dashboard remain visible to end
    users while others require branding of the cloud-provided user
    interface to meet corporate standards. This topic is discussed from
    both a business integration and technology integration perspective
    in Chapter 1 and Chapter 2, "Business Value of Incorporating Cloud
    into Your EA."

16. *How will the public cloud content we created be integrated with the system*
    management solution (products and governance) that I have in place for my
    existing IT content?

In general, the same tools that a company uses for system management today can be used in the public cloud environment. As part of installing the system management tools on your public cloud workload, a company should feed information from the cloud into its existing system management infrastructure to avoid having to maintain multiple system management implementations. This is one of the reasons why this book emphasizes building cloud into your EA, which encompasses system management and governance. You can find more information on this subject in Chapter 5, "What About Governance?."

17. *We understand the technical benefits of cloud and rapid provisioning and all; what are some example business benefits?*

The case studies shared in this appendix are intended to provide some example business benefits (of which the technical benefits are also incorporated). Some specific business advantages to using cloud are

■ Increased customer satisfaction due to rapid access to services and tools (e. g., social media) that are required to solve complex business problems

■ Increased client base and market share

■ Improved analyses and business intelligence

■ Self-service capabilities (end user empowerment)

■ Rapid problem solving and teamwork

■ Reduced operational costs

■ Improved business agility

■ Sustainable cloud usage and structured proliferation across your company

18. *What is the difference between cloud reference architecture and enterprise reference architecture?*

Cloud reference architecture emphasizes the architecture and components required to build a cloud solution. An enterprise reference architecture is derived from EA; it describes your enterprise strategy for designing and implementing solutions end to end and encompasses or references your cloud reference architecture.

19. *What are some contributors to unsuccessful cloud projects?*

The omission of a clearly defined cloud adoption strategy can lead to haphazard adoption of cloud solutions or an over proliferation of cloud environments as was discussed in the South African case study presented earlier in this chapter. This may not make the project unsuccessful per se, put it does contribute to a difficult portfolio to manage and unnecessary costs, both of which diminish your business agility and performance.

Lack of a clearly articulated and published service catalog and pricing model is a red flag for problems. This portfolio should be developed at the onset. Some clients are anxious to onboard cloud solutions and do not seem to give the pricing model much thought. Some do not understand the potential for profitability and should insist that providers team and discuss the possibilities.

As with traditional projects, mismanaged expectations between consumers and providers are contributors to related problems on cloud engagements. Clearly articulated service level requirements, service level agreements, and operational level agreements (SLAs, SLOs, and OLAs) are all significant and not only must be established but also governed.

Another contributor to unsuccessful projects is security, basics such as ensuring that your provider conducts ethical hacking of the virtual environments that they provision is often overlooked. Chapter 4 provides top-down analysis and approaches to developing your enterprise cloud adoption strategy; and Chapter 6 provides insights for addressing some security related matters.

20. *What is the role of the CIO when it comes to cloud?*

The CIO generally reports to the CEO or CFO and is responsible for ensuring that a vision and integrated business and IT strategy are established and executed appropriately within your organization. Your CIO might direct you to adopt specific cloud solutions, or she might assign this responsibility to your CTO and chief enterprise architect, but ultimately the CIO is (or should be) accountable.

21. *How does cloud fit within my SOA strategy?*

Cloud is an expansion and realization of your SOA strategy. Three points follow to further this topic.

First, there is a high degree of commonality between cloud and a service oriented architecture (SOA) strategy and as we progress toward an environment where almost everything is available as a service, we need to consider adding cloud to our overarching SOA strategy as an information, orchestration and integration channel and potentially as an Integration-as-a-Service capability.

Second, the essential characteristics for cloud (on-demand self-service, broad network access, resource pooling, rapid elasticity, and measured services) are optional for SOA and mandatory for cloud and cloud architectures require a set of capabilities and architectural building blocks (ABBs) to meet these characteristics.

Third, considering that SOA decomposes your business technology landscape into loosely coupled functional services, you can take advantage of established SOA decisions and leverage cloud to deploy or realize those identified business services. And just as with EA, you can expand your SOA governance model to incorporate cloud considerations.

Summary

Networking and collaborating with the competition to develop a partnership is one way to grow your business and one example of content discussed in this appendix. Understanding market opportunities and establishing adequate price points for cloud service offerings is another decision point. It is always good to connect with stakeholders to gain an appreciation of the motivators behind business decisions, as well as to gain an understanding of any experienced and projected benefits. The same is true when it comes to cloud-specific decision making. As a form of knowledge share for those that may be contemplating cloud adoption or looking to progress the use of cloud within your company, this appendix offers some referential case studies.

As we experience a turning point from an early adopter cloud mentality to a focus on enterprise sustainability, you probably have numerous questions about cloud and developing your strategy for adoption. Bearing this thought in mind, this appendix presents a list of 21 common questions asked and answered from our experience.

Endnotes

1. See http://www-01.ibm.com/software/webservers/workload-deployer/ for more information on CloudBurst and the appliance.

2. Virtual computing labs are described in depth at http://vcl.ncsu.edu/.

3. Isom, Pamela, 2011. "8 Ways to Strengthen Your Business Case for Using Cloud." EA Blogs. See http://eablogs.gotze.eu/2011/02/04/8-ways-to-strengthen-your-business-case-for-using-cloud/.

4. "Strengthening Your Business Case for Using Cloud." The Open Group. See https://www2.opengroup.org/ogsys/jsp/publications/PublicationDetails.jsp?publication id=12234.

5. Leese, John. "The Financial Benefits of Cloud Computing." Finance Director Europe (FDE). August 20, 2009. See http://www.the-financedirector.com/features/feature61743/.

6. "Cloud Computing." Electronic Privacy Information Center, Epic.org. See http://epic.org/privacy/cloudcomputing.

More on Cloud Business Trends

Everybody in this room understands that our nation's success depends on strengthening America's role as the world's engine of discovery and innovation.

We're the nation that put cars in driveways and computers in offices; the nation of Edison and the Wright brothers; of Google and Facebook. In America, innovation doesn't just change our lives. It is how we make our living.

—President Barack Obama

Initial discussions on cloud business trends commenced in the epilogue. This appendix continues the topic with a focus on innovation and thoughts pertaining to future usage of cloud computing.

Cloud Innovations

Innovation is a new way of doing something; a new product or service or method.

Cloud innovation relates to using cloud to renew or improve, and novelty is a consequence of the improvement.

Mobile and Cloud

You probably carry your mobile device everywhere and use your device for everything—well, almost everything. For many, mobile phones are becoming the primary portal for staying connected, learning, banking, and a way of life. Companies use cloud to track and measure business operations from a variety of mobile devices, and the integration of mobile with cloud is growing because of the convenience and your ability to use applications and data that does not have to be stored on your device. There is also the convenience of device independence since assets consumed reside in the cloud. Proprietary operating systems still present problems for some providers, and as a result there is an upswing to open source operating systems for greater interoperability.

This convergence can make things simpler. A case in point is both Google's and Amazon's innovative music programs that allow listeners to store music in the cloud. They essentially empower users to leverage cloud as an external hard drive with a positive caveat—the environment is managed and supported by someone else besides your company's IT department. You can expect mobile applications to continue to evolve and move to the cloud as opposed to having to get installed and run directly on your devices. A benefit being no downtimes due to software upgrades since this is taken care of for you by cloud resources.

Using cloud for access ubiquity and remote storage has other advantages. For instance, if you were to lose your mobile phone or your laptop, your applications and data would remain accessible, and all you would require is an ability to access the cloud environment. While we are not totally there (some applications remain associated with specific devices), I expect cloud to further ubiquity in the areas of access and connectivity, applications and data centers, as well as networks so that you are able to easily conduct business from any device, from any location, and at any time.

As mentioned in Appendix A, "Augmenting Your Delivery Model with Cloud," stakeholders are using social media and corporate applications, and there are explicit interests in accessing these applications from mobile devices. CIOs and technical leaders should do what they can to promote the use of mobile and ubiquity so that you empower employees to bring your own (BYO) technologies, such as smart phones and tablets. You should also count up the cost of not enabling such capability, which could mean losing key staff to competing companies.

Mobile banking is also on the rise. This includes everyday online functions and mobile wallets. Recent reports state that the use of mobile wallet technology among UK consumers has more than doubled in the last 12 months with more than one in ten people now making payments via their mobile, says "Mobile Life," a TNS research paper into use of mobiles in the UK. Mobile wallets allow consumers to use their phone like a debit or credit card to pay for items online.

Gamification and Serious Games

Gamification is the use or addition of game play mechanics to applications to address a business problem. Gamification is an emerging business trend to watch and engage. You will recognize application in programs such as frequent flyer initiatives where points, badges, levels, leader boards, and rewards are signals that a game of some nature is taking place.

For the purposes of this book, serious games and gamification are applied interchangeably. The "serious" adjective implies that the game-centric application is used by industries such as education, defense, and healthcare for business purposes. Although serious games can be entertaining, their main purpose is to investigate, educate, and advertise.

A well-executed serious game utilizes established scientific insights from design and psychology to successfully balance the development of skills and situational awareness with progressive disclosure of real-world challenges modeled within the game, building to proficiency within real-world systems, such as logistics. Serious games did not originate from video gaming, as one might think, but rather from game theory and understanding the social and human impact of one's decisions and actions on a situation or event.

Adding gamification to learning and end user experiences can facilitate growth in education as well as productivity in the workplace.

For example, the application of gaming technologies is known to demonstrate not only clear benefits in student engagement, attitude, and learning intensity, but it also encourages collaboration, healthy competition, and detailed learning.

Companies are adopting cloud to facilitate gaming experiences in both a consumer and provider capacity. Cloud provides an open marketplace of assets, tools, vendors, and expertise as well as a platform for hosting game-based applications, enabling rapid development, and deployment of applications that for example simulate customer experiences and the impacts of business process management decisions enabling you to exercise business process models in a serious game environment and ultimately optimize your operational effectiveness.

As with all cloud solutions, players access a secure cloud-based platform to play the game unless a nonconfidential environment is the preference. In a recent conference, Steve Ballmer reportedly cited what we all know: that cloud is the wave of the future. He went on to report how the gamebox Kinect's sensors register the body motions of its users without the need for a handheld device. He reportedly shared how friends using Kinect can interact with each other in cloud-based cyberspace.[1] This is an example of how game mechanics can be applied to serious situations such as three-dimensional (3D) simulations of medical emergencies and responses.

Adoption of cloud analytics is a business trend that is expected to continue to grow. Measurements in serious gaming environments must consider the human as well as the technological elements, such as metrics tracking of how well personnel are learning and engaging in gaming exercises, and instrumentation for monitoring the performance and utilization of applications and infrastructure hardware. Such instrumentation yields new insights, and the feedback needed to continuously improve scenarios that serious gamers seek to model in training and real life, as well as improving the quality of the playing experience. Table C.1 lists some example serious game motivators and solutions.

Table C.1 Serious Gaming Motivators and Example Providers

Motivators/Solutions	Business Challenge
Education Quest to Learn[2]	An example school that uses the underlying design principles of games to create highly immersive, gamelike learning experiences. Games and other forms of digital media serve another useful purpose at Quest: they serve to model the complexity and promise of "systems." Understanding and accounting for this complexity is a fundamental literacy of the twenty-first century.[3]
Education Science, Technology, Engineering and Math (STEM)	National STEM Video Game Challenge.[4] Aims to motivate interest in STEM learning among America's youth by tapping into students' natural passions for playing and making video games. Prizes offered to game developers who help foster education in the fields of science, technology, engineering, and math.

Table C.1   Serious Gaming Motivators and Example Providers

Motivators/Solutions	Business Challenge
Education Evoke[5]	The World Bank Institute has launched an online multi-player game, EVOKE, designed to empower young people all over the world, but especially in Africa, to start solving urgent social problems like hunger, poverty, disease, conflict, climate change, sustainable energy, lack of healthcare, and education.
Education Tabula Digita	Tabula Digita offers DimensionU Learning System, a universe of educational video games where students practice core K-12 subjects including math, literacy, science, and history. Focus is delivering innovative and effective technology-based educational tools for, middle and high school students.[6]
Business process management INNOV8 by IBM[7]	Evaluate existing traffic patterns and reroute traffic based on incoming metrics. Using a call center environment, develop more efficient ways to respond to customers. Evaluate a traditional supply chain model, balance supply and demand, and reduce environmental impact.
Knowledge share Cloud computing	Visualizes different cloud computing algorithms using serious games technologies.[8]
Military America's Army[9]	The military is an early adopter of serious games. The critical and hazardous nature of the work for which soldiers are trained requires a "virtually real" environment with learning and simulations that build, equip, and prepare teams for assignments.
Real-time strategy (RTS) Achron[10]	As published, Achron is "the world's first meta-time strategy game, a real-time strategy game where players and units can jump to and play at different times simultaneously and independently."
Save the Planet PowerUp[11]	Playing the game, students work together in teams to investigate the rich, 3D game environment and learn about the environmental disasters that threaten the game world and its inhabitants. Players take on the role of engineers, working together designing and building energy solutions to save the world.

Table C.1   Serious Gaming Motivators and Example Providers

Motivators/Solutions	Business Challenge
Smarter Planet CityOne[12]	Solve real-world business, environmental, and logistical problems. Learn how technology can revolutionize these industries. Explore ways to accelerate process change, integrate with trading partners, and control costs with a flexible IT infrastructure.

A case study on the subject of serious games is provided in Appendix B, "Cloud Case Studies and Common Questions."

Cloud Streaming

If you are familiar with video streaming technologies, you have experienced the buffer syndrome—delays that require you to patiently wait for images to load. And you have likely experienced image display issues on your mobile phones—where the images do not appear as they should. Cloud streaming is a video compression service that runs in a cloud data center. When graphics-intensive applications are made the cloud returns results as a video stream. The technology compresses video streams so that mobile devices are more receptive to graphics-intensive service requests; however, the process is seamless to the end user, and as far as they are concerned the mobile device is actually responding to service requests.

Cloud streaming is said to be able to allow streaming movies to be fast-forwarded and rewound in real time, while schools anywhere could gain easy access to software.[13] The technology is intended to make applications such as movie editing or architectural design tools accessible on Internet connected devices such as smart phones and tablets. Cloud streaming involves continuous checks of a network connection's quality, increasing the amount of video compression and adjusting bandwidth requirements as needed. Some providers of cloud streaming have reportedly negotiated with Internet carriers to ensure that data from cloud servers are carried directly on high-speed, high-capacity Internet backbones. An example cloud streaming service is OnLive.[14] The OnLive service allows the game content to be passed along the Internet to end users running OnLive clients on variety of operating systems.

Cloud Storefronts (a.k.a AppStores)

The trend that storefront providers use open source so that cloud applications can be used on numerous platforms has emerged as a business necessity. Consider the following: It has been reported that the number of native iPad apps has surpassed 100,000 and represents around 25 percent of the total number of applications in the AppStore, which as of this writing stands at more than 425,000.[15] These applications are distributed via the AppStore as third-party solutions that run on the provider's operating system (OS).[16]

Understandably, this business model presents problems for consumers as they could become bound to a provider. As an example, we look forward to shopping at the Kindle Store and being able to purchase books that may not be available yet by Amazon but are available in digital format at other AppStores.

The same is applicable to enterprise cloud applications. Open source standards adoption is the trend, and it should be. Providers should leverage open source so that consumers are not bound to a provider's dashboard because in many cases companies have user interface standards that cannot be replaced simply because they are interested in cloud services. In Chapter 5, "What About Governance?," you learned of key considerations for governing cloud service brokers; likewise in Chapter 6, "Mitigating Risk," you learned of key questions to ask your candidate providers when it comes to cloud adoption. Questioning and establishing policies for your potential AppStore, the variety of cloud solutions and services that will reside in the service catalog, interoperability, and the simplicity when it comes to using and maintaining the storefront is essential to your success.

An associated trend is the move away from requiring downloads to devices and instead applications are run remotely over the Internet where applications can be hosted by third-party providers in the case of brokered solutions, or they are hosted directly by the cloud providers. As discussed in this appendix, cloud enables service consumption across numerous devices and remote storage so that you do not have to download data onto your systems, fueling the concept of ubiquitous data centers.

Big Data

Information is growing at a staggering pace, and the increased velocity, volume, and variety of data brings challenges that cannot be met with legacy or traditional approaches. As the amount of data continues to grow a new term has been coined, Big Data, which refers to the large amount of data, the format of the data, and how it is managed. Managing and benefiting from this massive and growing amount of data is where cloud computing plays a role.

Competing and differentiating necessitates improved decision-making using information. Extracting insight from this enormous amount of data is the challenge. The Big Data phenomenon started from the Internet, as did the tools to manage it. Big Data has entered enterprises and with it a class of analytics described as massive scale analytics Although companies have handled large data sets before, we are now talking Internet scale. The type of data—unstructured, human generated and/or sensor generated—creates enormous opportunities for insights, innovation and differentiation.

The use of analytics, predictive and massive scale, fundamentally changes what is possible, enabling you to do things you cannot do today due to significant data volumes and associated complexities. In fact, the ease of leveraging Big Data's value and the magnitude of its value proposition varies. However, the arrival of cloud computing allows all companies to have access to platforms for massive scale analytics that might be CPU or I/O intensive. Companies need access to a platform that can handle structured (e.g., relational databases) and unstructured (e.g., videos, audio, blogs, etc.); and a platform that can accommodate a variety of workloads. Scalability and elasticity for data volumes at tens to hundreds of terabytes growing to pegabytes will be requirements for a platform. Analytics software supported by parallel analytics for performance will be required. Cloud computing will be the delivery model for many organizations taking advantage of the opportunities presented by Big Data and analytics. Adoption of cloud will allow organizations to bring together a variety of data, at huge volumes, and in a timely manner to generate insight. This is also where Big Data and cloud streaming merge as multiple data streams are analyzed from many sources live.

Natural Language

The IBM and *Jeopardy!* contest aired February 14, 15, and 16, 2011, on the *Jeopardy!* TV show between Watson and two of the most celebrated *Jeopardy!* champions of all time: Ken Jennings and Brad Rutter. In 2004, Ken won 74 games in a row. Brad is the biggest money winner in the history of the show. For nearly four years IBM scientists had been working on an advanced automatic Question Answering (QA) system, code-named "Watson." Watson is capable of analyzing and understanding rich natural language questions and answering them with enough precision, confidence, and speed to compete with *Jeopardy!* champions. *Jeopardy!* clues are written in rich natural language, requiring an understanding of subtle meaning, irony, riddles, and other complexities. The contest demonstrated that natural language processing can be used today.

The *Jeopardy!* challenge poses a different kind of problem than what is solved by a Web search. It demands that the computer deeply analyze the question to figure out exactly what is being asked, deeply analyze the available content to extract precise answers, and quickly compute a reliable answer in light of whatever supporting or refuting information it finds. IBM believes that an effective and general solution to this challenge can help drive the broader impact of automatic question answering in science and the enterprise. For example, such technology can be used to diagnose disease, handle technical support, and parse and understand vast tracts of legal documents.

Natural Language Processing (NLP) is the computerized approach to analyzing text that is based on both a set of computational techniques and a set of technologies. Its useful in that we can process huge amounts of data (e.g., books, research papers, Internet, etc.) in a mode that requires reasoning about questions, the answers uncovered, where a dialogue about the question can be held. Such a computer platform could extend its capabilities using analytics tools to empower much broader reasoning and higher quality responses. Cloud computing can provide the delivery model for leveraging such technology.

Summary

You can expect business models to evolve as your CIO and senior leaders explore how cloud can be most effectively used in your organization. This appendix provided some examples including the use of serious games to simulate business processes and cloud streaming for graphics-intensive "real-time" compute power.

Industry verticals (as discussed in Chapter 3, "The Life Cycle of Your Enterprise Cloud Adoption Strategy") are expected to continue to pursue private and community clouds because this most effectively meets their business models, but public cloud consumption will remain as well since this is a vehicle to grow and extend market share. Regulatory requirements may drive specialized cloud services; for example, in the healthcare and pharmaceutical industries, there is likely to be an emergence of cloud services that explicitly validate FDA compliance.

Numerous studies show that the adoption of cloud will continue to increase into well beyond the year 2015 followed with a tapering of adoption with a focus on more efficient use within the enterprise. Thus you can expect as well a shift from cost savings as the key business driver for cloud adoption to business capability such as advanced, complex business analytics.

Discussed in this appendix are six cloud business trends where an underlying theme for each is innovation and mobility:

- Mobile and cloud
- Gamification and serious games
- Cloud streaming
- AppStores
- Big Data
- Natural Language

In summary, the path forward for cloud is upward. Numerous uses for cloud are yet to be discovered; some examples were discussed in this appendix. In essence, the business benefits generally outweigh the business risks when it comes to cloud adoption and when the proper due diligence to prepare for the transition is conducted. How best might you sharpen your skills and prepare for the future? Consider operating as a strategic thinker, a thought leader, a visionary, and a roadmap developer that is sharp in business consultancy, IT transformation, and enterprise integration. On a more tactical level, learn to orchestrate cloud solutions across providers to optimize your business processes and solve problems. These skills will complement the automation, broad access, and self-service characteristics of cloud enabling you to take advantage of the capability in the appropriate manner and for the right business reasons.

Endnotes

1. Helman, Christopher. "Ballmer: Kinect Is the Future of Cloud Computing." Forbes.com. March 10, 2011. See http://blogs.forbes.com/christopherhelman/2011/03/10/ballmer-kinect-cloud-source-code/.

2. Quest to Learn. PBS Video. See http://video.pbs.org/video/1764943332/#.

3. Quest to Learn. See http://q2l.org/.

4. National Stem Video Game Challenge. See http://www.joanganzcooneycenter.org/Initiatives-31.html or http://www.whitehouse.gov/blog/2010/09/16/changing-equation-stem-education.

5. "World Bank Institute Launches Online Game EVOKE, a Crash Course in Changing the World." March 3, 2010. See http://web.worldbank.org/WBSITE/EXTERNAL/TOPICS/EXTEDUCATION/0,,contentMDK:22487657~menuPK:282391~pagePK:64020865~piPK:149114~theSitePK:282386,00.html.

6. DimensionU. See https://www.dimensionu.com/dimu/info/.

7. INNOV8 BPM Simulation Game. IBM. See http://www-01.ibm.com/software/solutions/soa/innov8/index.html.

8. "Cloud Computing Game." YouTube video. See http://www.youtube.com/watch?v=g2uq-psosF8.

9. America's Army. See http://www.americasarmy.com/.

10. Achron by Hazardous Software. See http://www.achrongame.com/site/gameplay.php.

11. PowerUp. See http://www.powerupthegame.org/home.html

12. CityOne. IBM. See http://www-01.ibm.com/software/solutions/soa/innov8/cityone/index.html.

13. "TR10: Cloud Streaming." MIT Technology Review. See http://www.www.techreview.com/video/?vid=691&channel=tr10.

14. OnLive is a cloud gaming system. The games are synchronized, rendered, and stored on remote servers (in the cloud) and delivered via the Internet. OnLive itself is not a platform. The games offered run off OnLive servers. See http://www.technologyreview.com/computing/37203/.

15. Athow, Desire. "iPad2 Fuelling Growth for Native iPad Apps." July 9, 2011. ITProPortal.com. See http://www.itproportal.com/2011/07/09/ipad-2-fuelling-growth-native-ipad-apps/.

16. Simonite, Tom. "App Stores Make Billions but Competition Is Growing." *MIT: Technology Review*. May/June 2011. See http://www.technologyreview.com/communications/37377/.

Glossary

A

AppStore
A service that enables and allows users to browse and purchase applications. *See also* marketplace.

asset management
A set of business practices that join financial, contractual, and inventory functions to support life cycle management and strategic decision making for the cloud environment. *See also* cloud portfolio management.

audit
An official inspection of an organization's cloud environment, including people, process, information, and technologies to ensure compliance. Audits are generally conducted by an independent body.

availability
The measure of the time a system or component is functional compared to the total time it is required or expected to function.

B

balance sheet

A statement of assets, liabilities, and capital of a business at a particular point in time. A balance sheet lists the balance of income and expenditures for a specific point in time such as at the end of its financial year.

Assets, liabilities, and ownership equity (or net worth) are core elements of the balance sheet.

bandwidth

The inbound and outbound network, data, and digital transfer rates to and from the cloud. Commonly expressed as bits per second (bps).

brand

Image. How a company or individual is presented.

business agility

The ability of a business to adapt efficiently and expediently to changes, including uncertainty in the business environment. A benefit of integrating cloud into your EA is business agility.

business architecture

The domain of an enterprise architecture (EA) related to architectural organization of the business including organization and processes.

business competency

A business's expertise, skills, talents, abilities, and experiences.

A core business competency is described as what a company perceives as central to its purpose (e. g., a business differentiator).

business intelligence (BI)

BI is a discipline and technology enablers that are used to analyze an organization's raw data. BI as a discipline encompasses activities such as sentiment analysis and data mining, online analytical processing, querying, and reporting. BI includes enablers such as data analytics, business performance management, data warehousing, dashboards, and key performance indicators (KPIs). Companies use BI for reasons such as to improve decision making, identify process improvements, streamline costs, and expand business growth.

business model

The plan implemented by a company to generate profits.

A business model is usually static in its representation and demonstrates what a company does; compared to business processes, which depict how a company conducts its business. For example, a restaurant's business model is to accelerate profits by cooking and preparing meals, while a business process is delivery of meals to customers with speed and quality. *See also* cloud business model.

business performance
The results of an organization's execution relative to its vision, objectives, targets, and metrics. A benefit of integrating cloud into your EA is sustained business performance.

business process
A sequence or flow of structured tasks, events, and activities that are applied in an enterprise to satisfy organizational and client objectives.

Business Process-as-a-Service (BPaaS)
BPaaS services are any business processes (horizontal or vertical) that are delivered using the cloud service model to internal or external consumers. Example services are employee benefits management and procurement processes. *See also* cloud service type.

business process outsourcing (BPO)
The contracting of business processes to a third-party or cloud service provider.

business support services (BSS)
The set of business-related cloud services that are exposed. These services are consumed and directly impact the user's experience. Example BSSs are the service offering catalog, billing, and pricing.

business value
The worth, both tangible and intangible of enterprise decisions.

buyer
The person(s) accountable for cloud adoption decisions and business investments. This role differs from procurers who obtain cloud solutions but are not accountable for cloud adoption decisions.

C

café style services
A menu of cloud choices is presented to consumers that balance standardized offerings and personal customizations.

capability
The measure of a person's or object's ability to perform a task, operation, or activity.

Capability Maturity Model Integration (CMMI)
CMMI is a process improvement approach that provides companies with the necessary capabilities for effective process improvement. CMMI can guide process improvements across projects, business divisions, or an enterprise.

CMMI can be applied to determine an organization's capability toward cloud adoption.

capacity
The potential or suitability of addressing business demands with cloud.

capacity management
A discipline that ensures IT infrastructure is provided at the right time and in the right amounts so that cloud is consumed in the most efficient manner.

capital expenditures (CAPEX)
Investments in asset purchases or upgrades such as cloud infrastructure, data centers, and computer systems. A capital expense occurs when the asset is newly purchased or if an investment improves the useful life of an existing capital asset.

cash flow
The movement of cash into and out of a business.

catalog of cloud services
An ordered list of cloud service offerings. *See also* cloud portfolio.

change management
The process of managing and controlling business and IT related changes in the environment. The objective is to allow or enable changes to the cloud with minimum or no service interruption and to ensure that all changes are carried out in a planned and authorized manner.

chief executive officer (CEO)
The highest ranking executive in an enterprise whose responsibilities include making major corporate decisions, managing the overall operations of a company, and operating as liaison to the board of directors on behalf of corporate stakeholders.

chief financial officer (CFO)
Executive in an enterprise who is responsible for the financial activities of an entire company.

chief information officer (CIO)
Executive in an enterprise who is responsible for information technology (IT) including management, implementation, and effective use of IT.

chief operating officer (COO)
Executive in an enterprise who is responsible for the operations of the company.

chief technology officer (CTO)
Executive in an enterprise who is responsible for the management of research and development (R&D) and adoption of the appropriate business technologies.

cloud
A business service model that enables consumption and delivery of business and IT services on a "pay for what you use" basis. According to NIST, cloud enables convenient, on-demand network access to a shared pool of configurable computing resources (e. g., networks, servers, storage, applications, and services) that can be rapidly provisioned and released with minimal management effort or service provider interaction. This cloud model promotes availability and is composed of five essential characteristics (on-demand self-service, broad network access, resource pooling, rapid elasticity, and measured service).

cloud adoption roadmap
A plan that matches short-term and long-term business goals with cloud adoption decisions and solutions to meet those goals.

cloud aggregator
A cloud service broker whose primary responsibility is to combine and present select cloud solutions from numerous vendors in an online community, AppStore, or marketplace. These services can be combined into new cloud services.

cloud application
Applications that reside in the cloud and the interfaces that administrators of the cloud can interact with and manage.

cloud business adoption patterns (CBAP)
Recurring types of cloud investments. Some examples are allocation, broker, resell, rebalancing, and trade.

cloud business model
The plan implemented by a company to generate profits using cloud computing.

cloud candidates
There are two types of cloud candidates. The first is cloud enablement candidates, which are the foundational building blocks for cloud adoption such as upgrades to antiquated billing and metering tools or ensuring that you have adequate network capacity, and the second is the actual cloud service such as a developer, test, or human resource management (HRM) cloud.

cloud characteristics
Features and qualities of a cloud.

Self-service, resource pooling, and broad network access are characteristics of cloud, while collaborative intelligence and sustainable cloud adoption decisions are characteristics of a well-defined and implemented enterprise cloud adoption strategy.

cloud consumer
A person or organization that makes use of cloud services to address business needs.

cloud deployment model
A description of how and where a cloud service should reside. Examples are public, private, hybrid, and community.

cloud portfolio
A repository of cloud solutions for a company.

cloud portfolio management
Knowledge of cloud attributes and control of deployments (on or off premise) for a company.

cloud provider
A person or organization that offers cloud-enabled services for consumption.

cloud risk management
The collection, assessment, prioritization, and response planning of risks associated with cloud adoption.

cloud roles and relationships
Analysis of roles to consider when it comes to cloud adoption and the relationship between the various roles.

cloud service broker
One who negotiates or brokers business relationships, often operating as an intermediary between cloud service providers and consumers. *See also* systems integrator (SI) and cloud service integrator.

cloud service creator
Person(s) who develop cloud services to be consumed end users. Some example creations are virtual images, storage images, and multitenant applications.

cloud service integrator
Designs, develops, and implements the interface (business and technology) between the customer's on-premise environment and off-premise cloud entities. *See also* systems integrator (SI) and cloud service broker.

cloud service type
The types of cloud services. Examples are CaaS, BPaaS, IaaS, PaaS, SaaS, and StaaS.

Cloud Standards Customer Council (CSCC)
An end user advocacy group dedicated to accelerating cloud's successful adoption, and drilling down into the standards, security and interoperability issues surrounding the transition to the cloud.

collective intelligence
A shared, large group intelligence that emerges from the collaboration and often competition of individuals and information sets. Collective intelligence is generally applied to promote innovation. IBM's Jam is an example collective intelligence enabler that is often applied in a cloud environment to support massive amounts of users.

communications service provider (CSP)
A service provider typically from the telecom industry that is the originator of cloud concepts such as business support services (BSS) and operational support services (OSS). CSPs are consumers as well as providers of cloud services.

community cloud
Provides a group with services that are shared such as healthcare or clinical clouds. In a community cloud setting, ownership of the cloud assets might be the organizations or a third party and the services can reside on or off premise.

company
Synonymous with an enterprise or organization of all sizes.

compliance
The act of adhering to a rule or policy.

Compute-as-a-Service (CaaS)
CaaS is an alternate reference to IaaS that is commonly used by communications service providers where specifically computing resources are acquired on-demand. *See also* cloud service type.

configuration management
The process of maintaining information about any component that must be managed to effectively deliver the cloud service and sustain performance over time.

cost take out
Elimination of costs.

D

decision parameters
A set of measurements and criteria that are evaluated to identify cloud candidates.

E

economic feasibility analysis
Cost benefit analysis of cloud investments.

economies of scale
The strategic advantages (usually associated with cost savings) that transpire due to the reusability and extensibility of cloud services.

end point
The target state objective of cloud adoption such as to reuse adopted SaaS services across the enterprise.

enterprise
Synonymous with a company or organizations of all sizes.

enterprise architecture (EA)
An integrated business and IT strategy.

EA is comprised of several domains that include business architecture, information systems architecture, infrastructure architecture, and governance.

enterprise cloud adoption strategy
An integrated business and IT strategy that guides cloud adoption decisions across the enterprise. This is one of the benefits of integrating cloud into your EA.

entry point
Where cloud adoption begins or commences; for instance, you might begin your adoption by consuming SaaS services for a specific division within your organization.

environmental management
Management of cloud environments to include development, test, systems integration, and production.

executive
Person(s) with senior management responsibility in an organization.

F

federation
Establishes a trust relationship between cloud providers on and off premise so that clouds can automatically access one another to fulfill a business request with single sign-on capability. This pattern allows enterprises to move workloads seamlessly across internal and external clouds.

FedRAMP
The Federal Risk and Authorization Management Program (in the USA).

financial management
Management of financial expenditures and savings relative to cloud adoption.

FISMA
The United States Federal Information Security Management Act of 2002.

G

gamification
The use of gaming elements, such as scoring reward issuance for the highest scores and techniques, such as the use of single and multiple players, to anticipate and resolve business challenges.

governance
The act of specifying decision rights and an accountability framework to encourage desirable behavior in the use of EA for effective adoption of cloud computing in an organization.

H

HIPAA
The Health Insurance Portability and Accountability Act of 1996.

HITECH
The Health Information Technology for Economic and Clinical Health Act was enacted as part of the American Recovery and Reinvestment Act of 2009 and signed into law on February 17, 2009. It promotes the adoption and effective use of health information technologies.

hybrid cloud
Combines multiple elements of public and private cloud, including any combination of providers and consumers, and might also contain multiple service types.

I–J

ideation
The capacity to and the act of forming valuable and often innovative courses of action for an enterprise.

implementation plan
Steps that must occur to successfully implement cloud projects. During implementation planning, consumers confirm providers, business solutions, and service level agreements that were strategically formed during transition planning. An implementation plan is a component of a transition plan.

income statement
A company's financial statement of profit and loss or revenues and expenses for a period of time.

Information Technology Infrastructure Library (ITIL)
A recognized collection of best practices for IT service management (ITSM).

Information Technology-as-a-Service (ITaaS)
The use of information technology to store, retrieve, and send information, with a mindset and capacity to offer end-to-end solutions that involve not only systems but also people and processes.

Infrastructure-as-a-Service (IaaS)
IaaS provides cloud service consumers with the ability to rent processing, storage, networks, and other fundamental computing resources

where the consumer is able to deploy and run arbitrary software, which can include operating systems and applications. *See also* cloud service type.

intelligent EA (IEA)
An IBM offering and capability that addresses the technological impacts of a Smarter Planet using EA. Core capabilities include information intelligence, cloud, green & beyond, and social computing. Examples of the fusion of cloud and EA are elaborated in this book.

IT budget
A financial plan that provides a forecast of expected expenditures and allocates financial resources to various organizational units within the IT organization.

K

key agility indicator (KAI)
A measurement of how well a business can adapt to change. KAI measures how well a company is able to sense and respond to market uncertainties. Example KAIs are time to collaborate across your enterprise and time to reflect market demands into your enterprise strategy. KAIs are not just measurements in time. For instance, the amount it costs to introduce a new product is an example KAI.

key performance indicator (KPI)
A measurement of how well you perform business as usual. Example KPIs are the rate of cloud adoption and the percentage of business processes that were optimized due to cloud adoption.

knowledge management (KM)
Processes to ensure that accurate and trustworthy information is available throughout the life cycle of the cloud. KM is typically accomplished with the use of a knowledge management system (KMS), which is a repository of shareable information that is consumable in and across the enterprise.

At the core of KM is the progression of Data $\Rightarrow$ Information $\Rightarrow$ Knowledge $\Rightarrow$ Wisdom.

L

large enterprise (LE)
Research indicates that the recognition of an SME in size can vary per country. In the United States (US) and Canada, for instance, SMEs include firms with fewer than 500 employees. For the purposes of this book, an LE is representative of 500 employees or more.

latency
Experienced delays when processing network data.

leaner
Derived from Lean Six Sigma principles, leaner focuses on process flow efficiencies and waste reduction, through the use of cloud.

life cycle
The phases of an enterprise cloud adoption strategy that range from the time it is conceived until the time it is retired from service.

M

marketplace
The space in which a market operates.

metering
A mechanism that measures cloud usage or consumption.

metric
An attribute (e.g., server utilization, energy consumption, or cloud usage) that can be measured.

multitenant
The cloud services multiple companies or client organizations.

N

National Institute of Standards and Technology (NIST)
An agency in the technology administration that makes measurements and sets standards as needed by industry or government programs.

net present value (NPV)
The difference between the present value of cash inflows and the present value of cash outflows.

network management
Processes, procedures, and tools that enable administration, monitoring, maintenance, and provisioning of the underlying cloud network. This includes network upgrades and tracking of resources on the network.

O

operational expenditures (OPEX)
The money a company spends on an ongoing, day-to-day basis to run a business or system. With cloud adoption it is possible that this amount can also be reduced.

operational support services (OSS)
The set of operational cloud services. These services are required to implement a cloud service. Example OSSs are service automation, provisioning, and configuration.

organization
Synonymous with an enterprise or company of all sizes.

P-Q

pattern
A solution or design that has been applied repeatedly. Prior to application the solution or design is a trend.

pay as you go
An arrangement where payment for cloud services is on a per-use basis.

payment options
The choice and arrangement made to pay for cloud services. Online payment processing through the use of credit cards in a secure environment and "pay as you go" are two example payment options.

performance/quality of service management
The ability to measure, monitor, and report the performance and quality of cloud services.

Platform-as-a-Service (PaaS)
PaaS services deliver compute infrastructure plus a predefined middleware stack that is typically structured for developers or advanced IT users. Providers can choose to offer a variety of service products that are configurable by the consumer. Examples include database, Web, or application server software. *See also* cloud service type.

practitioner
One who engages in and applies the skills of an occupation or profession (e.g., a cloud architect).

present value
The current value of a sum of money to be collected in the future.

pricing strategy
Strategy used to determine charges for products and services, such as the markup for cloud services that are offered through resellers.

private cloud
The cloud deployment model operated solely for a designated business. The consumer and provider generally exist within the same company; however, a private cloud can be managed by a third party. A private cloud is generally on premise but can reside off premise as long as it is operated solely for a designated business or sole tenancy. *See also* single tenant.

problem management (PM)
The resolution and prevention of incidents that affect the normal running of a business. PM involves root cause identification of defects to prevent incidents or reduce the impacts of occurrences. From a cloud perspective, the objective is to make sure services are error free and stable.

provisioning and release management
The process and automated distribution of software and hardware across the IT infrastructure such that cloud solutions are tested and quality assured prior to integration with existing infrastructure.

public cloud
The cloud deployment model that is made available to the public. The public cloud is owned by an organization selling cloud services and typically resides off premise with an ability for several tenants. *See also* multitenant.

R

regulatory compliance
Adherence to corporate and governmental laws and regulations in cloud undertakings.

reliability
The measure of the ability of a cloud component or system to consistently perform according to its specifications.

reliability availability serviceability (RAS)
The reliability of the cloud, its ability to respond to a failure, and its ability to undergo maintenance without service interruption.

resource pooling
An essential characteristic of cloud where resources are set aside (pooled) to respond to cloud service requests. With resource pooling, different physical and virtual resources are dynamically allocated to consumers based on anticipated and real-time demands.

return on investment (ROI)
ROI is a financial ratio that indicates the degree of profitability of a business. Simple cloud ROI is the result of calculating projected gains from cloud investments divided by the projected investment costs. The computation for ROI is ((total benefit − total cost) / (total cost) * 100). Consider an example where you expect to invest $2,500.00 in cloud services and support for year 1, and you project earnings of $10,000 after the first year as a result of your investment, then your projected ROI is 300 percent, computed as follows (($10,000 − $2,500) / 2500) * 100)) = 300 percent.

risk mitigation
The act of taking some kind of compensating control when a particular risk is probable or after an occurrence to reduce the business impact. Mitigation is typically applied to eliminate or reduce the chances of the occurrence.

risk response planning
Risk response planning is an aspect of managing risk. Responses are derived based on anticipated adverse effects of risk or opportunities presented as a result of an occurrence. Risk mitigation is an example risk response strategy.

S

scalability
The measure of a cloud service's ability to increase or decrease in performance and cost in response to changes in throughput or demand.

security management
The determination and implementation of security requirements, policies, and controls for business continuity and performance as cloud services are consumed across an enterprise.

self-service
A characteristic of cloud and a cloud business adoption pattern that is applied when selection of cloud services occurs by the consumer, without the help of an intermediary, at purchase.

seller
A person or organization accountable for the sale of cloud solutions.

serious games
A game designed for a primary purpose other than pure entertainment, such as immersive learning or business process improvements.

serviceability
The measure of the ease with which a cloud component or system can be maintained and repaired.

service level agreement
Describes the cloud service and documents service level targets. A cloud SLA should specify the responsibilities of the consumer and provider.

service oriented architecture (SOA)
A set of services that can be exposed to an organization and its customers. Technologists might describe SOA as an architecture comprising loosely coupled services, described by platform-agnostic interfaces, which can be discovered and invoked dynamically while business leaders might relate to SOA as common business services that can be consumed throughout an enterprise maximizing cost efficiencies due to business process and application optimization.

service request management
The workflow and orchestration of processes and governance such that a cloud service request is reliably submitted, routed, approved, monitored and delivered.

shared risk/reward
A business model that involves sharing the risks and rewards associated with cloud investments. For instance, both the consumer and provider might equally share the up-front costs of cloud undertakings at 50 percent just as both might share in the profits as they are generated.

single tenant
The cloud services a single company or client organization.

small medium business (SMB)
See small medium enterprise.

small medium enterprise (SME)
Research indicates that the recognition of an SME in size can vary per country. In the United States (US) and Canada, for instance, SMEs include firms with fewer than 500 employees, while the European Union (EU) defines a medium-sized enterprise as one with a headcount of 250,

a small enterprise as one with a headcount of fewer than 50, and a smaller or micro-enterprise as one with a maximum of 10 employees. For the purposes of this book, the US categorizations were applied to identify small, midsized, and large enterprises. *See also* large enterprise (LE).

Software-as-a-Service (SaaS)
SaaS provides cloud service consumers with the ability to rent and use predefined applications such as customer relationship management (CRM) and enterprise resource planning (ERP) that are made available in the cloud and accessible from various client devices. *See also* cloud service type.

stakeholder
An individual or entity that can affect or be affected by cloud adoption decisions.

Storage-as-a-Service (StaaS)
StaaS services are storage services made available via the cloud service model to internal or external consumers. An example StaaS is backup, archival, and recovery services. StaaS services reside within the IaaS domain. *See also* cloud service type.

strategy
The process of carefully analyzing the environment, assessing the capabilities of a company and its competitors, setting a target state, and planning a distinctive execution for a company's competitive advantage.

systems integrator (SI)
A company or individual that specializes in building complete computer systems by putting together cloud solutions from different vendors. SIs typically do not produce any original software but instead enable a company to use commercial off the shelf (COTS) solutions to meet business requirements. *See also* cloud service broker and cloud service integrator.

T

tenancy
Occupancy.

throughput
The amount of work that a computer can do in a given timeframe.

TM Forum
A global industry association focused on simplifying the complexity of running a service provider's business. The Forum serves as a unifying force, enabling more than 775 companies across 195 countries to solve critical business issues through access to a wealth of knowledge, intellectual capital, and standards.

TOGAF
The Open Group Architecture Framework.

total cost of ownership (TCO)
The process of determining direct and indirect costs of cloud adoption.

transition plan
The preparations required to ready an organization for cloud adoption and the required people, process, information, technology, and cultural changes. An implementation plan is a component of a transition plan.

U

up-front payment
Initial payment required to purchase cloud solutions. More common for private cloud adoption since investments in capital to build cloud environments might be required.

V

virtualization
The separation of the execution of an environment (application or operating system) from its underlying physical hardware. Virtualization in its simplest terms is a guest operating system or application running on a virtual machine.

virtual machine (VM)
An environment (usually an application or operating system) that is created and runs within a "host" environment. The VM emulates a physical machine and is a "guest" to the host.

W-Z

work artifacts
Tangible objects or work products that are produced during development and execution of the enterprise cloud adoption strategy to expedite and document activities. An example work artifact is a risk-response document. Unlike deliverables, work artifacts are not required to be delivered to clients.

workload
The type and amount of work assigned to and performed by the cloud.

workload management
Strategic distribution of the amount of computer processing required to complete a job (e.g., collective intelligence) across an enterprise and its cloud environments to optimize business performance.

work management
See workload management.

Index

E

E&U (energy and utilities) companies, 232

EA (enterprise architecture), 26
benefits of convergence, 29-34
implementation, 39-41
incorporation strategies, 26-29
life cycles, 45-46
gap analysis, 78-80
governance, 82-83
implementation planning, 81
initial planning phases, 46-47
target architecture, 61-70, 73-78
transition planning, 78-80
vision for cloud adoption, 49-59, 61
mapping, 38

ecosystems, specifying, 17-18
effectiveness, measurements of, 29
efficiencies, 248
storage, 140
emerging technologies, 235, 238
enablers, cloud, 61-70, 73-78
endorsements, executives, 53
energy and utilities companies, 232
enterprise
architecture. *See* EA
governance strategies, 53
integration, AppStore standards, 221
reference architecture case study, 277-278
resource planning applications, 247
enterprise adaptation, 137-146

Enterprise Architecture assessments, 60
Enterprise Architecture as Strategy, 105
Enterprise Cloud Adoption Strategy, 110
entry points, 5
environments, 47. *See also* architecture
frameworks, 105-116
governance, 104
innovation, 123-128
outsourcing, 118-119
ownership, 116-117
service brokers, 120-123
ERP (enterprise resource planning) applications, 247
evasiveness, 140
events, 64
examples of transition planning, 180-183
exception handling, 114
executives
communication, 108
endorsements, 53
ownership, 117
sponsorship, 49
expectations of adoption strategies, 2-3
clouds
defining outcomes, 13
determining utility opportunities, 15-16
developing metrics, 19
driving business innovation, 12
governance, 20
identifying use cases, 10-11

J–K–L

M

Is Your Company Ready for Cloud?

Choosing the Best Cloud Adoption Strategy for Your Business

Pamela K. Isom and Kerrie Holley

Safari

Books Online

FREE
Online Edition

Your purchase of *Is Your Company Ready for Cloud?* includes access to a free online edition for 45 days through the **Safari Books Online** subscription service. Nearly every IBM Press book is available online through **Safari Books Online**, along with thousands of books and videos from publishers such as Addison-Wesley Professional, Cisco Press, Exam Cram, O'Reilly Media, Prentice Hall, Que, and Sams.

Safari Books Online is a digital library providing searchable, on-demand access to thousands of technology, digital media, and professional development books and videos from leading publishers. With one monthly or yearly subscription price, you get unlimited access to learning tools and information on topics including mobile app and software development, tips and tricks on using your favorite gadgets, networking, project management, graphic design, and much more.

Activate your FREE Online Edition at
informit.com/safarifree

STEP 1: Enter the coupon code: JALGHFH.

STEP 2: New Safari users, complete the brief registration form. Safari subscribers, just log in.

If you have difficulty registering on Safari or accessing the online edition, please e-mail customer-service@safaribooksonline.com